BLACK MASS

Also by John Gray

Mill on Liberty: A Defense

Conceptions of Liberty in Political Philosophy
(ed. with Zbigniew Pelczynski)

Hayek on Liberty

Liberalism

Liberalisms: Essays in Political Philosophy

J. S. Mill, "On Liberty": In Focus (ed. with G. W. Smith)

*Beyond the New Right: Markets, Government
and the Common Environment*

Post-liberalism: Studies in Political Thought

*Enlightenment's Wake: Politics and Culture
at the Close of the Modern Age*

Isaiah Berlin

*After Social Democracy: Politics, Capitalism
and the Common Life*

Endgames: Questions in Late Modern Political Thought

False Dawn: The Delusions of Global Capitalism

Voltaire

Two Faces of Liberalism

Straw Dogs: Thoughts on Humans and Other Animals

Al Qaeda and What It Means to Be Modern

Heresies: Against Progress and Other Illusions

BLACK MASS

*Apocalyptic Religion
and the Death of Utopia*

JOHN GRAY

Farrar, Straus and Giroux
New York

Farrar, Straus and Giroux
19 Union Square West, New York, 10003

Printed in the United States of America
Originally published in 2007 by Allen Lane,
an imprint of Penguin Books, Great Britain
Published in the United States by Farrar, Straus and Giroux
First American edition, 2007

Library of Congress Cataloging-in-Publication Data
Gray, John, 1948–
    Black mass : apocalyptic religion and the death of utopia / John Gray.— 1st
American ed.
        p.   cm.
    Includes bibliographical references and index.
    ISBN-13: 978-0-374-10598-3 (hardcover : alk. paper)
    ISBN-10: 0-374-10598-7 (hardcover : alk. paper)
    1. Religion and politics.   2. Utopias.   3. Revolutions—Religious aspects.
4. Conservatism—Religious aspects.   5. World politics—20th century.
6. World politics—21st century.   I. Title.

BL65.P7 G69   2007
321'.07—dc22

                                                        2007028168

www.fsgbooks.com

1   3   5   7   9   10   8   6   4   2

THE SENATOR: This is an abyss into which it is better not to look.
THE COUNT: My friend, we are not free not to look.

Joseph de Maistre, *St Petersburg Dialogues*[1]

Black Mass, *df.* A sacrilegious ritual in which the Christian Mass is performed backwards.

Contents

Acknowledgements

Many people have helped me in writing this book. Norman Cohn gave me the immense benefit of his conversation, and I could not have developed the interpretation of modern politics and religion presented here without it. Conversations with Bryan Appleyard, Robert Colls, Michael Lind and Adam Philips have entered into the book in many ways. Simon Winder, my editor at Penguin, has given me invaluable suggestions and encouragement at every stage of the book's development. Tracy Bohan of the Wylie Agency UK in London, Eric Chinski at Farrar, Straus and Giroux in New York, and Nick Garrison, formerly of Doubleday Canada and now head of communications at the environmental company Zero Footprint, have been enormously helpful in giving me their comments. I am extremely grateful to David Rieff for his penetrating thoughts on a late draft. Responsibility for the book remains mine.

My biggest debt is to Mieko, who made the book possible.

John Gray

BLACK MASS

I

The Death of Utopia

Modern politics is a chapter in the history of religion. The greatest of the revolutionary upheavals that have shaped so much of the history of the past two centuries were episodes in the history of faith – moments in the long dissolution of Christianity and the rise of modern political religion. The world in which we find ourselves at the start of the new millennium is littered with the debris of utopian projects, which though they were framed in secular terms that denied the truth of religion were in fact vehicles for religious myths.

Communism and Nazism claimed to be based on science – in the case of communism the cod-science of historical materialism, in Nazism the farrago of 'scientific racism'. These claims were fraudulent but the use of pseudo-science did not stop with the collapse of totalitarianism that culminated with the dissolution of the USSR in December 1991. It continued in neo-conservative theories that claimed the world is converging on a single type of government and economic system – universal democracy, or a global free market. Despite the fact that it was presented in the trappings of social science, this belief that humanity was on the brink of a new era was only the most recent version of apocalyptic beliefs that go back to the most ancient times.

Jesus and his followers believed they lived in an End-Time when the evils of the world were about to pass away. Sickness and death, famine and hunger, war and oppression would all cease to exist after a world-shaking battle in which the forces of evil would be utterly destroyed. Such was the faith that inspired the first Christians, and though the End-Time was re-interpreted by later Christian thinkers as a metaphor for a spiritual change, visions of Apocalypse have haunted western life ever since those early beginnings.

During the Middle Ages, Europe was shaken by mass movements inspired by the belief that history was about to end and a new world be born. These medieval Christians believed that only God could bring about the new world, but faith in the End-Time did not wither away when Christianity began to decline. On the contrary, as Christianity waned the hope of an imminent End-Time became stronger and more militant. Modern revolutionaries such as the French Jacobins and the Russian Bolsheviks detested traditional religion, but their conviction that the crimes and follies of the past could be left behind in an all-encompassing transformation of human life was a secular reincarnation of early Christian beliefs. These modern revolutionaries were radical exponents of Enlightenment thinking, which aimed to replace religion with a scientific view of the world. Yet the radical Enlightenment belief that there can be a sudden break in history, after which the flaws of human society will be for ever abolished, is a by-product of Christianity.

The Enlightenment ideologies of the past centuries were very largely spilt theology. The history of the past century is not a tale of secular advance, as *bien-pensants* of Right and Left like to think. The Bolshevik and Nazi seizures of power were faith-based upheavals just as much as the Ayatollah Khomeini's theocratic insurrection in Iran. The very idea of revolution as a transforming event in history is owed to religion. Modern revolutionary movements are a continuation of religion by other means.

It is not only revolutionaries who have held to secular versions of religious beliefs. So too have liberal humanists, who see progress as a slow incremental struggle. The belief that the world is about to end and belief in gradual progress may seem to be opposites – one looking forward to the destruction of the world, the other to its improvement – but at bottom they are not so different. Whether they stress piecemeal change or revolutionary transformation, theories of progress are not scientific hypotheses. They are myths, which answer the human need for meaning.

Since the French Revolution a succession of utopian movements has transformed political life. Entire societies have been destroyed and the world changed for ever. The alteration envisioned by utopian thinkers has not come about, and for the most part their projects have produced results opposite to those they intended. That has not prevented similar projects being launched again and again right up to the start of the twenty-first century, when the world's most powerful state launched a campaign to export democracy to the Middle East and throughout the world.

Utopian projects reproduced religious myths that had inflamed mass movements of believers in the Middle Ages, and they kindled a similar violence. The secular terror of modern times is a mutant version of the violence that has accompanied Christianity throughout its history. For over 200 years the early Christian faith in an End-Time initiated by God was turned into a belief that Utopia could be achieved by human action. Clothed in science, early Christian myths of Apocalypse gave rise to a new kind of faith-based violence.

When the project of universal democracy ended in the blood-soaked streets of Iraq, this pattern began to be reversed. Utopianism suffered a heavy blow, but politics and war have not ceased to be vehicles for myth. Instead, primitive versions of religion are replacing the secular faith that has been lost. Apocalyptic religion shapes the policies of American president George W. Bush and his antagonist Mahmoud Ahmadinejad in Iran. Wherever it is happening, the revival of religion is mixed up with political conflicts, including an intensifying struggle over the Earth's shrinking reserves of natural resources; but there can be no doubt that religion is once again a power in its own right. With the death of Utopia, apocalyptic religion has re-emerged, naked and unadorned, as a force in world politics.

APOCALYPTIC POLITICS

'A new heaven and a new earth: for the first heaven and the first earth were passed away,' we read in Revelations. Cross out 'heaven', just keep the 'new earth', and you have the secret and the recipe of all utopian systems.

E. M. Cioran[1]

The religious roots of modern revolutionary movements were first systematically uncovered in Norman Cohn's seminal study *The Pursuit of the Millennium*.[2] It has often been noted that for its followers communism had many of the functions of a religion – a fact reflected in the title of a famous collection of essays by disillusioned ex-communists, *The God that Failed*, which was published not long after the start of the Cold War.[3] Cohn showed the similarities went much further than had been realized. At its height twentieth-century communism replicated many of the features of the millenarian movements that rocked Europe in late medieval times. Soviet communism was a modern millenarian revolution, and so – though the vision of the future that animated many Nazis was in some ways more negative – was Nazism.

It may be worth clarifying some key terms. Sometimes called chiliasts – a chiliad is anything containing a thousand parts, and Christian millenarians believe Jesus will return to the Earth and rule over it in a new kingdom for a thousand years – millenarians hold to an apocalyptic view of history. In common speech 'apocalyptic' denotes a catastrophic event, but in biblical terms it derives from the Greek word for unveiling – an apocalypse is a revelation in which mysteries that are written in heaven are revealed at the end of time, and for the Elect this means not catastrophe but salvation. Eschatology is the doctrine of last things and the end of the world (in Greek *eschatos* means 'last', or 'farthest'). As I have already indicated, early Christianity was an eschatological cult: Jesus and his first disciples believed that the world was destined for imminent destruction so that a new and perfect one could come into being. Eschatology does not always have this positive character – in some pagan traditions the end of the world is seen as meaning the death of the gods and final disaster. Despite the fact that the Nazis adopted a Christian demonology, negative eschatology of this kind was a strand in their ideology. However, it was a positive version of apocalyptic belief that fuelled medieval and secular millenarian movements, which expected an End-Time when the evils of the world would disappear for ever. (Millenarianism is sometimes distinguished from millennialism, with the former believing in the literal return of Christ and the latter looking forward to the arrival of some kind of holy kingdom. But there is no consistent pattern in the use of these terms, and except where otherwise indicated I will use them interchangeably.)

In the forms in which it has affected western societies millenarianism is a Christian inheritance. Most religions lack any conception of history as a story with a beginning and an end. Hindus and Buddhists view human life as a moment in a cosmic cycle; salvation means release from this unending round. Plato and his disciples in pre-Christian Europe viewed human life in much the same way. Ancient Judaism contained nothing resembling the idea that the world was about to come to an end. Christianity injected the belief that human history is a teleological process. The Greek word *telos* means 'end', a word that in English means both the terminus of a process and the goal or purpose that a process can serve. In thinking of history in teleological terms, Christians believed it had an end in both senses: history had a pre-determined purpose, and when that was achieved it would come to a close. Secular thinkers such as Marx and Fukuyama inherited this teleology, which underpins their talk of 'the end of history'. In that they view history as a movement, not necessarily inevitable but in the direction of a universal goal, theories of progress also rely on a teleological view. Standing behind all these conceptions is the belief that history must be understood not in terms of the causes of events but in terms of its purpose, which is the salvation of humanity. This idea entered western thought only with Christianity, and has shaped it ever since.

Millenarian movements may not be confined to the Christian West. In 1853 Hong Xiuquan, the leader of a movement called the Taiping Heavenly Army who believed himself to be the younger brother of Jesus, founded a utopian community in Nanjing that lasted until it was destroyed eleven years later after a conflict in which over twenty million people died.[4] The Taiping Rebellion is one of a number of Chinese uprisings moved by millenarian ideas, and while Christian missionaries may have brought these ideas to China, it may be the case that ideas of a similar kind were already present. Beliefs concerning an age of destruction followed by an era of peace guided by a celestial saviour may have existed in the country from the third century onwards.[5]

Whether or not they are uniquely western in origin, beliefs of this

5

kind have had a formative influence on western life. Medieval chiliasm reflected beliefs that can be traced back to the beginnings of Christianity. Modern political religions such as Jacobinism, Bolshevism and Nazism reproduced millenarian beliefs in the terms of science. If a simple definition of western civilization could be formulated it would have to be framed in terms of the central role of millenarian thinking.

Millenarian beliefs are one thing, millenarian movements another, and millenarian regimes something else again. Millenarian movements develop only in definite historical circumstances. Sometimes these are conditions of large-scale social dislocation, as in Tsarist Russia and Weimar Germany after the First World War; sometimes a single traumatic event, as happened in the US with 9/11. Movements of this kind are often linked with disasters. Millenarian beliefs are symptoms of a type of cognitive dissonance in which normal links between perception and reality have broken down.[6] In Russia and Germany, war and economic collapse produced full-fledged millenarian regimes, while in America an unprecedented terrorist attack produced a millenarian outbreak that included an unnecessary war and a shift in the Constitution. When and how millenarian beliefs become deciding forces in politics depends on the accidents of history.

Apocalyptic beliefs go back to the origins of Christianity and beyond. The recurrent appearance of these beliefs throughout the history of Christianity is not an incursion from outside the faith: it is a sign of something that was present from the start. The teaching of Jesus was grounded in the belief that humanity was in its final days. Eschatology was central to the movement he inspired. In this respect Jesus belonged in a Jewish apocalyptic tradition, but the radically dualistic view of the world that goes with apocalyptic beliefs is nowhere found in biblical Judaism. The central role of eschatology in the teaching of Jesus reflects the influence of other traditions.

Contemporary historical scholarship has shown beyond reasonable doubt that Jesus belonged in a heterodox current of charismatic Judaism.[7] The term 'Christian' that came to be applied to Jesus' followers comes from the Greek word *christos*, or 'the anointed one', which is also the meaning of 'messiah' in Hebrew and Aramaic. The term 'messiah' is rarely found in the Hebrew Bible and when it appears it is a title given to the king or a high priest. With the development of Christianity as a universal religion from the time of Paul onwards, 'the messiah' came to mean a divine figure sent by God to redeem all of humanity.

Originally a message directed only to other Jews, the teaching of Jesus was that the old world was about to come to an end and a new kingdom established. There would be unlimited abundance in the fruits of the earth. Those who dwell in the new kingdom – including the righteous dead, who will be raised back to life – would be rid of physical and mental ills. Living in a new world that is without corruption, they will be immortal. Jesus was sent to announce this new kingdom and rule over it. There is much that is original and striking in Jesus' ethical teaching. He not only defended the weak and powerless as other Jewish prophets had done, but he also opened his arms to the outcasts of the world. Yet the belief that a new kingdom was at hand was the heart of his message and was accepted as such by his disciples. The new kingdom did not arrive, and Jesus was arrested and executed by the Romans. The history of Christianity is a series of attempts to cope with this founding experience of eschatological disappointment.

Albert Schweitzer captured this predicament when he wrote:

In the knowledge that he is the coming son of man, Jesus lays hold of the wheel of the world to set it moving on that last revolution that is to bring all ordinary history to a close. It refuses to turn and he throws himself upon it. When it does turn it crushes him, instead of bringing the eschatological condition, that is, the condition of perfect faithfulness and the absence of guilt, he has destroyed these conditions.[8]

In fact, eschatological hope was not destroyed. Among his followers in the early Church the belief sprang up that Jesus rose from the dead and ascended into heaven. It was not long before an attempt was made to interpret Jesus' teaching of the end of the world as a metaphor for an inner change.

Already in St Paul there is the hint that the kingdom of heaven is an allegory of a spiritual change. It was Paul – a Hellenized Jew also called Saul of Tarsus – who more than anyone else turned the Jesus movement from a dissident Jewish sect into a universal religion. Paul shared the expectation of Jesus' original disciples that the world was about to come to an end, but he opened the way for a view of the End that applied to all humankind. A more systematic attempt to defuse the eschatological hopes that animated Jesus and his disciples was made by St Augustine (AD 354–430). Augustine began as a follower of the Manichean religion, which viewed evil as a permanent feature of the world, and his theology shows marked traces of this view. Whereas Mani believed the war between light and dark would go on for ever, the followers of Jesus looked forward to an End-Time in which evil would be permanently destroyed. Augustine believed that human beings were ineradicably flawed, and this doctrine of original sin became the cardinal tenet of Christian orthodoxy. Yet it may owe more to Mani than to Jesus.

Another major influence on Augustine's reformulation of Christian belief was Platonism. Much impressed by Plato's idea that spiritual things belong in an eternal realm, Augustine suggested that the end of time should be understood in spiritual terms – not as an event that will happen at some point in the future but as an inner transformation that can happen at any time. At the same time Augustine introduced into Christianity a categorical distinction between the City of Man and the City of God. Because human life is marked by original sin, the two cities can never be one. Evil has been at work in every human heart since the Fall of Man; it cannot be defeated in this world. This doctrine gave Christianity an anti-utopian bent it never completely lost, and Christians were spared the disillusionment that comes to all who expect any basic change in human affairs. In Augustinian terms, the belief that evil can be destroyed, which inspired medieval millenarians and resurfaced in the Bush administration, is highly unorthodox. Yet some such belief was a central feature of the apocalyptic cult to which the followers of Jesus belonged. The outbursts of chiliasm that recur throughout western history are heretical reversions to Christian origins.

By de-literalizing the hope of the End, Augustine preserved eschatology while reducing its risks. The kingdom of God existed in a realm out of time, and the inner transformation it symbolized could be realized at any point in history. With the denunciation of millennialism by the Council of Ephesus in 431 the Church adopted this Augustinian view, but that did not stop the eruption of chiliastic movements that harked back to the beliefs that inspired Jesus. Nor did it end the role of chiliasm in the Church itself. In the twelfth century Joachim of Flora (1132–1202) reversed Augustine's theology. Believing that he had gleaned an esoteric meaning from the scriptures, Joachim – a Cistercian abbot who had travelled in the Holy Land where he experienced some kind of spiritual illumination – turned the Christian doctrine of the Trinity into a philosophy of history in which humanity ascended through three stages. From the Age of the Father via the Age of the Son it would move to the Age of the Spirit – a time of universal brotherhood that would continue until the Last Judgement. Each of these ages had a leader, with Abraham at the head of the First and Jesus the Second. A new and final leader who embodied the third person of the divine trinity would inaugurate the Third Age, which Joachim expected to arrive in 1260. Joachim's trinitarian philosophy of history re-infused medieval Christianity with eschatological fervour, and versions of his three-phase scheme reappear in many later Christian thinkers. Taken up by a radical wing of the Franciscan order, Joachite prophecy inspired millenarian movements in southern Europe. In Germany it helped create a messianic cult around Emperor Frederick II, who after conquering the city in a crusade crowned himself king of Jerusalem and was denounced by Pope Gregory IX as the Antichrist.

The division of human history into three ages had a profound impact on secular thought. Hegel's view of the evolution of human freedom in three dialectical stages, Marx's theory of the movement from primitive communism through class society to global communism, Auguste Comte's Positivist vision of humankind's evolution from religious to metaphysical and scientific stages of development all reproduce the three-part scheme. The common division of history into three phases – ancient, medieval and modern – echoes the Joachite scheme. Even more strikingly, as will be seen in the next chapter, it was Joachim's prophecy of a third age that gave the Nazi state the name of the Third Reich. (Concepts such as ancient and modern have become indispensable terms of art, and I will use them even as I criticize the scheme of thought they express.)

In secular versions of the Apocalypse the new age comes about through human action. For Jesus and his disciples the new kingdom

9

could come about only through the will of God; but God's will was resisted by the power of evil, which they personified as Belial, or Satan. In this view of things the world is divided into good and evil forces; there is even a suggestion that humanity may be ruled by a diabolical power. Nothing like this can be found in the Hebrew Bible. Satan appears in the book of Job, but as an emissary of Yahweh, not as a personification of evil. A view of the world as a battle-ground between good and evil forces developed only in later Jewish apocalyptic traditions.

There are many similarities between the Zoroastrian religion of Zurvanism and Jewish apocalyptic beliefs of the kind recorded in the Dead Sea Scrolls, and Jewish apocalyptic thought most likely reflects the influence of Zoroastrianism. It seems to have been Zoroaster – an Iranian prophet also known as Zarathustra who lived some time between 1500 and 1200 BC – who first conceived of human life as a battle between light and darkness that could end in a victory for light. Zoroastrianism is one of the most peaceful religions in history. Nevertheless, through his formative influence on Judaism, Christianity and Islam, Zoroaster may be the ultimate source of the faith-based violence that has broken out again and again throughout western history.

Many traditions have seen human life as a war between good and evil, but they have taken for granted that the conflict will go on for ever. An unending alternation of light and dark is found in Egyptian myth. Some have expected the struggle to end in darkness – the eighth-century BC Greek poet Hesiod pictured human history as a process of decline from a primordial Golden Age to an age of iron in which humanity would be destroyed. If there is anything resembling a perfect society it is located in the past – it was never envisioned that the cosmic struggle could end in victory for light. Even Zoroaster may not have believed its triumph was preordained. Rather than announcing the end of the world, Zoroastrian texts call followers of the prophet to a struggle whose outcome remains in doubt. Even so, the belief that good *could* triumph was a new development in human thought, and as far as we can tell it came from Zoroaster.[9]

This dualistic view of the world was inherited by the religion of Mani – the later Iranian prophet born around AD 216 in Babylonia and martyred as a heretic by the Zoroastrian authorities in 277, whose teaching had such a deep influence on Augustine. Mani differed from Zoroaster in believing that a duality of light and dark is a permanent feature of the world. Manicheism spread as far as China, adopting some of the imagery and symbolism of Buddhism in the process. Throughout these transformations the Manichees retained their belief that evil could never be eradicated. On this point the religion of Mani differs radically from Zoroastrianism and from the teaching of Jesus.

Manichean dualism entered into Gnosticism, which despite being persecuted by Christianity reappeared in many different guises right up to modern times. Gnosticism is a tradition of forbidding complexity, but its central vision of a dark world governed by demonic forces had a profound impact on the history of religion. In the first two or three centuries after the death of Jesus there was a Gnostic current within Christianity, distinguished from others by its assertion that only those who shared in the secret teachings passed on by Jesus could be saved. The term Gnosticism comes from the Greek word *gnosis*, which means 'knowledge', and in the turbulent world of early Christianity, when nearly every aspect of Christian belief was intensely contested, Gnostics embodied the belief that salvation comes to those – perhaps only a few – who possess a type of esoteric spiritual insight and consists not in physical immortality in this world but in liberation from the human body and the material world. Though this set of beliefs had little in common with those of Jesus and was condemned by the early Church, it remained a strand in Christianity. Too little remains of their texts to be certain, but a type of Gnosticism seems to have resurfaced among the Cathars, who flourished in twelfth-century France until Pope Innocent III launched a crusade against them and (after a forty-year war in which around half a million people were killed) nearly erased them from history. However, Gnosticism was not destroyed. It survived and reinvented itself, appearing in many unexpected guises, including – according to Hans Jonas, author of a masterly study of Gnostic traditions – the philosophy of Martin Heidegger.[10]

Yet it was not Gnosticism that re-emerged in the repeated outbreaks of millenarianism that occurred throughout the history of

Christianity. It was the belief in a cosmic war between good and evil, a belief that had animated Jesus and his disciples, and which echoed the dualistic world-view of Zoroaster. Through its formative influence on western monotheism – of which Islam and modern political religions are integral parts – Zoroaster's view of the world shaped much of western thought and politics. When Nietzsche declared that good and evil are an invention of Zarathustra he may have been exaggerating, but he was not entirely wrong.

Christianity injected eschatology into the heart of western civilization, and despite Augustine it has reappeared time and again. Between the eleventh and sixteenth centuries, movements inspired by millenarian beliefs developed in England and Bohemia, France and Italy, Germany and Spain and many other parts of Europe. Whether the people they attracted were affected by war, plague or economic hardship, these movements thrived among groups who found themselves in a society they could no longer recognize or identify with. The most extraordinary was the Brethren of the Free Spirit, a network of adepts and disciples that extended across large areas of Europe for several centuries.[11] The Free Spirit may not have been only a Christian heresy. The Beghards, or holy beggars, as followers of the Free Spirit were sometimes known, wore robes similar to those of Sufis, who preached similar heterodox beliefs in twelfth-century Spain and elsewhere, and the Free Spirit may also have imbibed inspiration from surviving Gnostic traditions, which were never only Christian. In any event, before they were anything else – Christian or Muslim – the Brethren of the Free Spirit were mystics who believed they had access to a type of experience beyond ordinary understanding. This illumination was not, as the Church believed, a rare episode in the life of the believer granted by God as an act of grace. Those who had known this state became incapable of sin and could no longer be distinguished – in their own eyes – from God. Released from the moral ties that restrain ordinary humanity they could do as they willed. This sense of being divinely privileged was expressed in a condemnation of all established institutions – not only the Church but also the family and private property – as fetters on spiritual liberty.

It might be thought that mystical beliefs of this sort could not have much practical impact. In fact, interacting with millenarian beliefs about a coming End-Time, they helped fuel peasant revolts in several parts of late medieval Europe. In the town of Münster in north-west Germany this volatile mix gave birth to an experiment in communism. By the early part of the sixteenth century the Reformation that unseated the Catholic Church in parts of Europe was producing sects more radical than anything envisaged by Luther, whose theology pointed towards obedience to the emerging modern state, or by Calvin, who insisted on strict institutions of church governance. Chief among these sects were the Anabaptists, a movement aiming to recover the teachings of early Christianity. The sects who made up this movement encouraged the practice of rebaptism as a symbol of the believer's rejection of the Church and the prevailing social order. In early 1534, after converting large numbers of preachers, nuns and laypeople, the Anabaptists carried out their first armed uprising and seized control of Münster's town hall and marketplace. The city became an Anabaptist stronghold, with Lutherans fleeing while Anabaptists from nearby towns flocked in. It was announced that the rest of the Earth would be destroyed before Easter, but Münster would be saved to become the New Jerusalem.

Catholics and Lutherans were expelled while those who remained were rebaptised in the town square. The cathedral was sacked and its books burnt. Later, all books apart from the Bible were banned. The first steps to common ownership were taken. All money, gold and silver had to be handed over. The doors of houses had to be left open at all times. Under the leadership of a former apprentice tailor Jan Bockelson (otherwise known as John of Leyden) these measures were taken further. Private ownership was forbidden and direction of labour introduced along with capital punishment for a wide range of offences. Wives who refused to obey their husbands could be put to death – as could adulterers, who included anyone who married outside the Anabaptist community. This puritanical regime did not last. A form of polygamy was introduced under which it became a capital offence for a woman to remain unmarried. This did not last either – some women refused to comply and were executed. After that, easy divorce was allowed, leading to a version of free love.

In the autumn of 1534 Bockelson proclaimed himself king of Münster. He saw himself not as a worldly ruler but as a Messiah presiding over the world's last days. In an innovation that would be followed by the Jacobins he gave new names to streets and buildings and instituted a new calendar. Within days of the new order executions began, with women being prominent among those put to death. By now the town was under heavy siege from forces loyal to the Church, and the population was starving. Bockelson ordered spectacular celebrations for the distraction of his famished subjects – races, dances and theatrical performances. At the same time he banned unauthorized meetings. The famine continued, and in June 1535 the town's defences were penetrated. Bockelson was captured. After months of public humiliation he was tortured to death with red-hot irons in the town square.

The theocratic-communist regime John of Leyden installed in Münster bears all the marks of millenarianism. Norman Cohn identifies millenarian sects and movements as holding to an idea of salvation that has five distinctive features: it is *collective*, in that it is enjoyed by the community of the faithful; *terrestrial*, in that it is realized on earth rather than in heaven or in an after-life; *imminent*, in that it is bound to come soon and suddenly; *total*, in that it will not just improve life on earth but transform and perfect it; and *miraculous*, in that its coming is achieved or assisted by divine agency.[12]

Modern revolutionaries from the Jacobins onwards share these beliefs, but whereas the millenarians believed that only God could remake the world, modern revolutionaries imagined it could be reshaped by humanity alone. This is a notion as far-fetched as anything believed in medieval times. Perhaps for that reason it has always been presented as having the authority of science. Modern politics has been driven by the belief that humanity can be delivered from immemorial evils by the power of knowledge. In its most radical forms this belief underpinned the experiments in revolutionary utopianism that defined the last two centuries.

THE BIRTH OF UTOPIA

... people appeared who began devising ways of bringing
men together again, so that each individual, without ceasing
to prize himself above all others, might not thwart any
other, so that all might live in harmony. Wars were waged
for the sake of this notion. All the belligerents believed at
the same time that science, wisdom, and the instinct of
self-preservation would eventually compel men to unite in
a rational and harmonious society, and therefore, to speed
up the process in the meantime, 'the wise' strove with all
expedition to destroy 'the unwise' and those who failed to
grasp their idea, so they might not hinder its triumph.

Fyodor Dostoyevsky[13]

Utopia has not always been a revolutionary idea or even one that is overtly political. In many cultures and throughout most of history, humanity has been haunted by the thought of a perfect society; but it has interpreted this as a memory of a lost paradise rather than a glimpse of an achievable future. Plato placed his ideal republic in a Golden Age before history, and until around two hundred years ago perfect societies were imagined as being situated in an irrecoverable past or else in distant places not recorded on any map. Sir Thomas More, author of *Utopia* (1515) – a term he coined, meaning both 'a good place' and 'nowhere' – set his imagined community in a far-off land. Even when the idea of Utopia has been used as a tool of social reform it has not always been revolutionary. Many utopians have aimed not to over- turn society but to create an ideal community that society could use as a model. Utopianism was a movement of withdrawal from the world before it was an attempt to remake the world by force.

In the nineteenth century, utopian communities were established by a number of religious reformers and ethical socialists. John Humphrey Noyes (1811–86) – an ordained minister who believed he had reached a condition of sinless union with God – set up the Oneida community in upstate New York in 1848 to embody the principles of 'Christian perfectionism', 'Bible communism' and 'complex marriage'. In 1825 the British industrialist and socialist Robert Owen (1771–1858) purchased the town of Harmonie, Indiana, and set up New Harmony to embody the idea of communal living. Charles Fourier (1772–1837) – a French utopian socialist who looked forward to the appearance of new species, 'anti-lions' and 'anti-whales' that would exist solely to serve humans, and who (according to Nathaniel Hawthorne in his novel *The Blithedale Romance*) believed that a time would come in the progress of humanity when the sea would acquire the flavour of lemonade – advocated the establishment of 'phalansteres', communes whose members would practise a form of free love.

While they had an impact on radical thought, these utopian communities had very little influence on the societies that surrounded them. Opposed to common human inclinations and infected with the eccentricities of their founders, most of them failed in a generation or less. One might think that the disappearance of these communities is enough to establish their utopian character. But what is it that makes a community or a project utopian? There have been many attempts to define utopianism, and no single formula can cover all its varieties. Isaiah Berlin has written:

All the Utopias known to us are based on the discoverability and harmony of objectively true ends, true for all men, at all times and places. This holds of every ideal city, from Plato's Republic and his Laws, and Zeno's anarchist world, and the City of the Sun of Iambulus, to the Utopias of Thomas More and Campanella, Bacon and Harrington and Fénelon. The communist societies of Mably and Morelly, the state capitalism of Saint-Simon, the Phalansteres of Fourier, the various combinations of anarchism and collectivism of Owen and Godwin, Cabet, William Morris and Chernyshevsky, Bellamy, Hertzka and others (there is no lack of them in the nineteenth century) rest on three pillars of social optimism in the West ... that the central problems of men are, in the end, the same throughout history; that they are in principle soluble; and that the solutions form a harmonious whole ... this is common ground to the many varieties of reformist and revolutionary optimism, from Bacon to Condorcet, from the Communist Manifesto to modern technocrats, communists, anarchists and seekers after alternative societies.[14]

Contrary to Berlin, utopianism does not always involve a claim to objective knowledge of human needs. The history of religion contains many examples of communities aiming to embody an ideal of perfection that has come to them as a divine revelation. Such communities are based on faith rather than any claim to knowledge, but to the extent that their ideal of perfection is at odds with basic human traits they are still utopian. The theocratic-communist city-state set up by John of Leyden was one such religious utopia.

Berlin is right that a core feature of all utopias is a dream of ultimate harmony. Whether human ends are believed to be unchanging, as in Plato, or evolving, as in Marx, whether the nature of these ends is known through the scientific discovery of natural laws or accepted as a matter of faith, the normal conflicts of human life are left behind. Clashes of interest among individuals and social groups, antagonism between and within ideals of the good life, choices among evils – these conflicts, which are endemic in every society, are reduced to insignificance.

The pursuit of a condition of harmony defines utopian thought and discloses its basic unreality. Conflict is a universal feature of human life. It seems to be natural for human beings to want incompatible things – excitement and a quiet life, freedom and security, truth and a picture of the world that flatters their sense of self-importance. A conflict-free existence is impossible for humans, and wherever it is attempted the result is intolerable to them. If human dreams were achieved, the result would be worse than any aborted Utopia. Luckily, visions of an ideal world are never realized. At the same time, the prospect of a life without conflict has a powerful appeal. In effect it is the idea of perfection attributed in some traditions to God. In religion the idea of perfection answers a need for individual salvation. In politics it expresses a similar yearning, but it soon runs up against other human needs. Utopias are dreams of collective deliverance that in waking life are found to be nightmares.

Utopian projects are by their nature unachievable. As Hume put it: 'All plans of government which suppose great reformation in the manners of mankind are plainly imaginary.'[15] Hume's formula sounds definitive, but it is open to the objection of being too conservative. What counts as a 'great reformation in the manners of mankind', and is it true that such reformations are 'plainly imaginary'? Have not several such changes taken place in human history? Even if a 'plan of government' is unachievable, might not the attempt to achieve it make the world a better place? There is a school of thought that insists on the indispensable value of the utopian imagination. In this view, utopian thinking opens up vistas that would otherwise remain closed, expanding the range of human possibility. To remain within the boundaries of what is believed to be practicable is to abdicate hope and adopt an attitude of passive acceptance that amounts to complicity with oppression.

According to many who accept this view, the disastrous consequences of utopian projects – in Soviet Russia and Maoist China, for example – do not flow from the projects themselves. Western utopian theories are guiltless; it is Russian or Chinese traditions that are at fault. In the next chapter I examine in greater detail the idea that actually existing communism was a deformation of Marx's vision. At this point it need only be pointed out that Lenin's readiness to use terror to bring about a new world was in no sense new. The use of inhumane methods to achieve impossible ends is the essence of revolutionary utopianism. The Bolshevik Revolution was the culmination of a European revolutionary tradition, beginning with the Jacobins and to which Marx belonged, that accepted systematic terror as a legitimate means of transforming society.

Actually existing communism was not a noble humanist ideal corrupted by contact with backward peoples. Repression flowed from the ideal itself. In *The Communist Manifesto* Marx and Engels declared that communism was 'the riddle of history solved', but they were in no doubt that the solution would be reached only after much blood had been shed. Terror has been a feature not only of the Soviet and Maoist regimes but also of more recent communist movements such as the Shining Path in Peru,[16] which killed tens of thousands of people in pursuit of a world better than any that has ever existed. This vision animated every twentieth-century communist movement, and sustaining it led inescapably to repression.

It was not Marx's economic theory that led to this result. As an analyst of capitalism Marx has few rivals. It was Marx who understood before anyone else the advance of globalization that would render the national economies of the nineteenth century obsolete and destroy bourgeois life as known in the past. Perhaps only the Austrian economist Joseph Schumpeter, writing in the middle of the twentieth century, grasped the revolutionary character of capitalism quite as firmly. Marx perceived that capitalism is an economic system that unsettles every aspect of human life. Not only politics and government but also culture and society are continuously transformed under the impact of the anarchic energies of the market. Movements aiming to free up the market while reinstating 'traditional values' dominated much of late twentieth-century politics. While effectively reshaping society to serve the imperatives of the market, politicians such as Thatcher and Blair wanted at the same time to revive the virtues of bourgeois life. Yet, as Marx perceived, the actual effect of the un-fettered market is to overturn established social relationships and forms of ethical life – including those of bourgeois societies.

Marx showed how unreal are all visions of marrying the free market to bourgeois values. Far from being utopian, his account of capitalism is a vital corrective to the utopian visions that have distorted politics over the past generation. It is Marx's vision of the alternative to capitalism that is utopian. Though he understood capitalism better than most economists in his day or ours, Marx's conception of com-munism was dangerously impractical. Central planning was bound to fail: no one can know enough to plan a modern economy and no one is good enough to be entrusted with the power to govern it. Worse, Marx believed that with the arrival of communism the con-flicts of values that had existed throughout history would cease, and society could be organized around a single conception of the good life. It was a belief that was to have disastrous consequences, as will be seen when the Soviet experiment is examined in Chapter 2.

Today as in the twentieth century the dangers of utopianism are denied. Now as then it is believed that there is nothing to stop humans remaking themselves, and the world in which they live, as they please. This fantasy lies behind many aspects of contemporary culture, and in these circumstances it is *dystopian* thinking we most need. If we seek to understand our present condition we should turn to Huxley's *Brave New World* or Orwell's *1984*, Wells's *Island of Dr Moreau* or Philip K. Dick's *Do Androids Dream of Electric Sheep?*, Zamiatin's

We or Nabokov's *Bend Sinister*, Burroughs' *Naked Lunch* or Ballard's *Super-Cannes* – prescient glimpses of the ugly reality that results from pursuing unrealizable dreams.

The question remains how a utopia is to be recognized. How do we know when a project is unrealizable? Some of the greatest human advances were once believed to be impossible. The campaign to abolish slavery that began in the early nineteenth century was opposed on the ground that slavery will always be with us. Yet it was fortunately successful – the Slavery Abolition Act was passed in Britain in 1833 making slavery illegal throughout the British Empire, serfdom was abolished in Tsarist Russia in 1861 and in 1865 the Thirteenth Amendment was passed in the US making slavery illegal. These acts removed a barbarous practice and expanded human freedom. Does this not show the value of the utopian imagination? I think not. To seek to end slavery was not to pursue an unrealizable goal. Many societies have lacked slavery, and to abolish the institution was only to achieve a state of affairs others have taken for granted. At the same time, the condition of servitude was not abolished. During the twentieth century slave labour was used on a vast scale in Nazi Germany, Soviet Russia and Maoist China. Humans were not the tradable commodities they had been in chattel slavery; but they were resources that could be used at will, and exploited until they died. Slavery was reinvented in new forms, as horrible as any in the past. At the start of the twenty-first century, a form of chattel slavery has re-emerged in the form of human trafficking.

A project is utopian if there are no circumstances under which it can be realized. All the dreams of a society from which coercion and power have been for ever removed – Marxist or anarchist, liberal or technocratic – are utopian in the strong sense that they can never be achieved because they break down on the enduring contradictions of human needs. A project can also be utopian without being unrealizable under any circumstances – it is enough if it can be known to be impossible under any circumstances that can be brought about or foreseen. The project of engineering a western-style market economy in post-communist Russia fell into this category, and so did that of establishing liberal democracy in post-Saddam Iraq. In each case it was clear from the start that the necessary conditions of success were lacking and could not be created by any programme of action. A little insight into human nature and history was all that was needed to be able to know in advance that these experiments would end in a familiar mix of crime and farce.

Disasters of this magnitude do not come about as a result of ignorance, error or disinformation – though doubtless all three were at work. They are consequences of a type of thinking that has lost any sense of reality. Defining a sense of reality is a tricky business, but it is not difficult to know when it is lacking. For the utopian mind the defects of every known society are not signs of flaws in human nature. They are marks of universal repression – which, however, will soon be ended. History is a nightmare from which we must awake, and when we do we will find that human possibilities are limitless. To assess utopian projects as merely flawed exercises in rational policy-making is to miss the point. Such adventures are products of a view of the world, once found only in religious cults and revolutionary sects but for a time firmly established in western governments, that believes political action can bring about an alteration in the human condition.

As we understand it today, utopianism began to develop along with the retreat of Christian belief. Yet the utopian faith in a condition of future harmony is a Christian inheritance, and so is the modern idea of progress. Though it may seem at odds with the belief that the world is irredeemably evil and about to come to an end, an idea of progress has been latent in Christianity from early times, and it may be in the last book of the Christian Bible – St John's Revelation – that it is first advanced. As the American historian Ernest Lee Tuveson noted:

In the Revelation we see a great drama which joins angels, demons, monstrous villains, and the people of God in one great action. It involves the human race, which is inescapably divided into redeemed and condemned ... what redeems this frightful prediction is the confidence that good is, act by act, destroying evil. Mankind has suffered and still suffers many woes, but they are being eliminated ... Thus, strange as the idea may seem at first glance, the movement of the Revelation is in its way *progressive* – perhaps the first expression of the idea of history as progress.[17]

A hint of the idea of progress may be found in the Book of Revelation, and the early Christians believed they embodied something better than anything that existed in the ancient pagan and Jewish worlds. A belief in moral progress has always been part of Christianity, but it remained dormant until the Reformation. Puritans served as a vehicle for the idea – often called post-millennialism – that human effort could hasten the arrival of a perfect new world. In contrast with pre-millennialists who believe Jesus will *initiate* the Millennium, the Puritans believed that Jesus would come and rule over the world *after* the arrival of the Millennium – a Millennium generated as much by human effort as by divine will. Each is a version of millenarian belief.

The idea that the world must soon end and the idea that it is moving to a better condition look antithetical – after all, why strive to improve it when it is going to be destroyed in the near future? Yet both express a view of history that hardly exists outside cultures shaped by western monotheism. In the Book of Revelation history could be seen as a progressive movement *because* it was believed to have an end-point when evil would be overcome, and the same is true in theories such as Marxism. On the other hand theories of progress that claim to reject any belief in a final state of perfection turn out, on closer inspection, to retain the idea that history is a struggle between good and evil forces. Both these views take for granted that human salvation is worked out in history – a Christian myth without which the political religions of modern times could not have come into being.

Millenarian belief was at the heart of the Reformation, when it began to assume shapes that are closer to those found in modern revolutionary movements. Despite the opposition of John Calvin and Martin Luther, who led the rebellion against the authority of the Catholic Church, belief in an impending End-Time was rife among the more radical dissenting sects. Hundreds of thousands of agricultural and urban workers pillaged monasteries and demanded large-scale changes in society. They were supported in their struggle by prophetic divines such as Thomas Müntzer, a Protestant pastor who believed all their demands would be met in the imminent new world. In fact the Peasants' Revolt, which he led, was crushed, with Müntzer and around a hundred thousand others being killed in the process.

It was in seventeenth-century England that the millenarian currents of late medieval times started their mutation into modern revolutionary movements. All the main protagonists of the English Revolution were steeped in biblical prophecy, with figures as diverse as King James and Sir Walter Raleigh taking seriously the idea that the world would end in the near future.[18] If radical sects such as the Ranters carried on the millenarian traditions of the Middle Ages,[19] the Fifth Monarchy Men were 'the first organized millenarian political movement'.[20] There is in fact no clear dividing line between the two. The Fifth Monarchists were an anti-Cromwellian movement of anything between 20,000–40,000 armed men, taking their inspiration from the prophet Daniel and the Book of Revelation, who believed the existing order would pass away in 1666. So called in reference to Nebuchadnezzar's dream of a new divine kingdom coming into being after the four earthly kingdoms of ancient times, the Fifth Monarchy Men aimed to install divine rule in England. At a rank-and-file level the millenarian groups that were active in the English Revolution can be compared to the soldiers' Soviet that played such a key role in the early stages of the Russian Revolution.[21] Continuing a medieval chiliastic tradition, these groups began a modern revolutionary tradition of armed missionaries that was later embodied in the Jacobins and the Bolsheviks.

A common academic view sees such millenarian groups as primitive versions of later revolutionary movements. As the British historian Eric Hobsbawm has put it, millenarianism is 'an extremely useful phenomenon, which modern social and political movements can profitably utilize to spread their range of influence'.[22] In other words, millenarian beliefs are metaphors for the rational hopes that guided figures such as Lenin. The truth, I think, is the opposite. Though they were reactions against the existing social order, the secular hopes that inspired the most extreme modern revolutions were not only, or even mainly, demands for specific improvements in society. They were vehicles for apocalyptic myths. Rather than withering away in modern times, or evolving into more rational forms, movements driven by these myths have reappeared in new guises.

As new political movements began to take over, older types of millenarianism did not die out. The historian of English working-class movements E. P. Thompson noted:

The wilder sectaries of the English Revolution – Ranters and Fifth Mon-archy Men – were never totally extinguished, with their literal interpret-ations of the Book of Revelation and their anticipations of a New Jerusalem descending from above. The Muggletonians (or followers of Ludovic Mug-gleton) were still preaching in the fields and parks of London at the end of the eighteenth century . . . Any dramatic event, such as the Lisbon earth-quake of 1755, aroused apocalyptic expectations. There was, indeed, a millenarial instability at the heart of Methodism itself.[23]

Late eighteenth-century religious movements such as Methodism displayed many millenarian features. Whole villages in Yorkshire proclaimed they were 'saved'. At the start of the nineteenth century Joanna Southcott led a mass movement in which tens of thousands of people received from her a special seal, which ensured they would join the company of the Elect after the Millennium.[24]

Around the end of the eighteenth century apocalyptic movements existed side by side with dissenting sects that prepared the way for the secular belief in progress. William Godwin – the novelist and anarchist who promoted a belief in human perfectibility – was born in a family of Sandemanians, a small Christian sect, while Thomas Paine – who achieved fame as an ideologue of the American Revo-lution – began as a Quaker. Dissenting religious traditions interacted with English Jacobinism – some of Joanna Southcott's followers were former Jacobins, for example – until the Jacobin movement in England was destroyed in the wave of repression after the French Revolution.

Post-millennial beliefs were widely current by the start of the nine-teenth century. Christian thinkers who propagated these beliefs in-sisted that humanity served only as God's helper. Advancing scientific knowledge was welcomed as a means of realizing the divine plan. But the idea that human action can initiate a radical shift in history had been injected into western life. It was not long before post-millennialism mutated into the Enlightenment belief that humanity is an inherently progressive species.

The philosophers of the Enlightenment aimed to supplant Christi-anity, but they could do so only if they were able to satisfy the hopes it had implanted. As a result they could not admit – what pre-Christian thinkers took for granted – that human history has no overall meaning. Carl Becker – the American scholar whose book *The Heavenly City of the Eighteenth-Century Philosophers* (1932) showed how much Christianity shaped the Enlightenment – described the problem they faced:

In order to defeat Christian philosophy the Philosophers had to meet it on the level of certain common preconceptions. They could never rout the enemy by denying that human life is a significant drama – the notion was too widely, too unconsciously held, even by the Philosophers themselves, for that; but, admitting that human life is a significant drama, the Philosophers could claim that the Christian version of the drama was a false and pernicious one; and their best hope of displacing the Christian version lay in recasting it, and bringing it up to date.[25]

Many modern thinkers have tried to avoid a view of history as a battle of good and evil and instead presented it as a series of stages. In this view human knowledge advances in cumulative fashion, and so do improvements in ethics and politics: progress in science will be matched by progress in society, and history is a march to a better world. There is no mention here of any final battle, but it has proved impossible to avoid apocalyptic thinking. By maintaining that the crimes of history are the result of error, Enlightenment philosophers create a problem of evil as insoluble as any that confronts Christian theologians. Why are humans so fond of error? Why has growing knowledge been used to establish new kinds of tyranny and wage ever more destructive wars? In struggling to answer these questions Enlightenment thinkers cannot help falling back into a view of history as a battle between light and dark. The light may be that of knowledge and the darkness that of ignorance, but the view of the world is the same.

Modern political religions may reject Christianity, but they cannot do without demonology. The Jacobins, the Bolsheviks and the Nazis all believed vast conspiracies were mounted against them, as do radical Islamists today. It is never the flaws of human nature that stand in the way of Utopia. It is the workings of evil forces. Ultimately these dark forces will fail, but only after they have tried to block human advance by every kind of nefarious device. This is the classic millenarian syndrome, and in the forms in which they have shaped modern politics the millenarian and the utopian mentality are one and the same.[26]

During much of the nineteenth century, utopianism was embodied in voluntary communities that were often ridiculous but usually harmless. These communities lived in hopes of a fundamental alteration in human affairs, but they did not try to bring it about by force. Twentieth-century revolutionary movements were shaped by a different utopian tradition. It was the Jacobins who first conceived of terror as an instrument for perfecting humanity. Medieval Europe was no oasis of peace – it was wracked by almost continuous wars. Yet no one believed violence could perfect humanity. Belief in original sin stood immovably in the way. Millenarians were ready to use force to overthrow the power of the Church but none of them imagined that violence could bring about the Millennium – only God could do that. It was only with the Jacobins that it came to be believed that humanly initiated terror could create a new world.

The Jacobins began as a radical club, which soon exercised a powerful influence on the course of the French Revolution. Through leaders such as Maximilien Robespierre – himself a casualty of the Terror who was guillotined in 1794, and who in 1792 delivered a prophetic warning against the dangers of trying to export freedom by force of arms – they made terror an integral part of the revolutionary programme. Influenced by Rousseau's belief in innate human goodness, the Jacobins believed society had become corrupt as a result of repression but could be transformed by the methodical use of force. The Terror was necessary in order to defend the Revolution against internal and external enemies; but it was also a technique of civic education and an instrument of social engineering. To reject terror on moral grounds was unforgivable. As Robespierre put it in a speech to the National Convention in Paris on 26 February 1794, 'Pity is treason.' A higher form of human life was within reach – even a higher type of human being – but only once humanity had been purified by violence.

This faith in violence flowed into many later revolutionary currents. Nineteenth-century anarchists such as Nechayev and Bakunin, the Bolsheviks Lenin and Trotsky, anti-colonial thinkers such as Frantz

Fanon, the regimes of Mao and Pol Pot, the Baader-Meinhof Gang, the Italian Red Guard in the 1980s, radical Islamic movements and neo-conservative groups mesmerized by fantasies of creative destruction – these highly disparate elements are at one in their faith in the liberating power of violence. In this they are all disciples of the Jacobins.[27]

The French Terror of 1792–4 is the prototype for every subsequent millenarian revolution. Tens of thousands lost their lives through execution by revolutionary tribunals and death in prison. Once we include the deaths resulting from quashing the counter-revolutionary insurgency in the Vendée (a region of western France where counter-revolutionaries were killed by methods that included mass drowning) the human casualties of the Terror run far higher. In all, up to a third of the population of that region may have been slaughtered – a level of mass killing that can be compared with that which occurred in Pol Pot's Cambodia.[28] Like many revolutionaries after them the Jacobins introduced a new calendar to mark the new era they had begun. They were not mistaken in believing it marked a turning point in history. The era of political mass murder had arrived.

An Enlightenment thinker such as the Marquis de Condorcet – who died in prison a day after his arrest by Robespierre's Committee of Public Safety – may have been horrified by the manner in which his belief in human progress came to fuel political terror. Yet the fact that terror came to be used to promote Enlightenment ideals was not surprising. It followed from the belief that human life could be transformed by a human act of will. Why shrink from violence? Throughout history it had been used to sustain tyranny. In the hands of revolutionaries it could be used to liberate humanity.

From one point of view the Jacobins made a decisive break with Christianity. From another they offered, in a radically altered form, the Christian promise of universal salvation. Christianity implanted vast new moral hopes in the ancient world. Paganism was distinguished by its extreme moral modesty: it took as given that only a few people would ever live the good life. Socrates might argue that the wise person cannot be harmed; but Greek tragedy mocked the philosopher's reasoning and in any case Socrates never supposed most people could be wise. Again, Judaism is a historical religion; but it does not narrate the history of all humankind as a single story with an apocalyptic end. Christianity alone offered the prospect of salvation in a transfigured world – and offered it to everyone.

If Christianity sparked a hope of world-renewal that had not existed in the ancient world it also spawned a new type of violence. The Christian promise of universal salvation was inherited by its secular successors. But whereas in Christianity salvation was promised only in the life hereafter, modern political religions offer the prospect of salvation in the future – even, disastrously, the near future. In a seeming paradox, modern revolutionary movements renew the apocalyptic myths of early Christianity.

With the Jacobins, that utopianism became a revolutionary movement and modern secular religion a political force. Post-millennialist Christians propagated beliefs that mutated into the secular faith in progress; but so long as history was believed to be governed by providence there was no attempt to direct it by violence. While Christianity was unchallenged, Utopia was a dream pursued by marginal cults. The decline of Christianity and the rise of revolutionary utopianism go together. When Christianity was rejected, its eschatological hopes did not disappear. They were repressed, only to return as projects of universal emancipation.

THE UTOPIAN RIGHT AS A MODERN MILLENARIAN MOVEMENT

The enemy has got a face. He's called Satan. And we're going to destroy him.
Lt Colonel Gareth Brandl of the US Marines on leading his troops into the assault on the Iraqi city of Falluja[29]

In the last century utopianism was found mainly on the far Left. The Nazis attempted to realize a utopian vision that condemned much of humanity to enslavement or extermination, but for the most part the utopias that shaped politics were visions of human emancipation. Towards the end of the last century the pursuit of Utopia entered the political mainstream. In future only one kind of regime would be legitimate: American-style democratic capitalism – the final form of human government, as it was termed in the fleeting and now forgotten mood of hubris that followed the Soviet collapse. Led by the United States, western governments committed themselves to installing democracy throughout the world – an impossible dream that in many countries could only produce chaos. At the same time they launched a 'war against terror' that failed to distinguish between new threats and the normal conflicts of history. The Right was possessed by fantasies, and like the utopian visions of the last century – but far more quickly – its grandiose projects have crumbled into dust.

In the twentieth century it seemed utopian movements could come to power only in dictatorial regimes. Yet after 9/11 utopian thinking came to shape foreign policy in the world's pre-eminent democracy. In many ways the Bush administration behaved like a revolutionary regime. It was prepared to engage in pre-emptive attacks on sovereign states in order to achieve its goals, while at the same time it has been ready to erode long-established American freedoms. It established a concentration camp in Guantánamo whose inmates are beyond the reach of normal legal protection, denied the protection of *habeas corpus* to terrorist suspects, set up an apparatus of surveillance to monitor the population and authorized American officials to practise what in any other country would be defined as torture. Under the leadership of Tony Blair, Britain suffered, in a more limited way, a similar transformation.

Universal democracy and the 'war on terror' have proved to be dangerous delusions. Like utopian regimes in the past, governments will not admit they are attempting the impossible. They demand freedom from the constraints that have developed over many centuries to curb the exercise of power. In the twentieth century the result was totalitarianism – a system in which nearly every aspect of society was controlled by government. Today the result is a type of illiberal democracy in which elections take place against a background of diminished freedoms. As in earlier outbreaks of utopianism the achievements of the past have been damaged in the pursuit of an imaginary future.

Though its origins are in trends in thought and policy that developed earlier, rightwing utopianism was massively boosted by the collapse of communism. The communist regimes were meant to be the advance guard of a new type of society that would replace all earlier models. The western states that emerged as victors in the Cold War embarked on a similar project. With a triumphal America in the lead they committed themselves to building a worldwide economic system. Having rendered every other economic system obsolete, global capitalism would bring about the end of history.

In fact, as could be foreseen, history resumed on traditional lines. In intellectual terms the Cold War was a competition between two ideologies, Marxism and liberalism, that had a great deal in common. Though they saw one another as mortal enemies they differed chiefly on the question of which economic system was best suited to achieve goals they shared. Both were Enlightenment ideologies that looked forward to a universal civilization. Both interpreted history in reductive terms, viewing technological and economic development as primary and religion as a secondary factor of dwindling importance. Given these similarities it was only to be expected that the collapse of communism should be seen as a victory for western liberalism, but the actual effect was to render the ideological conflict that had dominated world politics throughout much of the second half of the twentieth century irrelevant.

With the world no longer divided by an obsolete controversy, the nations that were under communist rule returned to their diverse histories. Most eastern European countries became normal democratic states. In Russia a new type of authoritarianism has emerged under the aegis of a ruling elite drawn from the former Soviet intelligence services, which shows signs of being more enduring than the semi-liberal regime that emerged under western auspices immediately after the Soviet collapse. In the Balkans nationalism has reappeared, with war and ethnic cleansing in its wake. Central Asia has become the site of a new Great Game, with the world's energy-thirsty powers vying for control of oil and natural gas against a background of dictatorial regimes and rising Islamic militancy.

Let us be clear: this is no return to stability. The post-Cold War world was one in which the geo-political patterns set in place after the Second World War were breaking up, and American defeat in Iraq has set in motion a further reconfiguration of global politics. The result of the attempt to project American-style democracy worldwide has been a steep decline in American power. For the first time since the 1930s, undemocratic regimes are the rising stars in the international system, while the US has ceased to be the pivotal player in some of the system's most important conflicts. It is China not the US that is central in the crisis in North Korea, and without the engagement of Iran and Syria there can be no peace in Iraq. America has become a great power like others in history, and like them faces dilemmas that are only partly soluble.

The Bush administration's campaign for global democracy has been seen in much of the world as a self-serving rationale for American interests, and the two are clearly intertwined. Many of America's military involvements have been moves in an ongoing resource war. One goal of the American invasion of Iraq was to control the country's oil reserves, and an American attack on Iran would have control over the natural resources of the Gulf as one of its objectives. Side by side with its idealistic rhetoric, the United States has pursued geo-political strategies to secure control of energy supplies. Yet it would be wrong to dismiss Bush's talk of universal democracy as mere hypocrisy. For a time American power became a vehicle for an attempt to remake the world. The disaster that continues to unfold in Iraq is not the result of policy being shaped by corporate interests, or of any conspiracy. It is a testimony to the power of faith.

Communism collapsed but utopianism did not disappear. It was given a new lease on life and came to power in the world's most powerful state. How did this happen? How did Utopia – once found mainly on the Left – come to power through the Right? It was a development that signalled a fundamental shift in politics, and if we are to understand it we need to look beyond the past few years. Without the 9/11 attacks the neo-conservatives in the Bush administration could not have achieved their dominance and the war on Iraq could not have been launched, but lying behind these events are political changes that occurred over the past thirty years. During this period traditional conservatism ceased to exist. Like the far Left in the past the Right that developed from the 1980s onwards saw humanity advancing from darkness to light by way of the fires of war and revolution.

The transformation that overtook the Right was profound. Ever since the French Revolution it has defined itself by opposition to utopian schemes. Its philosophy was summarized by Britain's greatest twentieth-century painter, Francis Bacon – also an acute observer of politics and culture – when he remarked that he voted for the Right because it made the best of a bad job. In the past the Right stood for a realistic acceptance of human frailty and a corresponding scepticism regarding the prospect of progress. Change was not always resisted, but any idea of history as a march towards the sunlit uplands was firmly rejected. Politics was seen as a way of coping with the fact of human imperfection. Often this view was grounded in the Christian doctrine of original sin, but a version of the same idea can be found in conservative thinkers with no such beliefs. Whether religious or not, the Right understood that the flaws of human nature could not be overcome.

During the past generation the Right abandoned this philosophy of imperfection and embraced the pursuit of Utopia. In its militant faith in progress, the Right accepted a radical strand of Enlightenment thinking that renewed, in altered forms, some of the core myths of Christianity. Like other modern revolutionary movements, the Utopian Right was a vehicle for beliefs that go back to medieval times and beyond.

Rightwing utopianism started as a secular movement. The neo-liberals who shaped western policies in the 1990s were mostly *bien-pensant* economists with a naive faith in their version of reason. The advance of the free market might need to be helped on its way – by the structural adjustment programmes that were imposed by the International Monetary Fund on many emerging countries, for example; but it would spread and be accepted on account of the growing prosperity it brought. This innocent creed was ill-suited to the harsh realities of the post-Cold War world, and it was not long before it was replaced by the more militant faith of neo-conservatism. Neo-conservatives understood that free markets would not spread throughout the world in a peaceful process – it would have to be assisted by the intensive application of military force. The post-Cold War world would be an era of blood and iron, not peace.

As an intellectual movement neo-conservatism originated on the

Left, and in some ways it is a reversion to a radical kind of Enlightenment thinking that has disappeared in Europe. Europe is not without
its own illusions – such as the idea that the diverse countries that
compose it can somehow be welded into a federal super-state capable
of acting as a rival power to the United States – but it has abandoned
the belief that human life can be remade by force. Even in France –
the home of the Jacobins – faith in revolution was killed off by the
history of the twentieth century, but when it died in Europe it did not
vanish from the world. In a flight that would have delighted Hegel
it migrated to America where it settled on the neo-conservative
Right. Neo-conservatives are noted for their disdain for Europe but
one of their achievements is to have injected a defunct European
revolutionary tradition into the heart of American political life.[30]

In Europe conservatism arose as a reaction against the Enlightenment project of remaking society on an ideal model – a reaction that
was continued by the American authors of the *Federalist Papers*, who
viewed government as a means of coping with human imperfection
rather than as an instrument for re-creating society. In contrast,
neo-conservatives have been distinguished by their belligerent optimism, which links them with a powerful utopian current in Enlightenment thinking and with the Christian fundamentalist faith that evil
can be defeated. In the US the Utopian Right has been able to draw
both on religious traditions that expect imminent catastrophe and on
secular hopes of continuing progress. One reason for its rise was its
ability to mobilize these conflicting systems of belief. Beyond the
political shifts of the past generation and the traumatic events of the
last few years the Utopian Right achieved ascendancy by remobilizing
some of humanity's most ancient – and most dangerous – myths.

As the Utopian Right became more militant it became less secular,
and at its height in America it had many of the features of a millenarian movement. In the early 1990s neo-conservatives joined forces
in a strategic alliance with Christian fundamentalists, and in the
aftermath of the 9/11 terrorist attacks American politics acquired an
unmistakably apocalyptic tone. Declaring that the United States was
at risk from the forces of evil, Bush launched a campaign to eradicate
terrorism throughout the world. Two years later he declared his
intention of exporting American democracy to the Middle East and

other parts of the world. Each of these projects was unrealizable. When pursued together they were a recipe for disaster. This fact was well understood in the major branches of American government. The State Department, the uniformed military in the Pentagon and the CIA all resisted these policies or tried to temper them with a dose of realism. For the most part they failed and the juggernaut rolled on.

The belief that evil can be removed from human life has assumed many shapes, of which post-millennialism is only one. Many of the theo-conservatives who have been George W. Bush's power base expect an End to come about by divine intervention. They view the world's conflicts – especially those in biblical lands – as preludes to Armageddon, a final battle in which the struggle of light and dark will be concluded. Others expect to be delivered from these trials in a Rapture in which they ascend into heaven. In both cases the imperfect world in which humanity has lived will soon pass away.

The peculiar quality of the view of the world that came to power in the Bush administration is not that it is obsessed with evil. It is that it does not finally believe in evil. Referring to the 9/11 terrorist attacks president Bush announced: 'Our responsibility to history is clear: to answer these attacks and rid the world of evil.'[31] In terms of established Christian doctrine this is a thoroughly heterodox declaration. Since Augustine the mainstream of Christian thought has rejected the temptation of moral absolutism in politics: the kingdom of heaven is not of this earth; no human institution can claim to embody good.

A venerable cliché has it that Bush's view of things is Manichean; but the followers of Mani were subtle thinkers who accepted that evil could never be eliminated. Talk of ending evil is no more Manichean than it is Augustinian. It is an expression of Christian post-millennialism, which harks back to the belief of the first Christians that the blemishes of human life can be wiped away in a benign catastrophe.

The political violence of the modern West can only be understood as an eschatological phenomenon. Western civilization contains many traditions that are not implicated in this way. In the ancient world pagan philosophers did not aim to convert humanity by force any more than the Hebrew prophets did. Throughout western history there have been sceptics such as Michel de Montaigne who viewed doubt as the essence of civilization. Within the Enlightenment there have been thinkers who rejected any idea of a permanent transformation in human affairs. But these strands have rarely been dominant – the world has never been dotted with statues of Thomas Hobbes or Benedict Spinoza, for example. The most powerful western traditions have been those that looked to alter the very nature of human life – a project that has always been given to violence.

Contemporary liberal thinkers tend to view the totalitarian movements of the last century as anomalies in western history, and there is a similar tendency among conservatives regarding the millenarian frenzies of the Middle Ages. These outbreaks of mass killing are seen as departures from the peaceful norms of a civilization that is good, healthy and harmonious. Not all the world's evils come from 'the West' – however that amorphous concept is defined. Humans are an extremely violent species; there are plenty of examples of mass killing in non-western societies. Where the West is distinctive is in using force and terror to alter history and perfect humanity. The chiliastic passions that convulsed late medieval Europe and which reappeared in the twentieth century are not aberrations from a pristine western tradition. They go back all the way, and they continue today. In the twentieth century they were embodied in secular regimes that aimed to remake humanity by force.

2

Enlightenment and Terror in the Twentieth Century

To destroy a city, a state, an empire even, is an essentially finite act; but to attempt the total annihilation – the liquidation – of so ubiquitous but so theoretically or ideologically defined an entity as a social class or racial abstraction is quite another, and one impossible even in conception to a mind not conditioned by western habits of thought.

Edmund Stillman and William Pfaff[1]

The twenty-first century has been a time of terror, and it is easy to imagine that in this it is different from the one that has just ended. In fact terror was practised during the last century on a scale unequalled at any other time in history, but unlike the terror that is most feared today much of it was done in the service of secular hopes. The totalitarian regimes of the last century embodied some of the Enlightenment's boldest dreams. Some of their worst crimes were done in the service of progressive ideals, while even regimes that viewed themselves as enemies of Enlightenment values attempted a project of transforming humanity by using the power of science, whose origins are in Enlightenment thinking.

The role of the Enlightenment in twentieth-century terror remains a blind spot in western perception. Libraries are stocked with books insisting that mass repression in Stalinist Russia and Maoist China was a by-product of traditions of despotism. The implication is that it is the people of the countries that were subject to communist rule that are to blame, while the communist ideology is innocent of any role in the crimes these regimes committed. A similar lesson has been drawn from the catastrophe that has ensued as a result of the Bush administration's project of regime change in Iraq: it is not the responsibility of those who conceived and implemented the project, whose goals and intentions remain irreproachable. The fault lies with the Iraqis, a lesser breed that has spurned the freedom it was nobly offered.

There is more than a hint of racism in this way of thinking. During the last century mass repression was practised in countries with vastly different histories and traditions whose only common feature was the fact that they were subjects of a utopian experiment. The machinery of terror – show trials, mass imprisonment and state control of political and cultural life through a ubiquitous secret police – existed in every communist regime. Mongolia and East Germany, Cuba and Bulgaria, Romania and North Korea, Eastern Germany and Soviet Central Asia all suffered similar types of repression. The type of government these countries had before they became subject to communist rule – democratic or otherwise – made very little difference. Czechoslovakia was a model democracy before the Second World War but that did not prevent it becoming a totalitarian dictatorship after the communist takeover. The strength of the Church in Poland may have prevented the imposition of full-scale totalitarianism, but like every other communist country it suffered periods of intense repression. If communist regimes had been established in France or Italy, Britain or Scandinavia the result would have been no different.

The apparent similarities between countries with communist regimes imposed on them stem from their shared fates rather than their earlier histories. While some communist regimes made advances in social welfare, all experienced mass repression along with endemic corruption and environmental devastation. Terror in these and other communist countries was partly a response to these failures and the resulting lack of popular legitimacy of the regimes, but it was also a continuation of a European revolutionary tradition. The communist regimes were established in pursuit of a utopian ideal whose origins lie in the heart of the Enlightenment. Though the fact is less widely recognized, the Nazis were also in some ways children of the Enlightenment. They had only scorn for Enlightenment ideals of human freedom and equality, but they continued a powerful illiberal strand in

37

Enlightenment thinking and made use of an influential Enlightenment ideology of 'scientific racism'.

The last century witnessed many atrocities that owed nothing to Enlightenment thinking. Though it was facilitated by the history of colonialism in the country and by the policies of France – the chief former colonial power – the genocide that claimed a million lives in Rwanda in 1994 was also a struggle for land and water. Rivalry for resources has often been a factor in genocide, as have national and tribal enmities. So has sheer predatory greed. The genocide committed in the Belgian Congo by agents of King Leopold II when he ruled it as his personal fiefdom between 1885 and 1908 eventually claimed somewhere between eight and ten million people, who perished from murder, exhaustion, starvation, disease and a collapsing birth rate. Though he justified his enterprise in terms of spreading progress and Christianity, Leopold's goal was not ideological. It was his personal enrichment and that of his business associates.[2]

It is not terror of this kind that marks off the twentieth century from earlier times. At its worst, twentieth-century terror was used with the aim of transforming human life. The peculiar quality of twentieth-century terror is not its scale – unprecedented though that was. It is that its goal was to perfect human life – an objective integral to totalitarianism.

There is a school of thought that mistrusts the concept of totalitarianism, and it is true that the picture of it propagated by thinkers after the Second World War was over-simple. Hannah Arendt blurred important differences between Nazism and communism. Communism was a radical version of an ideal of equality in which all humankind could share, while Nazism excluded most of humanity and condemned a section of it to death. The Stalinist regime murdered many more people than the Nazis. Entire peoples such as the Volga Germans and the Crimean Tatars were subject to deportations that were genocidal in their effects, and there were sections of the Gulag from which it was practically impossible to emerge alive. Even so, there were no extermination camps in the former USSR. Arendt also portrayed totalitarian states as impersonal machines in which individual responsibility was practically non-existent.[3] In fact, life in totalitarian regimes was endemic chaos. Terror was an integral part of the system but it did not happen without personal decisions. People became accomplices in Nazi crimes for the pettiest reasons – in the case of Eichmann, careerism. It would have been better to speak of the banality of the evildoers than of the banality of evil. The crimes they committed were not banal and flowed from beliefs that were integral to the regime in which they occurred.[4]

The pursuit of Utopia need not end in totalitarianism. So long as it is confined to voluntary communities it tends to be self-limiting – though when combined with apocalyptic beliefs, as in the Jonestown Massacre in which around a thousand people committed mass suicide in Guyana in 1978, the end can be violent. It is when state power is used to remake society that the slide to totalitarianism begins. The fact that the utopian project can only be promoted by dismantling existing social institutions leads to a programme that goes well beyond anything attempted by traditional tyrannies. If totalitarianism does not result it is because the regime is overthrown or breaks down, or else utopian commitment wanes and the system lapses into authoritarianism. When a utopian ideology captures power in a democracy, as happened for a time during the Bush administration, there is a loss of freedom as the power of government is used to mask the failings of the utopian project. Unless a determined attempt is made to reverse the trend, some type of illiberal democracy is the result.

Many criteria have been used to mark off totalitarianism from other kinds of repressive regime. One test is the extent of state control of the whole of society, which is a by-product of the attempt to remake human life. Bolshevism and Nazism were vehicles for such a project, while – despite the fact that the term 'totalitarian' first came into use in Italy during the Mussolini era – Italian fascism was not. Nor – despite being at times extremely violent – was the clerical fascism of central and eastern Europe between the two world wars. There are plenty of very nasty regimes that cannot be described as totalitarian. Pre-modern theocracies used fear to enforce religious orthodoxy, but they did not aim to remodel humanity any more than did traditional tyrannies. Leninism and Nazism aimed to achieve such a transformation. Describing these regimes as totalitarian reflects this fact.

SOVIET COMMUNISM: A MODERN MILLENARIAN REVOLUTION

Bolshevism as a social phenomenon is to be reckoned as a religion, not as an ordinary political movement.

Bertrand Russell[5]

In the last pages of his pamphlet 'Literature and Revolution', published in 1923, Leon Trotsky gives a glimpse of the transformation in human life he believed was within reach. He writes not about changes in society but an alteration in human nature. The change he anticipates will be in the biology of the human species. In the future, he writes,

Even purely physiologic life will become subject to collective experiments. The human species, the coagulated Homo sapiens, will once more enter into a state of radical transformation, and, in his own hands, will become an object of the most complicated methods of artificial selection and psycho-physical training . . . It is difficult to predict the extent of self-government which the man of the future may reach or the heights to which he may carry his technique. Social construction and psycho-physical self-education will become two aspects of one and the same process. All the arts – literature, drama, painting, music and architecture will lend this process beautiful form. More correctly, the shell in which the cultural construction and self-education of Communist man will be enclosed, will develop all the vital elements of contemporary art to the highest level. Man will become immeasurably stronger, wiser and subtler; his body will become more harmonized, his movements more rhythmic, his voice more musical. The forms of life will become dynamically dramatic. The average human type will rise to the heights of an Aristotle, a Goethe, or a Marx. And above this ridge new peaks will rise.[6]

In Trotsky's view history is the process in which humanity gains control of itself and the world. Just as there are no limits to the growth of human knowledge so there is no limit to human advance in ethics and politics. If there are flaws in human nature science can correct them. This is the true meaning of perfectibility in radical Enlightenment thought: not so much a condition of static perfection as a vision of unbounded human possibility. Trotsky's vision in which science is used to perfect humanity expresses a recurrent modern fantasy. The belief that science can free humankind from its natural limitations, perhaps even make it immortal, thrives today in cults such as cryogenics, transhumanism and Extropianism that acknowledge their debts to the Enlightenment.[7]

From the start the Bolsheviks aimed to create a new type of human being. Unlike the Nazis they did not see this new humanity in racial terms, but like the Nazis they were ready to employ science and pseudo-science in an attempt to achieve their goal. Human nature was to be altered so that 'socialist man' could come into being. Such a project was impossible with the scientific knowledge that was available at the time, but the Bolsheviks were ready to use any method, no matter how inhuman, and adopt any theory however dubious that promised to deliver the transformation of which they dreamt. From the early twenties onwards the Soviet regime harassed genuine scientists. Later, as in Nazi Germany, science was perverted for the purposes of terror. By the late thirties human subjects – German and Japanese prisoners of war, soldiers and diplomats, Poles, Koreans and Chinese, political prisoners and 'nationalists' of all kinds (including Jews) – were being used in medical experiments in the Lubyanka prison in the centre of Moscow. Despite attempts to resist the process, science became an integral part of the totalitarian state.[8]

The role of Trofim Lysenko (1898–1976) is well known. Lysenko propagated a version of the Lamarckian theory of evolution, which differed from the Darwinian theory that was accepted by most scientists at the time in claiming that acquired characteristics could be inherited. Lamarck's theory seemed to open up the possibility that human nature could be progressively improved. Inasmuch as it appeared to extend human power over the natural world, Lamarckism chimed with Marxism, and with Stalin's support Lysenko was made head of the Soviet Academy of Agricultural Sciences. He was also given free rein in farming, where he claimed to be able to breed new high-yielding strains of wheat. Lysenko's experiments in agriculture were disastrous, adding to the collapse in food production that accompanied collectivization. His hare-brained ideas retarded the development of biology in the USSR until well into the 1960s and had an even longer influence in Maoist China.

Less well known is the work of Ilya Ivanov, who in the mid-twenties was charged by Stalin with the task of crossbreeding apes with humans. Stalin was not interested in filling the world with replicas of Aristotle and Goethe. He wanted a new breed of soldier – 'a new invincible human being', highly resistant to pain, that needed little food or sleep. Ivanov was a horse-breeder who made his reputation in Tsarist times by pioneering the artificial insemination of racehorses, but acting on Stalin's instructions he turned his attention to primate research. He travelled to West Africa to conduct trials impregnating chimpanzees and set up a research institute in Georgia, Stalin's birthplace, where humans were impregnated with ape sperm. A number of experiments were attempted, but unsurprisingly all of them failed. Ivanov was arrested, sentenced to a term of imprisonment that was commuted and then exiled to Kazakhstan, where he died in 1931. An obituary appeared by the Russian psychologist Ivan Pavlov, who achieved worldwide fame via a series of experiments applying methods of behavioural conditioning to dogs, praising Ivanov's life and work.[9]

Stalin's requirements for the new human being were coarsely practical. Yet they embody a project of developing a superior type of human being that recurs time and again in Enlightenment thinkers. It is sometimes questioned whether there ever was such a thing as 'the Enlightenment project'.[10] Certainly the Enlightenment was a heterogeneous and often contradictory movement. A wide range of beliefs can be found amongst Enlightenment thinkers – atheist and Deist, liberal and anti-liberal, communist and pro-market, egalitarian and racist. Much of the Enlightenment's history consists of rabid disputes among rival doctrinaires. Yet it cannot be denied that a radical version of Enlightenment thinking came to power with the Bolsheviks, which aimed to alter human life irrevocably.

In Russia there have always been many who looked to Europe to redeem the country from backwardness. When the great Counter-Enlightenment thinker Joseph de Maistre went to live in Russia he declared that he wanted to live among people who had not been 'scribbled on by philosophers'. To his disappointment he found in St Petersburg an elite that spoke French, revered Voltaire and looked to the *philosophes* for inspiration. Throughout the nineteenth century Russian thinkers continued to look to Europe. Bakunin the anarchist, Plekhanov the orthodox Marxist, Turgenev the Anglophile liberal – all were convinced that Russia's future lay in merging into the universal civilization they saw emerging in Europe. So were the Bolsheviks who created the Soviet state. When they talked of turning Russia into a modern state, Lenin and Trotsky spoke in a European voice.

It has become a commonplace that Russia's misfortune was that the Enlightenment never triumphed in the country. In this view the Soviet regime was a Slavic version of 'oriental despotism', and the unprecedented repression it practised was a development of traditional Muscovite tyranny. In Europe Russia has long been seen as a semi-Asiatic country – a perception reinforced by the Marquis de Custine's famous journal recording his travels in Russia in 1839 in which he argued that Russians were predisposed to servility.[11] Theories of oriental despotism have long been current among Marxists seeking to explain why Marx's ideas had the disastrous results they did in Russia and China. The idea of oriental despotism goes back to Marx himself, who postulated the existence of an 'Asiatic mode of production'. Later Marxian scholars such as Karl Wittfogel applied it to Russia and China, arguing that totalitarianism in these countries was a product of Asiatic traditions.[12]

As Nekrich and Heller summarize this conventional wisdom:

Western historians draw a direct line from Ivan Vasilievich (Ivan the Terrible) to Joseph Vissarionovich (Stalin) or from Malyuta Skuratov, head of Ivan the Terrible's bodyguard and secret police force, to Yuri Andropov . . . thus demonstrating that from the time of the Scythians Russia was inexorably heading for the October Revolution and Soviet power. It was inherent in the national character of the Russian people. Nowhere else, these scholars think, would such a thing be possible.[13]

It is true that Russia never belonged fully in the West. Eastern Orthodoxy defined itself in opposition to western Christianity, and there was nothing in Russia akin to the Reformation or the Renaissance. From the time of the fall of Constantinople to the Ottomans in 1543 the idea developed that Moscow was destined to be a 'third Rome' that would lead the Christian world from the east. In the nineteenth century an influential group of Slavophil thinkers argued on similar lines and suggested that Russia's difference from the West was a virtue. Rejecting western individualism they maintained that Russian folk traditions embodied a superior form of life. This anti-western strand of thought developed into a belief in Russia's unique role in world history that may have helped sustain the communist regime. The Russian religious philosopher Nikolai Berdyaev believed that Russian communism 'is more traditional than is commonly thought and is a transformation and deformation of the old Russian messianic idea'.[14] Certainly there were messianic strands in Bolshevism. Anatoli Lunacharsky, a Bolshevik who was expelled from the party by Lenin for ideological deviancy but who later became Soviet Minister of Education, noted these points of affinity in a book on *Socialism and Religion* in 1907 and commented on the way in which Christian ideas about the Day of Judgement and Christ's millennial reign had been reproduced in socialism.[15] It is also true that the Revolution inspired apocalyptic hopes in Russia. In 1918 the Symbolist poet Alexander Blok published 'The Twelve', in which a band of twelve Red Guards march through the streets of Petrograd led by the figure of Christ under a red flag. Secular and religious forms of messianism are not mutually exclusive – they joined forces in the American Utopian Right, for example. For a time it may have seemed to a few that the new Soviet regime embodied a Russian messianic tradition. But reactionary Russian messianism was not an expansionist creed. For the most part it saw Russia as a redoubt of virtue in a fallen world. It was not this anti-western messianism that came to power in Russia with the October Revolution.

The Bolsheviks wanted to surpass the West by achieving its most radical ideals. They did not aim to emulate actually existing western societies (as late Tsarism did with some success). Lenin wanted to transplant the core institutions of western capitalism, such as work discipline and the factory system, into Russia. He was an ardent missionary for two of the most advanced capitalist techniques – 'Taylorism', the American technique of 'scientific management', and 'Fordism', American assembly-line mass production. As the Bolshevik leader described his programme, 'The combination of the Russian revolutionary sweep with American efficiency is the essence of Leninism.'[16] In a similar way Trotsky demanded the 'militarization of labour' – a work system in which the discipline of the capitalist factory was carried to a higher level. But Bolshevik goals went far beyond installing the work discipline and techniques of mass production of western capitalism. Central among them was realizing the Enlightenment utopia that the Jacobins and the Paris Commune failed to achieve. Russia's misfortune was not in failing to absorb the Enlightenment but in being exposed to the Enlightenment in one of its most virulent forms.

Contrary to the views of most western historians, there are few strands of continuity linking Tsarism with Bolshevism. Lenin came to power as a result of a conjunction of accidents. If Russia had withdrawn from the First World War, the Germans had not given Lenin their support, Kerensky's Menshevik provisional government had been more competent or the military coup attempted against the Mensheviks by General Kornilov in September 1917 had not failed, the Bolshevik Revolution would not have occurred. Terror of the kind practised by Lenin cannot be explained by Russian traditions, or by the conditions that prevailed at the time the Bolshevik regime came to power. Civil war and foreign military intervention created an environment in which the survival of the new regime was threatened from the start; but the brunt of the terror it unleashed was directed against popular rebellion. The aim was not only to remain in power. It was to alter and reshape Russia irreversibly. Starting with the Jacobins in late eighteenth-century France and continuing in the Paris Commune, terror has been used in this way wherever a revolutionary dictatorship has been bent on achieving utopian goals. The Bolsheviks aimed to make an Enlightenment project that had failed in France succeed in Russia. In believing that Russia had to be made over on a European model they were not unusual. Where they were distinctive was in their belief that this required terror, and here they were avowed disciples of the Jacobins. Whatever other purposes it may have served – such as the defence of Bolshevik power against foreign intervention and popular rebellion – Lenin's use of terror flowed from his commitment to this revolutionary project.

Lenin presented his vision of the society he aimed to achieve in his book *State and Revolution*. He wrote this utopian tract in August–September 1917 while in hiding in Finland from the Russian Provisional Government, and he originally meant it to appear under a pseudonym. History moved faster than he expected and copies appeared under his own name in 1918, with a second edition appearing a year later. Lenin attached some importance to the book, instructing that if he were killed it must still be published at all costs. It remains the best guide to his picture of the future.

State and Revolution is firmly rooted in the thought of Marx. Citing the idea of the dictatorship of the proletariat that Marx coined in a letter of 1852, Lenin uses the Paris Commune of 1870–71 as the model for the revolutionary government of Russia and the world. In future there would be no state in the sense understood in modern times. Standing armies and police forces would be abolished. Everyone would take part in government. Public officials would enjoy no privileges and receive a worker's income. Lenin did not imagine that the installation of this new order would occur without a struggle. A small minority would resist, and the suppression of this resistance was the principal function of the new state. Lenin left no doubt that the new regime would have nothing in common with bourgeois democracy. As he put it in a note published in 1920: 'The scientific term "dictatorship" means nothing more or less than authority untrammelled by any laws, absolutely unrestricted by any rules whatever, and based directly on force.'[17]

In *State and Revolution* Lenin asserts that in a proletarian dictatorship there would be no need for coercion of the masses, for the new regime would exist only to serve them. At the same time the dictatorship would need to act ruthlessly against its enemies. Here again Lenin was only repeating Marx. In their address to the Communist League in London in March 1850, Marx and Engels are clear that terror will be an integral part of the revolution:

Above all, during and immediately after the struggle the workers, so far as it is at all possible, must oppose bourgeois attempts at pacification and force the democrats to carry out their terroristic phrases ... Far from opposing so-called excesses – instances of popular vengeance against hated individuals or against public buildings with which hateful memories are associated – the workers' party must not only tolerate these actions but give them direction.[18]

While Lenin – following Marx – maintained terror would only be used against remnants of the old order, it was actually turned most severely on workers and peasants. In part this can be explained by the circumstances in which the Bolsheviks seized power. The October Revolution was a by-product of the First World War and of the ensuing chaos in Russia. The new Soviet regime faced several years of civil war that could easily have ended in victory for their opponents, generally referred to as the Whites. Some type of authoritarian rule may have been unavoidable in these conditions. But they cannot account for the scale and intensity of Bolshevik repression, which was the result of attempting to reconstruct society on an unworkable model.

From its beginnings the Soviet state was involved in hostage-taking, mass executions and the establishment of concentration camps, none of which existed in late Tsarist Russia. When the Socialist Revolutionary Fanny Kaplan wounded Lenin in an assassination attempt on 30 August 1918, the Cheka – the Extraordinary Commission conceived by Lenin in the aftermath of the October Revolution and founded in December 1917 – was ordered to carry out a 'merciless mass terror'. Hundreds were executed. A system of hostages was set up to ensure obedience in suspect groups – an innovation Trotsky, one of the pioneers of twentieth-century state terror, later defended.[19] It was Trotsky who established concentration camps in June 1918, initially for the detention of Czechs fighting against the Red Army and then for former Tsarist officers who refused to join it. Repression was soon extended to peasants who were subjected to forcible grain requisitioning. In 1921 the revolt of a few thousand sailors in Kronstadt was suppressed by around 50,000 Red Army troops (a repressive measure Trotsky – the founder of the Red Army – also defended).[20] Most of the sailors ended up in camps, where many died. From 1918 onwards a rash of peasant revolts spread across much of Russia, and from 1920 to 1921 the civil war became a peasant insurgency. The Bolsheviks were determined to crush peasant resistance. Entire villages were deported to the Russian north, and at the end of 1921 around 80 per cent of the people being held in camps were peasants or workers.[21]

It is commonly believed that the Soviet security apparatus was inherited from late Tsarism. Certainly Peter the Great used the forced labour of convicts – not least in building St Petersburg, an enduring Russian symbol of modernity. Yet on the eve of revolution in 1916 only 28,600 convicts were serving sentences of forced labour.[22] There is a huge disparity between the size of the penal and security apparatus in Tsarist Russia and that established by the Bolsheviks. In 1895 the Okhrana (Department of Police) had only 161 full-time members. Including operatives working in other departments it may have reached around 15,000 by October 1916. In comparison, the Cheka had a minimum of 37,000 operatives in 1919 and in 1921 reached over a quarter of a million. There is a similar disparity between the numbers of executions. During the late Tsarist period from 1866 to 1917 there were around 14,000 executions, while in the early Soviet period from 1917 to 1923 the Cheka carried out around 200,000 executions.[23]

The techniques of repression employed by the Bolsheviks owed more to recent western practice than to the Tsarist past. In creating the camps they were following a European colonial model. Concentration camps were used by Spain to quell insurgents in colonial Cuba at the end of the nineteenth century and by the British in South Africa during the Boer War. Around the same time they were established in German South-West Africa, when the German authorities committed genocide on the Herero tribe. (The first imperial commissioner of German South-West Africa was the father of Hermann Goering, and medical experiments were carried out on indigenous people by two of the teachers of Joseph Mengele.[24])

The Bolshevik repression of intellectual freedom was also of a different order from anything that had existed before in Russia. In the past, a number of writers and political activists had been sent into exile. The radical writer Alexander Herzen left Russia for Paris, London and Italy. Lenin spent time in Siberia and much of his life in Switzerland, Germany, Britain and other European countries. However, it was only after the Bolshevik seizure of power that Russian intellectuals experienced mass deportation. In the autumn of 1922, two ships sailed from Petrograd containing some of the most creative members of the Russian intelligentsia – writers, philosophers, literary critics, theologians, historians and others – that Lenin had selected for involuntary emigration. Arrested by the political police, the GPU, these eminent Russian figures were deported (along with their families) because they were out of tune with the new regime. The episode passed almost unnoticed at the time and was barely mentioned during the Cold War. The expellees settled in Paris, Berlin, Prague and other European cities, some of them – like Nikolai Berdyaev – establishing a new life, many others vanishing into poverty and obscurity. Lesley Chamberlain, who has given the first comprehensive account of the mass deportation, notes that this neglect 'is all the more astonishing, since it was Lenin himself, the leader of the Bolsheviks and the founder of the Soviet Union, who masterminded the deportation and chose many of his victims by name'. She comments that 'Though they could never have described themselves that way, the 1922 expellees were the first dissidents from Soviet totalitarianism.'[25] It is a description that captures the novelty of Lenin's regime.

The methods of repression used by the Bolsheviks were not an inheritance from Tsarism. They were new, and they were adopted in the pursuit of utopian goals. The central role of the security apparatus in the new Soviet state was required by its project of remaking society – an aspiration no traditional tyranny has had, and which the Tsars certainly lacked. As has been correctly noted, 'Prior to the appearance of the Soviet party-state, history offered few, if any, precedents of a millenarian, security-focused system.'[26] To call the Soviet state a tyranny is to apply an antique typology to a system that was radically modern.

Western opinion followed the Bolsheviks in seeing the Soviet regime as an attempt to realize the ideals of the French Revolution. It is a telling fact that Soviet communism was most popular in the West when terror was at its height. After visiting the Soviet Union in 1934 – when around five million people had perished in the Ukrainian famine – the British Labourite intellectual Harold Laski declared: 'Never in history has man attained the same level of perfection as in the Soviet regime.' In much the same vein, in 1935 the renowned Fabians Sidney and Beatrice Webb published a book entitled *Soviet*

Communism: A New Civilisation? (In later editions of the book the question mark was dropped.) For these western enthusiasts Stalinism was the highest point in human progress. The American literary critic Edmund Wilson went still further. In the Soviet Union, he wrote, 'I felt as though I were in a moral sanctuary, where the light never stops shining.'[27] Western progressive intellectuals were never in any doubt that the USSR was a regime dedicated to Enlightenment ideals. They would have been horrified at the suggestion that the Soviet state was no more than Tsarist despotism in a new guise. It was only when it was clear that the Soviet system had failed to achieve any of its goals that its use of terror was explained as a Tsarist inheritance.

For the most part western opinion saw in the Stalinist Soviet Union an image of its utopian fantasies, and it projected the same image on to Maoist China, where the human cost of communism was even greater. Some thirty-eight million people perished between 1958 and 1961 in the Great Leap Forward. As Jung Chang and Jon Halliday have written: 'This was the greatest famine of the twentieth century – and of all recorded human history. Mao knowingly starved and worked these millions of people to death.'[28] As they did in the Soviet Union, the peasants suffered most from a policy – alien to Chinese traditions – that aimed to subjugate the natural environment to human ends. Around a hundred million were coerced into working on irrigation projects. Often without proper tools, they used doors and planks taken from their homes to construct dams, reservoirs and canals – most of which collapsed or were abandoned. In a spectacular display of the Promethean spirit sparrows were deemed pests fit only for extermination. The peasants were ordered to wave sticks and brooms so that the birds would fall exhausted from the sky and could be killed. The result was a plague of insects. A secret message had then to be sent to the Soviet embassy in Beijing requesting that hundreds of thousands of sparrows be sent as soon as possible from the Soviet Far East.[29]

The cultural cost of the Maoist regime was evident in the Great Proletarian Revolution of 1966–7. Like the Bolsheviks, Mao saw the persistence of the past as the chief obstacle to building a new future. China's ancient traditions had to be wiped from memory. In effect the Maoist regime declared war on Chinese civilization. Yet it was during the Cultural Revolution – a politically engineered mass frenzy that had an undeniable millenarian dimension – that the regime achieved its highest level of popularity in the west. As with Stalinism, western opinion saw Mao's regime as dedicated to an Enlightenment ideal of universal emancipation: terror was a necessary phase in the conversion of an Asiatic tyranny to western ideals of freedom and progress. Again, it was only when its catastrophic results could no longer be denied that Chinese communism was condemned as a form of oriental despotism. Rather than being results of an attempt to apply a modern western ideology, the crimes of the Maoist regime could then safely be seen as vestiges of traditional barbarism. When Maoism was abandoned, western opinion interpreted its rejection as the beginning of a process of westernization, when in fact – as in the case of the collapse of the Soviet system – it was the opposite. Post-Mao China rejected a western ideology not in order to adopt another one, but in order to carve out a path of development that owed little to any western model. Given China's worsening ecological problems and the social dislocation that has accompanied the phasing out of the 'iron rice bowl', which ensured lifetime employment and basic welfare for most of the population, the upshot remains in doubt; but the period in which China struggled to implement a western ideology is over.

Wherever it has come to power communism has meant a radical break with the past. Late Tsarism had far more in common with *fin de siècle* Prussia than with the Soviet system.[30] The late Tsarist period had dark blemishes – it witnessed many pogroms, for example – but in terms of its overall record it compares favourably with many countries in the world today and it was incomparably less repressive than the Soviet regime. In employing terror as an instrument of social engineering the Bolsheviks were self-consciously continuing the Jacobin tradition. Just as the Jacobins had liquidated the remnants of the old regime it was necessary to eliminate residues of reaction that could be found in all sections of Russian society. As Nekrich and Heller have written: 'Lenin was obsessed with two historical precedents: first, the Jacobins, who were defeated because they did not guillotine enough people; and second, the Paris Commune, which was defeated because its leaders did not shoot enough people.'[31]

The safety of the revolution required active measures against human remnants of the past. One of the first acts of the regime announced in January 1918 was to create a new category of 'disenfranchised person' whose members could be deprived of rights – including the right to food. Around five million people fell into this category and were subject to a class-based system of rationing created later that year. It was against this background of the disenfranchisement of whole categories of people that the Great Terror took place. As Kołakowski, author of the definitive study of the rise and collapse of Marxism, has put it, 'Stalinism was the natural and obvious continuation of the system of government established by Lenin and Trotsky.'[32] The millions of deaths that accompanied Stalin's policies of agricultural collectivization were larger than anything contemplated by Lenin but they were a consequence of policies that Lenin began. In turn, Lenin's policies were genuine attempts to realize Marxian communism.

Despite Marx's repudiation of utopian thinking, his vision of communism is itself thoroughly utopian. As I noted in the last chapter, no one can ever know enough to plan the course of an advanced economy. But the utopian quality of Marx's ideal does not come only from the impossible demands it makes on the knowledge of the planners. It arises even more from the clash between the ideal of harmony and the diversity of human values. Central planning involves an enormous concentration of power, without – as Lenin made clear in his 'scientific' definition of proletarian dictatorship – any institutional checks. A system of arbitrary rule of this kind is bound to encounter resistance. The values of the regime will surely not be those of everyone or even the majority. Most people will continue to be attached to things – religion, nationality or family – the regime sees as atavistic. Others will cherish activities – such as aesthetic contemplation or romantic love – that make no contribution to social reconstruction. Whether they actively resist the new regime or – like Dr Zhivago in Boris Pasternak's novel – simply insist on going their own way, there will be many who do not share the regime's vision of the good life. While every Utopia claims to embody the best life for all of humankind, it is never more than one ideal among many. A society without private property or money may seem idyllic to some people but to others it looks like a vision of hell. For some it may seem obvious that a world ruled by altruism would be best, while for others it would be insufferably insipid. All societies contain divergent ideals of life. When a utopian regime collides with this fact the result can only be repression or defeat. Utopianism does not *cause* totalitarianism – for a totalitarian regime to come into being many other factors are necessary – but totalitarianism follows whenever the dream of a life without conflict is consistently pursued through the use of state power.

The Bolsheviks were practitioners of what Karl Popper described as utopian social engineering, which aims to reconstruct society by altering it all at once.[33] For the utopian social engineer it is not enough to reform institutions piecemeal. Society as it presently exists is beyond redemption. It must be destroyed in order to create a new way of life. One difficulty of utopian social engineering is that it contains no method for correcting mistakes. The theory that guides the construction of Utopia is taken to be infallible; any deviation from it is treated as error or treason. There may be tactical retreats and switches of direction – as when in 1921 Lenin abandoned War Communism and adopted the New Economic Policy allowing peasants to keep their own grain – but the utopian model remains beyond criticism. However, given the fact of human fallibility the model is sure to contain flaws, some of which may be fatal. The result of persisting in the attempt to realize it is bound to be a society very different from the one that was envisaged. This is not a process confined to the Soviet Union and other communist states. It is evident in Iraq, where a hardly less ambitious attempt at utopian engineering was made. Predictably, the failure of the project has been ascribed to deficiencies in its execution and the recalcitrance of the Iraqi people rather than any defects in the project itself.

Destroying an existing social order for the sake of an ideal is irrational, as Popper argued. Where Popper went astray was in supposing that by demonstrating the irrationality of utopianism he had disposed of it. To dissect the errors in Marxian theory that underpinned Lenin's *State and Revolution* may be useful, but the utopian mentality is not nurtured on falsifiable social theories. It feeds on myths, which cannot be refuted. For Lenin and Trotsky, terror was a way of remaking society and shaping a new type of human being.

The goal of the new Soviet regime was a world where humanity would flourish as never before. In order to achieve this end it was ready to sacrifice millions of human lives. The Bolsheviks believed the new world could come into being only after the destruction of the old.

Russia under Soviet rule did witness something like an apocalypse. While no aspect of life was untouched, the change was most complete in the camps. Varlam Shalamov, who spent seventeen years working in the mines of Kolyma – a section of the Gulag, finally covering a tenth of Soviet territory, in which around a third of the inmates died every year – described the events following the arrival in the camp of bulldozers donated under the American Lend-Lease programme. Meant to assist in the war against Nazism, the bulldozers were used to dispose of thousands of frozen bodies that emerged when mass graves dating from an earlier period of camp life were uncovered:

These graves, enormous stone pits, were filled to the brim with corpses. The bodies had not decayed; they were just bare skeletons over which stretched dirty, scratched skin bitten all over by lice.

The north resisted with all its strength this work of man, not accepting the corpses into its bowels. Defeated, humbled, retreating, stone promised to forget nothing, to wait and preserve its secret. The severe winters, the hot summers, the winds, the six years of rain had not wrenched the dead men from the stone. The earth opened, baring its subterranean storerooms, for they contained not only gold and lead, tungsten and uranium but also undecaying human bodies.

These human bodies slid down the slope, perhaps attempting to rise . . .[34]

While it had apocalyptic consequences the Bolshevik revolution failed to usher in the Millennium. Tens of millions died for nothing. Even now the number of deaths resulting from forced collectivization cannot be known with certainty, but Stalin boasted to Churchill that it reached ten million. Robert Conquest has estimated the overall number of deaths in the Great Terror at around twice that figure – an estimate that is likely to be fairly accurate.[35] The toll in broken lives was incalculably larger. The land itself was scarred with man-made deserts and dead or dying lakes and rivers. The Stalinist Soviet Union became the site of the largest humanly induced ecological disasters – probably only surpassed by those in Maoist China.[36]

The Soviet Union survived the Second World War, in which its people made a decisive contribution to defeating Nazism. In the period immediately after the war there were some who anticipated a thaw in the Stalinist system; but in fact millions who had fought heroically ended up in the Gulag. The Cold War years saw several attempts at liberalization, including Khrushchev's attack on Stalin's 'cult of personality' at the party congress in 1956; but when a systematic attempt was made to renew the Soviet Union under Mikhail Gorbachev it collapsed. By then the Soviet system was an empty shell held together by corruption and inertia, and though it maintained peace throughout its vast territories and supplied a kind of security to its citizens that they were later to lose, it had little popular legitimacy. Even the Soviet elite lacked the will to defend the system, and when Gorbachev's naive effort at reform triggered its collapse a state founded on terror fell apart without violence in a débâcle unprecedented in history. In the chaos that followed, the new humanity that the Soviet regime had been founded to create was nowhere to be seen. Human life had been altered, but in a process that had more in common with the alteration described in Kafka's *Metamorphosis* than with anything dreamt by Marx, Lenin or Trotsky.

NAZISM AND THE ENLIGHTENMENT

Hitler and the Third Reich were the gruesome and incongruous consummation of an age which, as none other, believed in progress and felt assured it was being achieved.

Lewis Namier[37]

Like Bolshevism, Nazism was a European phenomenon. This may seem obvious, but the implication – that the origins of Nazism are in western civilization – is still resisted. Yet the Nazis did not come from a faraway land. Developing in the chaos of the interwar years, they were driven by beliefs that had been circulating in Europe for many centuries. The crimes of Nazism cannot be explained (as some have tried to explain the crimes of communism) as products of backwardness. They emanated from some of Europe's most cherished traditions and implemented some of its most advanced ideas.

The Enlightenment played an indispensable role in the development of Nazism. Nazism is often presented as a movement that was opposed to the Enlightenment, and it is true that many Nazis thought of themselves as its enemies. They claimed to have learnt lessons from a body of thinkers belonging to a movement Isaiah Berlin called the Counter-Enlightenment – a diverse group that included reactionaries such as Joseph de Maistre and Romantics such as J. G. Herder.[38] Nazi ideologues picked from these and other Counter-Enlightenment thinkers whatever they found useful – as they did with the thinkers of the Enlightenment. In both cases they were able to draw on powerful currents of anti-liberal thought. The argument advanced by some members of the neo-Marxist Frankfurt School, which says that Nazism was a logical development of Enlightenment thinking, is much overstated; but there is more than a grain of truth in it.[39]

An academic cliché has it that the Nazis were extreme Romantics who exalted emotion over reason. However, the idea that Nazism was a hyperbolic version of the Romantic Movement is at best an oversimplification. What the Nazis owed to the Romantics was a belief also shared by many Enlightenment thinkers – the idea that society had once been an organic whole and could be so again at some time in the future. Romantic thinkers had different ideas about where this organic society existed – some looked to medieval Christendom, others to ancient Greece, still others to faraway countries of which they knew nothing. Wherever they thought they had found it, their vision of society was a chimera. No society has ever been a harmonious whole, and with its suspicion of conflict and diversity the idea of organic community is always liable to be used against minorities. There is a clear link between integral nationalism of this Romantic kind and Nazism. While the Nazis celebrated conflict, they believed that the *Volk* – the people – was a seamless whole that fell from unity only when corrupted by alien minorities. The peoples of the world were not equals, and the hierarchy that should exist among them could be secured only by force. But within the German *Volk* there would be a condition of perfect harmony.[40]

The belief that society should be an organic whole is far from being only a Romantic idea, however. The fantasy of seamless community is as much a feature of Enlightenment thinking as of the Counter-Enlightenment. Like Fichte and other German thinkers of the nationalist Right, Marx condemned trade and disparaged individualism. Like the Romantics he condemned the division of labour as inhuman. Like them he looked to the remote past for a society in which humanity was not alienated or repressed. He found it in a prehistoric condition of 'primitive communism', which he believed had once been universal (but of which no trace has ever been found). No less than the thinkers of the Counter-Enlightenment, Marx promoted a myth of organic community.

If Enlightenment thinkers shared some of the worst ideas of the Counter-Enlightenment, the Counter-Enlightenment contained much that was at odds with Nazi ideology. Consider Herder and de Maistre. Each rejected the Enlightenment project but neither was in any sense a proto-Nazi. Herder never accepted any kind of hierarchy among cultures or races (as some key Enlightenment thinkers did). On the contrary he affirmed that there are many cultures, each in some way unique, which cannot be ranked on a single scale of value. De Maistre would have been horrified by the Nazis' atheism and by their doctrines of racial superiority. At the most important points, Nazi ideology and Counter-Enlightenment thought are opposed.

A connection can be traced between Nazi ideology and Nietzsche, but it is with Nietzsche in his role as an Enlightenment thinker. The genealogy that traces Nazism back to Nietzsche is suspect, if only because it was promoted by his Nazi sister, Elizabeth Forster-Nietzsche (1846–1935) – who looked after Nietzsche in his last years and whose funeral Hitler attended. Even so there are points of affinity, and they are found in the areas where Nietzsche is closest to the Enlightenment. Nietzsche was a lifelong admirer of Voltaire – the celebrated Enlightenment rationalist – and like Voltaire he despised Rousseau's exaltation of emotion over reason. While Nietzsche appears as a Romantic in a popular stereotype, he was in fact a thinker who took a radical version of the Enlightenment project to its conclusion.[41]

Unlike his early intellectual idol Arthur Schopenhauer, who turned his back on Christianity and mounted a devastating criticism of modern humanism, Nietzsche never escaped from the Christian-humanist world-view he attacked. His idea of the Superman shows him trying to construct a new redemptive myth that would give meaning to history in much the same way that other Enlightenment thinkers did. But as the *fin de siècle* Viennese wit Karl Kraus observed, 'The superman is a premature ideal, one that presupposes man.'[42] The idea of the *Übermensch* is an exaggerated version of modern humanism and shows what Nietzsche had in common not only with the Nazis but also with Lenin and Trotsky.

The links between liberal values and the Enlightenment that many people today are keen to stress are more tenuous than they believe. Voltaire may be the exemplary Enlightenment thinker.[43] Yet he saw the liberal state as only one of the vehicles through which human progress could be achieved; in many circumstances, he believed, enlightened despotism was more effective. For Voltaire as for many other Enlightenment thinkers, liberal values are useful when they promote progress, irrelevant or obstructive when they do not. Of course there are many conceptions of progress. Among Enlightenment thinkers of the Left, liberal society was seen as a valuable stage on the way to a higher phase of human development, while among Enlightenment thinkers of the Right it was viewed as a condition of chaos that at best served as a transition point from one social order to another. For Marx, progress was conceived in terms that applied to humankind as a whole, while for those Enlightenment thinkers who subscribed to 'scientific racism' it excluded most of the species. Either way, liberal values were destined for the rubbish heap.

The French Positivists were among the most influential Enlightenment thinkers, and they were thoroughgoing anti-liberals.[44] The founders of Positivism, Henri de Saint-Simon and Auguste Comte, looked forward to a society akin to that which existed (they imagined) in the Middle Ages, but based on science rather than revealed religion. Saint-Simon and Comte viewed history as a process in which humanity passed through successive stages – from the religious to the metaphysical, and then on to the scientific or 'positive'. In this process there were 'organic' and 'critical' phases – times when well-ordered societies existed and times when society was in chaos and disarray. The liberal era belonged in the latter category. Saint-Simon and Comte were bitterly hostile to liberalism, and they transmitted this animus to generations of radical thinkers on the Right and the Left. The society of the future would be technocratic and hierarchical. It would be held together by a new religion – the Religion of Humanity, in which the human species would be worshipped as the Supreme Being.

It may seem that the Positivists diverged from the mainstream of Enlightenment thinking – for example, in their admiration for the medieval Church.[45] But what they admired in the Church was not the faith it embodied. It was the Church's power in unifying society, which the Religion of Humanity tried (without success) to emulate. They believed the growth of knowledge was the driving force of ethical and political progress and celebrated science and technology for expanding human power. Rejecting traditional religions they founded a humanist cult of reason. This was the creed of the eighteenth-century *philosophes* restated for the nineteenth century. If the Positivists were distinctive it was not in their attitude to religion – many Enlightenment savants including Voltaire cherished the absurd project of a 'rational religion' – but in their belief that, as human knowledge advanced, human conflict would wither away. Science would reveal the true ends of human action, and – though why this was so was never explained – they would be found to be harmonious. This was the archetypal utopian idea in a modern guise, and it was vastly influential. In the late nineteenth century it shaped Marx's view that under communism the government of men would be replaced by the administration of things. It inspired Herbert Spencer's dream of a future society based on *laissez-faire* industrialism, and in a later version it inspired Hayek's delusive vision of a spontaneous social order created by the free market.

In the early twentieth century Positivist ideas were embraced by the far Right. Charles Maurras, the anti-Semitic ideologue of the Vichy regime, was a lifelong admirer of Comte. The Positivists were committed to developing a science of society and invented the term 'sociology'; but they were insistent that such a science must be based in human physiology. Like many Enlightenment thinkers at the time, Comte was a devotee of phrenology – the nineteenth-century pseudo-science that claimed to be able to identify the mental and moral faculties of people and their tendency to criminality by studying the shape of their skulls – and believed that physiological characteristics can explain much of human behaviour. This was also the view of the founder of modern psychology, Francis Galton, who was a strong supporter of positive eugenics. In criminology, similar views were advanced by Cesare Lombroso, who developed a pseudo-science of 'craniometry' based on skull and facial contours to assist courts in their deliberations about guilt and innocence At this point we are not far from Nazi 'racial science'.

Ideas of natural human inequality are not aberrations in the western tradition. A general, though not specifically racist, belief that humans are divided into distinct groups with innately unequal abilities goes back to Aristotle, who defended slavery on the ground that some humans are born natural slaves. For Aristotle hierarchy in society was not – as the ancient Greek Sophists argued – a product of power and convention. Every living thing had a natural purpose that dictated what it needed to flourish. The natural end of humanity was philo-sophical inquiry, but only a very few humans – male property-owning Greeks – were suited to this activity, and the mass of humanity – women, slaves and barbarians – would flourish as their instruments. The best life was for the few and the rest were 'living tools'.

If the belief in innate human inequality reaches back to classical Greek philosophy, it was revived in the Enlightenment, when it began to take on some of the qualities of racism. John Locke was a Christian committed to the idea that humans are created equal, but he devoted a good deal of intellectual energy to justifying the seizure of the lands of indigenous people in America. Richard Popkin writes:

Locke, who was one of the architects of English colonial policy – he drafted the Constitution of the Carolinas, for example – saw Indians and Africans as failing to mix their labours with the land. As a result of this failing they had no right to property. They had lost their liberty 'by some Act that deserves Death' (opposing the Europeans) and hence could be enslaved.[46]

A number of Enlightenment luminaries were explicit in expressing their belief in natural inequality, with some claiming that humanity actually comprised several different species. Voltaire subscribed to a secular version of the pre-Adamite theory advanced by some Christian theologians that suggested that Jews were pre-Adamites, remnants of an older species that existed before Adam was created. It was

Immanuel Kant – after Voltaire the supreme Enlightenment figure and, unlike Voltaire, a great philosopher – who more than any other thinker gave intellectual legitimacy to the concept of race. Kant was in the forefront of the science of anthropology that was emerging in Europe and maintained that there are innate differences between the races. While he judged whites to have all the attributes required for progress towards perfection, he represents Africans as being predisposed to slavery, observing in his *Observations on the Feeling of the Beautiful and the Sublime* (1764), 'The Negroes of Africa have by nature no feeling that rises above the trifling.'[47] Asians, on the other hand, he viewed as civilized but static – a view that John Stuart Mill endorsed when in *On Liberty* (1859) he referred to China as a stagnant civilization, declaring: '. . . they have become stationary – have remained so for thousands of years; and if they are ever to be improved it must be by foreigners'.[48] Here Mill echoed the view of India held by his father, James Mill, who argued in his *History of British India* that the inhabitants of the sub-continent could only achieve progress by abandoning their languages and religions. A similar picture of India was presented by Marx, who defended colonial rule as a means of overcoming the torpor of village life. Whether the disabilities of other peoples were innate (as was believed in the case of Africans) or due to cultural backwardness (as was supposed to be true of Asians), the remedy was the same. All had to be turned into Europeans, if necessary by force.

Beliefs of this kind are found in many Enlightenment thinkers. It is frequently argued on their behalf that they were creatures of their time, but it is hardly a compelling defence. These Enlightenment thinkers not only voiced the prejudices of their age – a failing for which they might be forgiven were it not for the fact that they so often claimed to be much wiser than their contemporaries – they also claimed the authority of reason for them. Before the Enlightenment, racist attitudes rarely aspired to the dignity of theory. Even Aristotle, who defended slavery and the subordination of women as part of the natural order, did not develop a theory that maintained that humanity was composed of distinct and unequal racial groups. Racial prejudice may be immemorial, but racism is a product of the Enlightenment.

Many of those who subscribed to a belief in racial inequality believed that social reform could compensate for the innate disadvantages of inferior breeds. Ultimately all human beings could participate in the universal civilization of the future – but only by giving up their own ways of life and adopting European ways. This was 'a form of liberal racism, making the best of European experience the model for everyone, and the eventual perfection of mankind consisting in everyone becoming creative Europeans'.[49] Liberal racism left open the possibility of the forcible destruction of other cultures, and even – if all else failed – genocide. If any culture resisted it would be an obstacle to the coming universal civilization. In that case it would be an obstacle to progress and a candidate for elimination. When H. G. Wells asked himself what would be the fate in the World-State of the 'swarms of black and yellow and brown people who do not come into the needs of efficiency' he replied: 'Well, the world is not a charitable institution, and I take it they will have to go. The whole tenor and meaning of the world, I take it, is that they have to go.'[50] Among progressive thinkers at the time, such ideas were commonplace. The peculiar achievement of Enlightenment racism was to give genocide the blessing of science and civilization. Mass murder could be justified by faux-Darwinian ideas of survival of the fittest, and the destruction of entire peoples could be welcomed as a part of the advance of the species.

Nazi policies of extermination did not come from nowhere. They drew on powerful currents in the Enlightenment and used as models policies in operation in many countries, including the world's leading liberal democracy. Programmes aiming to sterilize the unfit were underway the United States. Hitler admired these programmes and also admired America's genocidal treatment of indigenous peoples: he 'often praised to his inner circle the efficiency of America's extermination – by starvation and uneven combat – of the "Red Savages" who could not be tamed by captivity'.[51] The Nazi leader was not unusual in holding these views. Ideas of 'racial hygiene' were by no means confined to the far Right. A belief in positive eugenics as a means to progress was widely accepted. As Richard Evans has put it:

Seeing that Hitler offered them a unique opportunity to put their ideas into practice, leading racial hygienists began to bring their doctrines into line with those of the Nazis in areas where they had so far failed to conform. A sizeable majority, to be sure, were too closely associated with political ideas and organizations on the left to survive as members of the Racial Hygiene Society ... Writing personally to Hitler in April 1933, Alfred Ploetz, the moving spirit of the eugenics movement for the past forty years, explained that since he was now in his seventies, he was too old to take a leading part in the practical implementation of the principles of racial hygiene in the new Reich, but he gave his backing to the Reich Chancellor's policies all the same.[52]

There were many who shared the Nazi belief in 'racial science'. The Nazis were distinctive chiefly in the extremity of their ambitions. They wanted an overhaul of society in which traditional values were destroyed. Whatever the conservative groups that initially supported Hitler may have hoped, Nazism never aimed to restore a traditional social order. Defeatist European intellectuals who saw it as a revolutionary movement – such as Pierre Drieu La Rochelle, the French collaborator who praised the Nazis for what they had in common with the Jacobins[53] – were nearer the mark. The Nazis wanted a permanent revolution in which different social groups and branches of government competed with one another in a parody of Darwinian natural selection. But – as with the Bolsheviks – Nazi goals went beyond any political transformation. They included the use of science to produce a mutation in the species.

The eighty thousand inmates of mental hospitals who were killed by gassing were murdered in the name of science. The thousands of gay men who ended up in concentration camps (where around half of them perished[54]) were classified as incorrigible degenerates. 'Criminal biologists' had long categorized the quarter of a million Gypsies who perished during the Nazi period as belonging to a dangerous racial type. The belief that Slavs also belonged to an inferior racial group allowed the Nazis to view with equanimity the vast loss of life they inflicted in Poland, the Soviet Union and Yugoslavia.

Without doubt 'racial science' opened the way for the Nazis' supreme crime. The theory that humanity was divided into distinct racial groups that ought not to intermarry gave the imprimatur of reason to fantasies of pollution. The idea that these groups were innately unequal sanctioned the enslavement of those deemed to belong on the lower rungs of the hierarchy. Without the construction of race as a scientific category the project of annihilating European Jewry could scarcely have been formulated. Anti-Semitism is coeval with the appearance of Christianity as a distinct religion: Jews were persecuted from the time of Rome's conversion from paganism and throughout the Christian Middle Ages, while medieval anti-Semitism was reproduced in the Reformation by Luther. However, while anti-Semitism has ancient Christian roots, the project of exterminating Jews is modern. If the Holocaust required modern technology and the modern state in order to be executed, it also required the modern idea of race to be conceived.

Hitler's goal of exterminating the Jews could not have been formulated without using ideas derived from a modern pseudo-science. Even so, it is impossible to account for the Holocaust solely in terms of racist ideology. No other group was selected for complete extermination, and none was hunted down with such systematic intensity. Whether they were Yiddish poets or medical doctors, university professors or Hasidic teachers, scientists or artists, tradesmen and merchants, men, women or children, Jews were threatened and stigmatized, driven from civil life and their property stolen, beaten and murdered in state-inspired violence, consigned to concentration camps and finally singled out for a fate no other section of humanity has had to suffer.

If a historical comparison can be made, it is with the attribution of demonic power to Jews in medieval Europe. As Norman Cohn has put it, 'the drive to exterminate the Jews sprang from a quasi-demonological superstition.'[55] A belief in the diabolical powers of Jews was a major feature in the millenarian mass movements of the late Middle Ages. Jews were shown in pictures as devils with the horns of a goat, while attempts were made by the Church to force Jews to wear horns on their hats. Satan was given what were considered to be Jewish features and described as 'the father of the Jews'. Synagogues were believed to be places where Satan was worshipped in the form of a cat or a toad. Jews were seen as agents of the Devil, whose goal was the destruction of Christendom, even of the world. Documents such as the *Protocols of the Elders of Zion* – a hugely influential forgery that probably emanated from the foreign branch of the Tsarist secret service – reproduced these fantasies and turned them into a paranoid vision of a worldwide Jewish conspiracy.

The singularity of the Nazi attempt to annihilate the Jews comes not only from the scale of the crime but also from the extremity of its goal. Jews were seen as the embodiment of evil and their extermination as a means of saving the world. Nazi anti-Semitism was a fusion of a modern racist ideology with a Christian tradition of demonology. Eschatological myth and perverted science came together to produce a crime without precedent in history.

Like the millenarian movements of medieval times, Nazism emerged against a background of social disruption. Mass unemployment, hyperinflation and the humiliating impact of the Great War produced a wrenching sense of insecurity and loss of identity among Germans. As Michael Burleigh has written, the 1914–18 conflict

... created the emotional effervescence which Emil Durkheim regarded as integral to religious experience. The Great War and its disturbed aftermath led to an intensified revival of this pseudo-religious strain in politics, which exerted its maximum appeal in times of extreme crisis, just as medieval millenarians, or the belief that the thousand-year interval before the Day of Judgement was at hand, had thrived before in times of sudden change and social dislocation.[56]

The similarities between Nazism and medieval millenarianism were recognized by a number of observers at the time. Eva Klemperer, the wife of the philologist and diarist Victor Klemperer, compared Hitler with John of Leyden, and so did Friedrich Reck-Malleczewen, the aristocratic author of an anti-Nazi book entitled *History of a Mass Lunacy*, published in 1937.[57] Around the same time the British foreign correspondent F. A. Voigt identified the central role of eschatology in Nazism:

Every transcendental eschatology proclaims the end of this world. But *secular* eschatology is always caught in its own contradiction. It projects into the *past* a vision of what *never was*, it conceives what *is* in terms of what *is not*, and the *future* in terms of what can *never be*. The remoter past becomes a mystical or mythical Age of Innocence, a Golden or a Heroic Age, an Age of Primitive Communism or of resplendent manly Virtue. The Future is the Classless Society, Eternal Peace, or Salvation by Race – the Kingdom of Heaven on Earth.[58]

In a study that is too little known, James Rhodes has provided a systematic examination of Nazism as a modern millenarian movement. Like the Anabaptists and other medieval millenarians, the Nazis were possessed by a vision of disaster followed by a new world. Seeing themselves as victims of catastrophes, they experienced sudden revelations that explained their sufferings, which they believed were the work of evil forces. They believed they had been called to struggle against these forces, to defeat them and rid the world of them in short, titanic wars.[59]

This millenarian syndrome of impending catastrophe, the existential threat of evil, brief cataclysmic battles and an ensuing paradise can be seen in many modern political movements (including the Armageddonite wing of the American Right). It fits the Nazis closely and shows the poverty of any account of Hitler's movement that sees it simply as a reaction to social conditions. Nazism was a modern political religion, and while it made use of pseudo-science it also drew heavily on myth. The *Volk* was not just the biological unit of racist ideology. It was a mystical entity, which could confer immortality on those who participated in it. Using the Kantian term 'Ding-an-sich', which means ultimate reality or the thing-in-itself, Goebbels declared that 'Ding-an-sich is the *Volk*', and produced a poem in which the semi-divine qualities ascribed to the *Volk* are clear:

I arise, I have power
To wake the dead. They awakened out of deep sleep,
Only a few at first but then more and more. The ranks fill up, a host arises,
A *Volk*, a community.[60]

Without the vengeful war reparations of the Versailles settlement and the chaos of the interwar German economy, the Nazis would most likely have remained a fringe movement. They remained popular for as long as they did because they delivered material benefits to large sections of the German population. The efficiency of Hitler's war machine may have been exaggerated, but Nazi economic policies were not dissimilar to those advocated by Keynes (as Keynes himself recognized) and delivered full employment in the run-up to the war. The popularity of the Nazis was sustained in the first years of the war by military success and the orgy of looting that it permitted in occupied Europe. Delivering these benefits to the German population was a major part of the Nazis' strategy to gain and maintain power.

At the same time the Nazis mobilized a potent mix of beliefs. Nazi ideology differs from that of most other utopian and millenarian movements in that it was largely negative. Nazi eschatology was a debased imitation of pagan traditions that allowed the possibility of a final disaster without any prospect of future renewal. This negative eschatology was linked with a sort of negative utopianism, which focused on the obstacles to future paradise more than on its content. The Nazis' eschatology may have been less important than their demonology, which came from Christian sources (not least the Lutheran tradition). The world was threatened by demonic forces, which were embodied in Jews. The present time and the recent past were evil beyond redemption. The one hope lay in catastrophe – only after an all-destroying event could the German *Volk* ascend to a condition of mystical harmony.

The name of the Nazi regime derived from Christian apocalyptic traditions. The 'Third Reich' comes from Joachim of Flora's prophecy of a Third Age, passed on to modern times by Anabaptist Christians and popularized in interwar Germany by Moeller van den Bruck in his book *Das Dritte Reich* (*The Third Empire*, 1923). A 'revolutionary conservative' in the manner of Oswald Spengler (whose book *The Decline of the West* had a huge impact in the 1920s), van den Bruck believed that the problems of interwar Germany were not only political and economic but also cultural and spiritual. He had a strong interest in Dostoyevsky, co-editing a German translation of *The Brothers Karamazov* with the émigré Russian writer Dmitri Merezhkovsky, himself the author of a book of apocalyptic speculation.[61] Both writers were sympathetic to Dostoyevsky's fantasy of Russia as a 'third Rome' that could produce spiritual renewal in Europe, and van den Bruck visited Russia in 1912. With these beliefs one would expect him to be sympathetic to the emerging Nazi movement. Yet – perhaps because he seems not to have shared their anti-Semitism – he and the Nazis never joined forces. On meeting Hitler in 1922 van den Bruck was repelled by the Nazi leader's 'proletarian primitivity'. Later the Nazis repudiated van den Bruck's ideas, but a signed copy of his book was found in Hitler's bunker and for a time van den Bruck supplied a scheme of thought that matched the Nazis' sense of apocalyptic crisis and historical destiny. If the Holy Roman Empire was the first Reich and the united German Empire ruled by the Hohenzollerns (1871–1918) the second, the third would be the Nazi state that would last for a thousand years.

It is wrong to see the Nazis as coming from outside the western tradition. Some Nazis saw themselves as anti-western, and it was a view adopted by some of their opponents, such as the once widely read but now almost forgotten writer Aurel Kolnai, who saw Nazism as part of a 'war against the West'. A Catholic convert, Kolnai defined 'the West' in terms of Christianity,[62] and it is true that some of the most courageous opponents of the Nazis were devout Christians; for example, Claus von Stauffenberg, a pivotal figure in the July 1944 plot to assassinate Hitler, was a pious Catholic. However, while many leading Nazis were hostile to Christianity and some Christians resolute anti-Nazis, it is also true that Nazism continued some Christian traditions. Eric Voegelin, a German scholar who fled Nazi Germany in 1938 and whose work has done much to illuminate the nature of modern political religion, recognized that 'Hitler's millennial prophecy authentically derives from Joachitic speculation, mediated in Germany through the Anabaptist wing of the Reformation and through the Johannine Christianity of Fichte, Hegel and Schelling.' As he summarized this development, 'The superman marks the end of a road on which we find such figures as the "godded man" of English Reformation mystics ... A line of gradual transformation connects medieval with contemporary gnosticism.'[63]

Voegelin understood Nazism as being – like communism – a contemporary revival of Gnosticism. There can be no doubt that Gnostic beliefs have had a far-reaching influence in shaping western thought, and there may well have been Gnostic influences on medieval millenarian movements, but there are few points of affinity between Gnosticism and modern millenarianism. Like the Manicheans, with whom they had much in common, the Gnostics were subtle thinkers. They did not look to an End-Time in which the Elect would be collectively saved, but understood salvation as an individual achievement that involved release from time rather than its end. Again, few if any Gnostic thinkers envisioned a world in which human life is no longer subject to evil. While it undoubtedly had an influence, the impact of Gnosticism on modern political religion was not formative. The decisive influence was the faith in the End that shaped Christianity from its origins. In expecting a final struggle between good and evil forces, medieval millenarians harked back to this eschatological faith, as did modern totalitarian movements.

TERROR AND THE WESTERN TRADITION

> The figure of the lonely metaphysical terrorist who blew himself up with his bomb appeared in Russia at the end of the nineteenth century ... The real genesis of al-Qaeda violence has more to do with a Western tradition of individual and pessimistic revolt for an elusive ideal world than with the Koranic conception of martyrdom.   Olivier Roy[64]

Nazism and communism are products of the modern West. So too – though the fact is denied by its followers and by western opinion – is radical Islam. The intellectual founder of radical Islam is Sayyid Qutb, an Egyptian intellectual executed by Nasser in 1966. Qutb's writings show the influence of many European thinkers, particularly Nietzsche, and they are full of ideas lifted from the Bolshevik tradition. Qutb's conception of a revolutionary vanguard dedicated to the overthrow of corrupt Islamic regimes and the establishment of a society without formal power structures owes nothing to Islamic theology and a great deal to Lenin. His view of revolutionary violence as a purifying force has more in common with the Jacobins than it does with the twelfth-century Assassins. The Assassins devoted themselves to killing rulers they believed had deviated from the true path of Islam; but they did not believe that terror could be used to perfect humanity, nor did they see self-destruction in suicide attacks as a token of personal purity. Such views arose only in the twentieth century when Islamic thinkers came under European influence. Ali Shariati – the predecessor of Ayatollah Khomeini as leader of Iranian fundamentalists in exile during the reign of the Shah – defended martyrdom as a central practice in Islam, but his conception of martyrdom as a type of chosen death came from modern western philosophy. The fundamentalist redefinition of Shi'ism advanced by Shariati invoked an idea of existential choice derived from Heidegger.[65]

Islamist movements think of violence as a means of creating a new world, and in this they belong not in the medieval past but the modern West. Talk of 'Islamo-fascism' obscures the larger debts of Islamism to western thought. It is not only fascists who have believed that violence can give birth to a new society. So did Lenin and Bakunin, and radical Islam could with equal accuracy be called Islamo-Leninism or Islamo-anarchism. However the closest affinity is with the illiberal theory of popular sovereignty expounded by Rousseau and applied by Robespierre in the French Terror, and radical Islam may be best described as Islamo-Jacobinism.

Radical Islam is a modern revolutionary ideology, but it is also a millenarian movement with Islamic roots. Like Christianity, Islam has always contained a powerful eschatological element. Both Sunni and Shia Islam contain a Mahdist tradition that anticipates the arrival of a divinely guided teacher who will re-order the world – a tradition that Bin Laden has exploited when projecting his image as a prophet-leader.[66] Some scholars question the orthodoxy of Mahdist beliefs but they exemplify a conception of history that is clearly Islamic. As one contemporary Islamic scholar has written: 'The Mahdist "event" ... is History as eschatology, giving history a progressive nature.'[67] The apocalyptic beliefs of president Ahmadinejad of Iran are a version of this view of history.

In thinking of history in this way Islam shares common ground with Christianity and with the secular creeds of the modern West. It is misleading to represent Islam and 'the West' as forming civilizations that have nothing in common. Christianity and Islam are integral parts of western monotheism, and as such they share a view of history that marks them off from the rest of the world. Both are militant faiths that seek to convert all humankind. Other religions have been implicated in twentieth-century violence – the state cult of Shinto in Japan during the militarist period and Hindu nationalism in contemporary India, for example. But only Christianity and Islam have engendered movements that are committed to the systematic use of force to achieve universal goals. At the same time the notion that Islam lies outside 'the West' neglects Islam's positive contributions. It was Islamic cultures that preserved the inheritance of Aristotle and developed much of the mathematics and science that Europe later used. In the medieval kingdoms of Moorish Spain, Islamic rulers provided shelter for persecuted Christians and Jews when Christian Europe was mired in religious conflict. To erase these Islamic achievements from the western canon misrepresents history.

The belief that Islam developed outside or against western civilization leads to a mistaken view of Islamist movements as being directed against 'the West'. In fact the chief objective of Islamist jihad is to overthrow what are seen as infidel governments in Islamic countries. Qutb's goal was to topple Nasser, while Osama Bin Laden has always viewed the destruction of the House of Saud as his major objective. Islamist movements seek the destruction of secularist regimes such as Baathist Syria and Iraq (where the work of destruction was done for them by the American-led invasion). The Palestinian Sunni Islamist organization Hamas began by attacking Fatah and the PLO, which are secular in orientation. To the extent that the US has intervened in these struggles, Islamist movements have been drawn into conflict with western governments, but this has not always been so. Throughout the Cold War western governments viewed Islamist movements as instruments in the struggle against communism. The Afghan mujahadeen were western-armed, trained and financed, with al-Qaeda being among the organizations the West assisted. The Reagan administration developed close contacts with Ayatollah Khomeini's Iran in order to contain Soviet influence in the Gulf, and the use of Islamist movements as western proxies continued after the Cold War had ended. The Taliban regime in Afghanistan had friendly relations with the United States until 9/11. As Ahmed Rashid, one of the best-informed writers on the subject, has noted,

Between 1994 and 1996, the USA supported the Taliban politically through its allies Pakistan and Saudi Arabia, essentially because Washington viewed the Taliban as anti-Iranian, anti-Shia and pro-Western . . . [Many US diplomats] saw them as messianic do-gooders – like born-again Christians in the American Bible Belt.[68]

If western governments have often been able to use Islamists as allies it is partly because Islamists have not seen western power as their principal enemy. Though it harboured al-Qaeda, the Taliban regime was at war not with the West but with the people and culture of Afghanistan – banning songbirds and kite-flying because they distracted the population from religious observance, and rejecting the authority of tribal law. The Taliban were an extreme manifestation of 'salafism', the family of fundamentalist movements that aim to return to the original purity of Islam. In other countries such as Yemen (where its followers have attacked the privileges accorded to descendants of the Prophet) and Saudi Arabia (where a version is embodied in the powerful Wahhabi clergy), salafism has been intensely hostile to local cultures. Wherever salafism has taken root it has attempted to counter the influence of Sufism, which has been more tolerant of indigenous practices.

In all its varieties radical Islam is a movement of rejection of traditional cultures – whether Islamic or 'western'. Islamists talk of restoring a caliphate – a form of Islamic government that claims to go back to the Prophet (though the succession was contested almost from the beginning) that was last embodied in the Ottoman Empire. Yet Islamist movements recruit some of their most active members in highly advanced societies – notably amongst deracinated Muslims in western Europe. Islamism is a by-product of the conflicts that go with accelerating globalization.[69]

A clash of civilizations may yet occur, but thinking of radical Islam in terms of cultural conflicts mistakes its true character. If it aims to achieve a traditional goal – the *ummah*, or universal community of

Muslims – it does so by waging war on traditional Islamic societies. Like other modern political religions, radical Islam is a hybrid of apocalyptic myth and utopian hope, and in this it is unmistakably western.

Of course, 'the West' stands for nothing fixed. Its boundaries shift with cultural changes and geo-political events. There are those who think the medieval world was a synthesis of the whole of western civilization, but to think of 'the West' in this way is to leave out the inheritance of pagan polytheism and tragic drama, Greek philosophy and the lamentations of Job, the inheritance of Rome and Islamic science. During the Cold War the countries of the Soviet bloc were described as being outside the West or opposed to it though their governments subscribed to a European ideology. Later, post-communist Russia was expected to become part of 'the West' despite the fact that it had rejected this ideology and resumed an older identity of which anti-western Orthodox Christianity was an important part.

Nowadays 'the West' defines itself in terms of liberal democracy and human rights.[70] The implication is that the totalitarian movements of the last century formed no part of the West, when in truth these movements renewed some of the oldest western traditions. If anything defines 'the West' it is the pursuit of salvation in history. It is historical teleology – the belief that history has a built-in purpose or goal – rather than traditions of democracy or tolerance, that sets western civilization apart from all others. By itself this does not produce mass terror – other conditions including large-scale social dislocation are required before that can come about. The crimes of the twentieth century were not inevitable. They involved all kinds of historical accidents and individual decisions. Again, there is nothing peculiarly western about mass murder. What is unique to the modern West is the formative role of the faith that violence can save the world. Totalitarian terror in the last century was part of a western project of taking history by storm. The twenty-first century began with another attempt at this project, with the Right taking over from the Left as the vehicle of revolutionary change.

3

Utopia Enters the Mainstream

The ultimate similarity between Marxist and bourgeois
optimism, despite the initial catastrophism of the former,
is, in fact, the most telling proof of the unity of modern
culture.   Reinhold Niebuhr[1]

A belief that a single economic and political system was coming into
being throughout the world began to shape the policies of western
governments from the late 1980s onwards. An expression of the
Enlightenment faith that humanity is evolving towards a universal
civilization that, in a different form, shaped communist regimes, it
was strengthened rather than weakened by the Soviet collapse. A
confident expectation that liberal democracy was spreading worldwide dominated the nineties, and the events of 9/11 triggered an
attempt to accelerate the process throughout the Middle East. If the
débâcle in Iraq has undermined these hopes the rise of authoritarian
Russia and China has shattered the assumption that post-communist
countries are bound to take western institutions as their model. Yet,
despite this refutation by history, the myth that humanity is moving
towards adopting the same values and institutions remains embedded
in western consciousness.

It is a belief that has been defended in many theories of modernization, but it is instructive to recall the many incompatible forms this
ultimate convergence has been expected to take. Marx was certain it
would end in communism, Herbert Spencer and F. A. Hayek that its
terminus would be the global free market, Auguste Comte was for
universal technocracy and Francis Fukuyama 'global democratic capi-

talism'. None of these end-points was reached, but that has not dented the certainty that some version of western institutions will eventually be accepted everywhere – indeed, with every historical refutation it is more adamantly asserted. The communist collapse was a decisive falsification of historical teleology, but it was followed by another version of the same belief that history is moving towards a species-wide civilization. Similarly, disaster in Iraq has only buttressed the conviction that the world faces a generational 'Long War' to defeat terrorism and establish western government everywhere. History continues to be seen as a process with a built-in goal.

Theories of modernization are not scientific hypotheses but theodicies – narratives of providence and redemption – presented in the jargon of social science. The beliefs that dominated the last two decades were residues of the faith in providence that supported classical political economy. Detached from religion and at the same time purged of the doubts that haunted its classical exponents, the belief in the market as a divine ordinance became a secular ideology of universal progress that in the late twentieth century was embraced by international institutions.

The conviction that humanity was entering a new era did not begin in the upper reaches of world politics. As damagingly utopian as any earlier grand design for humanity, this late twentieth-century faith in a global free market was born more humbly, in the struggle to replace the failing post-war settlement in Britain.

Margaret Thatcher and the Death of Conservatism

The end of history? The beginning of nonsense!
Margaret Thatcher on Francis Fukuyama[2]

Margaret Thatcher did not start as a revolutionary, and there was little that was utopian in the cast of mind she brought to her first government. 'Thatcherism' is a term coined by the Left that gives her policies an ideological flavour they did not always possess. Her early programme was a demanding yet realistic agenda whose most important requirements she implemented. Judged in terms of her original aims, Thatcher was a successful reforming prime minister – one of several in a long British tradition. She began as a leader like de Gaulle, focusing on national issues. By the time she was toppled she had come to see the policies she had implemented in Britain as a model for a global programme.

Thatcher became a neo-liberal only towards the end of the 1980s, but the origins of the neo-liberal period in Britain were in the economic crisis of the seventies. Neo-liberalism refers to a body of thought that claims to return to liberal values in their original form – which, neo-liberals believe, requires strictly limited government and an unfettered free market. Despite its claim to scientific rationality, neo-liberalism is rooted in a teleological interpretation of history as a process with a preordained destination, and in this as in other respects it has a close affinity with Marxism. Just as Marxists underestimate the importance of historical accidents in the establishment of the communist regime in Russia, neo-liberals overlook the role of chance in the rise of Margaret Thatcher.

Thatcher became leader of the Conservative party at a time when the post-war settlement in Britain was ceasing to be viable. Her central task was to dismantle it and set up a new framework for the British economy. Labour governments had tried to do this and failed. Thatcher succeeded because she approached the job with a winning mix of ruthlessness and caution. The result was a far-reaching change in British life that created a society different from any she envisioned or desired.

It is a truism of politics that policies often have consequences different from those that are expected. In Thatcher's case the discrepancy was exceptional. She was bent on destroying socialism in Britain, so that – in the words of a crass slogan that circulated among the rightwing think tanks in the eighties – 'Labour will never rule again'. Instead she brought the Conservative party to the brink of collapse and destroyed conservatism as a political project in Britain. As she thrust market forces into every corner of British life with the aim of 'rolling back the frontiers of the state', the state grew ever stronger. Just as constructing the free market in early Victorian England required a large-scale exercise of state power, so did restoring a partial version of it towards the end of the twentieth century. Victorian *laissez-faire* was engineered by a series of parliamentary acts that enclosed what had up to that time been common land, creating private property where none had existed before – a process that involved mass coercion. It was a change that could only be brought about by highly centralized government, and the same was true of Thatcher's programme. The unavoidable result of attempting to reinvent the free market was a highly invasive state.[3]

The price of Thatcher's success was a society in many ways the opposite of the one she wanted. Her goal of unshackling the free market was achievable, and to a measurable degree it was realized; but her belief that she could free up the market while shrinking the state was utopian, and so was her aim of reinstating bourgeois values. Utopia is a projection into the future of a model of society that cannot be realized, but it need not be a society that has never existed. It may be a society that once did exist – if not in exactly the form in which it is fondly remembered – but which history has since passed by. In a television interview in January 1983 Thatcher declared her admiration for Victorian values and her belief that they could be revived. Actually, the country of Thatcher's nostalgic dreams was more like the Britain of the fifties, but the idea that unleashing market forces could re-create this lost idyll was strikingly paradoxical. The conservative Britain of the fifties was a by-product of Labour collectivism. Thatcher tore up the foundations of the country to which she dreamt of returning. Already semi-defunct when she came to power in 1979, it had vanished from memory when she left in 1990. In attempting to restore the past she erased its last traces.

Thatcher propagated an individualist ethos of personal responsibility, but in the type of society that is needed to service the free market old-fashioned virtues of saving and planning for the future are no longer profitable. A makeshift lifestyle is well suited to the incessant mobility of latter-day capitalism. Chronic debt has proved to be a mark of prudence, and a readiness to gamble is more useful than diligent application to the job in hand. Though an earlier generation of social theorists anticipated that as capitalism developed it would foster *embourgeoisement* – the spread of a middle-class ethos throughout society – it has done the opposite. Most of the population belong in a new proletariat, with high levels of income but nothing resembling a long-term career. The deliquescence of bourgeois society has come about not through the abolition of capitalism but as a result of capitalism operating without restraint.

Neo-liberals see the advance of the free market as an unstoppable historical process, which no human agency promoted and none can prevent. Yet it was Thatcher who advanced it in Britain and it is only in retrospect that her rise to power looks inevitable. The accidental quality of her ascendancy can be seen in the people and events, many now forgotten, that made it possible. If Tory prime minister Edward Heath had not called a general election on the issue of who governed the country and in so doing lost the support of much of his party; if the party chairman and old-style grandee Willie Whitelaw had not been loyal to Heath and refused to stand as leader; if the volatile member of parliament and rightwing ideologue Keith Joseph had not given a public lecture in which he seemed to favour eugenic policies aimed at discouraging the poor from having children and thereby disqualified himself from standing for leadership of the party; if former party chairman Edward du Cann had not abruptly withdrawn from the leadership race; if Thatcher's campaign for the leadership had not been skilfully orchestrated by Airey Neave, the MP, wartime escaper and connoisseur of special operations who was later assassinated by the IRA – if any of these circumstances had been different Thatcher would very likely not have become leader of the Conservative party. Again, if the Labour prime minister James Callaghan had not delayed calling a general election until 1979 when the government was deeply unpopular, or if Thatcher had not been advised on public relations by the advertising firm led by Charles and Maurice Saatchi, which produced the killer campaign slogan 'Labour isn't working' – then she might well not have become prime minister.

Thatcher's coming to power turned on the fall of a leaf. Once in office her agenda was imposed by history. British politics was shaped by memories of industrial conflict and government defeat. The three-day week, which prime minister Edward Heath introduced in response to industrial unrest in December 1973, the miners' strike that ejected him from power in the spring of 1974, the winter of discontent that paralysed the Labour administration in 1978–9, when refuse disposal, petrol supplies and for a time the burial of corpses were disrupted by strike action – these events, symbolic at once of national decline and the chronic weakness of government, shaped Thatcher's political outlook and her initial policies more than any ideology.

The agenda of Thatcher's first government contained few of the policies that later became neo-liberal orthodoxy. The general election manifesto of April 1979 did not mention privatization, a term that came into use only in the eighties. One state-owned corporation (the National Freight Company) was earmarked for selling off and a commitment made to start selling off council houses, but there was no talk of bringing market mechanisms into public services. There was a promise to end the closed shop and restrict industrial picketing, but this went with a commitment to consult the trade unions on public-sector pay claims. Remarkably in view of Thatcher's later policies, the German system of wage-determination was singled out for praise. Looked at from the perspective of Thatcher's reputation for scorning consensus this was an incongruously moderate document. Yet the effect of Thatcher's early policies was to bury the post-war settlement and with it British social democracy.

A major influence in shaping Thatcher's early agenda was Sir John Hoskyns, a businessman who by 1978 had become the chief strategist in her private office. In the autumn of 1977 Hoskyns presented Thatcher with a paper, 'Stepping Stones', which set the objectives with which she came to power.[4] The paper was a diagnosis of the forces underlying the current British malaise and recommended curbing union power, controlling inflation and securing balanced budgets. An archetypal early Thatcherite, Hoskyns displayed the characteristics of that breed, well summarized by Hugo Young: 'a fierce pessimism about the past, millennialist optimism about the future and a belief in the business imperative as the sole agent of economic recovery'.[5] These attitudes marked Thatcher off from the other leading politicians of her party and the rest of the British political class at that time. From the start she displayed some of the qualities of a missionary; but in the early days she did not aim to save the world, only Britain.

Post-war policy in Britain was based on the belief that steady economic growth could be promoted by a combination of deficit financing and lax monetary policy. Whether John Maynard Keynes would have endorsed the mix may be open to question, but a generation of politicians, civil servants and academic economists viewed this 'Keynesian' combination as an infallible recipe for economic growth. Yet by the 1970s growth was faltering and unemployment and inflation were rising, while industry was locked into a series of destructive wage disputes. On the wilder fringes of the Right there was talk of something like a communist state coming to power. There was never any danger of this happening – the risk in the seventies was Britain would become a country more like Argentina than anywhere in the Soviet bloc. Still, the crisis was real. The old ways had stopped working.

Margaret Thatcher was not the first leading British politician to accept that the post-war settlement was no longer viable. It was Denis Healey, the Chancellor of the Exchequer in James Callaghan's Labour government, who thrust this fact into the centre of British politics. Throughout the mid-seventies Healey tried to persuade his party that the post-war settlement no longer worked, but Labour's strong links with the trade unions and the opposition of much of its membership thwarted the shift in policy Healey wanted. Thatcher also faced entrenched opposition. Her overriding priority was to alter the system of collective wage bargaining that governed much of British industry. This meant a showdown with the trade unions, and after the miners' strike of 1984–5 their power was broken. British corporatism – the triumvirate of government, trade unions and employers that had managed the economy since the Second World War – ceased to exist. Henceforth the economy would grow within a new framework that ensured low inflation and a flexible labour market. The social costs of putting this framework in place were high, involving a period in which unemployment rose steeply and a long-term increase in economic inequality, but in political terms it was a resounding success. Thatcher's vision of the kind of government and society that would come about when something like the free market had been reinvented was chimerical and utopian; but the deregulation of market forces she engineered formed the basis of a new settlement that was sufficiently productive to be generally accepted, and is likely to remain in force until history renders it irrelevant.[6]

Thatcher's successful challenge to the British consensus did not satisfy her ambitions. Like de Gaulle she had come to see herself as embodying the nation. Unlike the General, she launched a wide-ranging assault on national institutions. She regarded local government with particular scorn, and prompted by the rightwing think tanks she adopted the 'poll tax', a flat-rate local levy that was deeply unpopular. The poll tax sowed deep doubts about Thatcher's leadership in her own party and among the public, but her hostility to Europe may have been a more significant factor in the coup that brought about her downfall in 1990. It was the irrational extremity of her European policy that led Geoffrey Howe to resign as deputy prime minister and triggered a leadership challenge from Michael Heseltine. It was hostility to Heseltine's pro-European stance that led the Thatcherite wing of the party to mount the all-out effort to prevent him succeeding as leader, which resulted in the election of John Major. It was Major's attempt to mend relations with Europe that led to his joining the European Exchange Rate Mechanism at the wrong rate – a decision that rebounded when sterling was ejected from the mechanism on 'Black Wednesday' in September 1992. Major's government never recovered, civil war broke out among Conservatives on Europe, and the Conservative party became an ungovernable rabble.

Thatcher's successors struggled for nearly a decade to understand what made their party unelectable. Clearly a number of decisions and events had contributed to this result, including the coup that toppled Thatcher in 1990. But Conservative unpopularity had deeper causes, and it was only when David Cameron became leader that the party was forced to accept that the obstacle to electoral success was conservatism itself. Post-Thatcher Britain is a less cohesive society than the one she inherited, but it is also more tolerant – unbothered about 'family values', no longer pervasively homophobic, less deeply racist and (though markedly more unequal) not so fixated on issues of class. While he relegated Thatcher to the history books Cameron accepted the society she had, contrary to her intentions, helped create. By burying Thatcher while embracing post-Thatcher Britain he made his party once again a contender for power.

Though it was an episode in the microcosm of British politics, the destruction of conservatism that resulted from Thatcherite policies was part of a larger trend. The application of neo-liberal ideas has provoked a backlash in many countries. In post-communist Poland and Hungary the triumph of the New Right has been followed by a resurgence of the Old Right, which while attacking the excesses of the free market has revived some of the worst features of the past. Integral cultural nationalism and the old poison of anti-Semitism have returned in much of post-communist Europe. In western Europe the far Right has undertaken a process of modernization as a result of which it has become a key player in democratic politics. Few European far-Right parties any longer hold to an interwar agenda of protectionism. In northern Italy and Switzerland they promote a high-tech economy linked with the rest of the world by global free trade but insulated from the world's disorders by a ban on immigration. By fastening on immigration the far Right has been able to tap into the discontent of the casualties of globalization in rich countries – unskilled workers and middle managers whose work can be done more cheaply in emerging economies. By identifying itself with these groups the radical Right has been able to shape the political agenda in many countries, even where – as in France and Austria – it has declined in electoral terms. In countries with no tradition of far-Right politics new types of populism have developed. In Holland the ex-Marxist politician Pim Fortuyn, who was assassinated by a crazed animal rights activist, embodied a combination of libertarianism on issues of personal morality with xenophobic hostility to immigrants (particularly Muslims). In America the Right has splintered between neo-conservative ideologues and paleo-conservative nativists. The common factor in these disparate currents is that conservatism has ceased to be a coherent political project. The links it requires with the past have been severed. Any attempt to revive them can only be atavistic, and when conservative parties resist the temptation of reaction they become vehicles for a progressive agenda that easily degenerates into utopianism.

Thatcher's career illustrates this development. She never shared the belief that the fall of communism heralded an era of peace, and she ridiculed Francis Fukuyama's declaration that history had ended. Yet by 1989 she accepted Fukuyama's view that one type of government was the model for all the rest. Believing that contemporary America embodied the virtues of Britain in the past, she convinced herself that the United States could become at the end of the twentieth century what she believed Britain had been in the late nineteenth century – the final guarantor of progress throughout the world. For Thatcher as for Fukuyama this meant that a version of American 'democratic capitalism' could be replicated everywhere. From being a reformer she had become an ideologue. This was partly hubris – the inordinate confidence in their own rectitude that is the occupational vice of leaders who have achieved success against the odds – but it also reflected her beliefs. Thatcher was always a firm believer in human progress, and if she had anything like a personal philosophy it was not Tory but Whig. The eighteenth-century Whigs viewed the emergence of English liberty as the result of providential design. It was a belief the Tory David Hume mocked in his *History of England*, where he showed the crucial role of chance events. This sceptical cast of mind was alien to Thatcher, and she came to view the mix of policies she had implemented as a cure for a specifically British disease as an all-purpose panacea. By the time she was ejected from Downing Street the loose set of attitudes and beliefs with which she had begun her career had hardened into a closed system.

The neo-liberal world-view that Thatcher accepted by the end of the 1980s was a successor-ideology to Marxism. Ideological thinking tends to adopt a one-size-fits-all approach to society, and so it was at the end of the eighties, when the close of the Cold War gave neo-liberal ideas a catastrophic boost. Led by Thatcher, western governments told the countries of the former Soviet bloc that if they wanted prosperity they had to import the free market. The notion that one set of policies could have the same beneficent results in the widely different countries of the former Soviet bloc was absurd, but it was of a piece with the mind-set in the International Monetary Fund that had imposed similar policies on highly dissimilar countries such as Indonesia, Nigeria and Peru. Along with the bureaucrats of the IMF, emissaries were dispatched to post-communist lands carrying the same draft constitution in their briefcases. No matter how discrepant the countries they descended upon these neo-liberal ideologues tried to impose the same model on them all.

While the fall of the Soviet Union was an advance for human freedom, its impact on peace was always going to be mixed. War and ethnic cleansing have gone with the transition from dictatorship in many countries. Though the communist collapse itself occurred with remarkably little violence, there was never any reason to think the post-communist world would depart from this pattern. More sober western policies might have mitigated the dangers, but in the triumphal climate of the time there was no taste for realism. Instead a utopian outlook came to be accepted by mainstream political parties.

Utopian thinking is most dangerous when it is least recognized. The emergence in the 1990s of a centrist version of utopianism illustrates this fact. First with neo-liberal economic policies in Russia and then with humanitarian military intervention in the Balkans, western governments embarked on courses of action that had no prospect of success. They were unprepared when the spread of democracy triggered ethnic nationalism in former Yugoslavia, separatism in Chechnya and Islamism in former Soviet Central Asia. Democracy and free markets were supposed to bring peace in their wake, not crime and violence.

Without realizing the fact, western governments had absorbed a utopian outlook. Governments of Left and Right believed that resurgent nationalism and ethnic and religious conflicts were passing local difficulties in the universal advance towards a new world order. Realistic thought was disabled by the return to power of an ideology that had been discarded over a century before.

THE RISE AND FALL OF NEO-LIBERALISM

Modern professors of economics and of ethics operate in disciplines which have been secularized to the point where the religious elements and implications which were once an integral part of them have been painstakingly eliminated.

Jacob Viner[7]

By the end of the 1980s a doctrinaire form of liberalism had conquered the Conservative party. In the nineties it extended its influence to Labour. Blair accepted not only the new framework of policy that Thatcher had imposed in place of the post-war settlement but also the neo-liberal style of thinking that had grown up around it.

New Labour's embrace of neo-liberalism was first of all a response to Thatcher's political success. When Blair became Labour leader in 1994 his party had been out of power for a decade and a half. He swallowed Thatcher's faith in the market as an elixir that would revivify the party and bring it back to power. The infusion seemed to have the desired effect, and Blair – along with Gordon Brown, Labour Chancellor and his rival for the leadership – accepted neo-liberal economics. Yet Blair was always closer to neo-conservative thinking, and after the 9/11 attacks he shifted decisively to neo-conservatism.

Versions of neo-liberal ideas have shaped policy in Britain and many other countries from the late eighties to the present day. Neo-liberalism encompasses several schools of thinking, but they have some key beliefs in common. Neo-liberals believe that the most important condition of individual liberty is the free market. The scope of government must be strictly limited. Democracy may be desirable but it must be limited to protect market freedoms. The free market is the most productive economic system and therefore tends to be emulated throughout the world. Free markets are not only the most efficient way of organizing the economy but also the most peaceful. As they expand, the sources of human conflict are reduced. In a global free market war and tyranny will disappear. Humanity will advance to unprecedented heights.

With minor variations F. A. Hayek, Milton Friedman and a host of lesser lights all subscribed to these beliefs. All were exponents of a late twentieth-century Enlightenment ideology whose basic tenets – despite being advanced as the results of scientific inquiry – are rooted in religious faith. Neo-liberals aimed to recover the lost purity of liberalism before its pollution by collectivist thinking, and like all fundamentalists they ended up with a caricature of the tradition they seek to revive. Neo-liberalism was a late twentieth-century parody of classical political economy. The classical economists of the eighteenth century believed all societies pass through definite stages of development leading to a single destination – a commercial civilization based on market exchange – but they had a clear understanding of the flaws of market societies. Lacking this insight, neo-liberals turned classical economics into a utopian ideology.

The classical economists themselves had serious doubts about the commercial society they saw coming into being around them. For Adam Smith commercial society was the best kind of human association, but it was highly imperfect. At times he refers to the market – or the 'system of natural liberty', as he often calls it – as being a Utopia; but he means that it is the best achievable system, not that it is without serious flaws. While he was impressed by the productivity of free markets, Adam Smith feared their moral hazards. Workers did not need to be well educated to perform the simple repetitive tasks required of them in the factories that were being set up in the north of England, while the anonymous cities that were springing up around the factories did not encourage virtue. In the long run this posed a risk to commercial civilization. Smith's anxieties echoed those of earlier thinkers in a civic republican tradition and influenced later critics of capitalism. Marx's theory of the alienating effects of wage-labour owes a good deal to Smith's insights into the flaws of commercial societies. Caricatured by twentieth-century ideologues as a market missionary, Smith was in fact an early theorist of the cultural contradictions of capitalism.[8] Smith's Utopia is '. . . an imperfect utopia, or, differently put, a utopia suited for imperfect creatures'.[9] Imperfect as it may be, the system of natural liberty is not easily achieved. Unlike neo-liberals in the late twentieth century, Smith was sceptical of schemes of market reform. Such hopes as he had for his Utopia being realized rested on his religious beliefs.

Smith had little in common with secular evangelists for the free market like Hayek and Friedman. He viewed the emergence of commercial society as the work of divine providence. His conception of the 'invisible hand' – a system of hidden adjustments whereby the miscellaneous exchanges of the market promote the common good – was spelt out in unequivocally theistic terms. The invisible hand was God working through the medium of human sentiments, and human reason played a small role in this process. The market did not develop because human beings understood its advantages. It emerged as a by-product of instincts God had implanted in them. Like other thinkers of the Scottish Enlightenment, Smith understood that human behaviour is governed by emotion and convention far more than by reason, and like them he was suspicious of the intellect when it operated without regard for sentiment. The American economic historian Jacob Viner has summarized Smith's standpoint:

The sentiments are innate to man; that is, man is endowed with them by providence. Under normal circumstances, the sentiments are infallible. It is reason which is fallible. Greatest of all in degree of fallibility is the speculative reason of the moral philosopher, unless the legislator is on a still lower level. Man, however, tends to attribute to the human reason what is really the wisdom of the Author of Nature as reflected in the sentiments.[10]

A conception of providence underpins the idea of a natural system of liberty advanced by Smith, and liberal thought as a whole is shaped by Christian beliefs. It was only in the mid-nineteenth century that liberalism came to be linked with secular thought. Since that time many attempts have been made to detach it from its origins, but liberalism remains an offshoot of Christianity.

In the early nineteenth century the chief argument for free trade was that tariffs thwart the divine design. In the most common formula, God scattered resources throughout the world so that widely separated peoples might come into close relations through trade and in this way recognize one another as brothers. Free trade was a means to brotherhood under the law of God. In the 1840s Richard Cobden waged a successful campaign against the protectionist Corn Laws in Britain with the slogan 'Free Trade is the International Law of God'. For him this was not metaphor but literal truth. Later economists tried to reformulate the case for universal free trade in secular terms of comparative advantage, but they have never been very successful. A great deal of economic theory consists of attempts to deduce free markets from dubious axioms of rational choice. The resulting body of thought is markedly more dogmatic than Smith's faith-based political economy. The free market became a religion only when its basis in religion was denied.[11]

The idea that the free market is grounded in science is central in the thought of Herbert Spencer (1820–1903). Born into a dissenting Methodist family that was strongly anticlerical (with some Quaker connections) but firmly Christian in its beliefs, Spencer became an agnostic and spent his life trying to reformulate a version of Smith's system of natural liberty in scientific terms. An eccentric personality who produced part of his vast corpus of writings while travelling back and forth on the Channel ferry wearing earmuffs as a protection against noise pollution, Spencer became one of the most influential thinkers of the late nineteenth century, with a large following in the United States. It was chiefly his idea of social evolution that brought him this renown. In seeking a scientific basis for ethics, Spencer was much influenced by Comte, but while Comte invoked science to attack liberal values Spencer used science to defend them. In each case the science was bogus.

Spencer was the most influential exponent of Social Darwinism, a system of ideas that owes little to Charles Darwin – it was Spencer not Darwin who coined the phrase 'survival of the fittest'. For Spencer society evolves and its evolution can have only one end, the free market, or – as he called it following Comte – industrialism. 'Industrial' societies faced competition from 'militant' societies – socialist and nationalist regimes – which attempted to organize the economy on a basis of command. Spencer had no doubt the free market would prevail, but he never specified any mechanism that would ensure this result. Spencer's silence was not surprising. Market-based societies may be more productive than others. That does not mean they will be adopted everywhere. Even where they exist they may be abandoned – as Spencer himself observed with dismay, a type of *dirigisme* had replaced *laissez-faire* in Britain by the end of the nineteenth century. His theory of social evolution struggled to explain this fact, which planted a large question mark over his whole system of ideas.[12]

For most of his life Spencer was able to persuade himself that history was going his way. Faced with the rise of imperialism and protectionism towards the end of the nineteenth century he fell into despair. Some of his disciples were not so tender-minded. Sidney and Beatrice Webb shared Spencer's view that more productive economic systems win out over less productive ones. Like him they could not help noticing that *laissez-faire* was in retreat, and they concluded that Soviet collectivism was more productive than western capitalism. The Webbs' embrace of Stalinism illustrates a flaw in all evolutionary theories of society. Social evolution is nearly always believed to lead to a single type of society, but history – like natural selection – has no overall direction or predetermined end-state. In practice, theorists of social evolution end up backing current trends. That is not far from equating might with right and often turns out to be a bad bet.

Towards the end of the twentieth century collectivism was in retreat. Neo-liberals believed a global free market was on the horizon; when it triumphed, peace and prosperity would be universal. This was the message of religious campaigners for free trade such as Cobden and John Bright. However, neo-liberals presented it as a fact established by social science – in this case the putative science of economics. Several different schools of economic theory were represented in the neo-liberal movement. Heavily influenced by Positivism, the Chicago School maintained that economics was a science containing universal laws just like the natural sciences, while the Austrian School maintained that the methods of natural science could not be applied to society. This was a fundamental disagreement, but it in no way dampened their enthusiasm for the free market; that was a tenet of their creed that could not be questioned. How it was justified did not matter.

The most ambitious and influential neo-liberal ideologue was F. A. Hayek (1899–1992). He grew up in the last years of the Habsburg Empire, viewing it correctly as in some ways a model liberal regime. He hated nationalism, rightly seeing in it a force of great destructive power, but he saw it as a reversion to tribalism. He failed to see that – like Nazism, communism and Jacobinism – nationalism is a modern phenomenon. He was a trenchant opponent of scientism – the mistaken application of the methods of the natural sciences to human affairs. Yet his defence of the free market was itself a type of scientism. In the 1930s he engaged in an extended debate on the origins of the Great Depression with J. M. Keynes, which Keynes – a more penetrating thinker as well as being more skilful in orchestrating opinion – won without difficulty. In the 1940s he gave up economics for social philosophy, but not before developing a powerful critique of central planning. Mainstream economists believed that under suitable conditions central planning could be highly productive. Against this consensus Hayek argued that it was inherently unworkable.

The core of Hayek's argument was that the planners could never possess the knowledge they need to organize economic life efficiently. Like the philosopher of science Michael Polanyi – who visited the University of Chicago at the start of the 1950s when Hayek was a professor there – Hayek argued that knowledge of society is mostly embodied in practices. The price mechanism is a response to this problem – it enables us to use widely dispersed knowledge that is completely available to no one. Hayek overlooked the distortions to which free markets are prone, and exaggerated when he suggested that centralized economic planning was impossible – the British command economy worked pretty well during the Second World War, for example. But he identified an insuperable obstacle to economic planning of the sort that was advocated by Marx and attempted in the Soviet bloc, Maoist China, Cuba and other communist countries. Even where some of the planners' objectives were achieved – as in sections of the Soviet military-industrial complex – it was against the background of colossal waste. At a time when the majority of economists had no doubt that central economic planning could produce a level of prosperity comparable with that of market-based systems, Hayek showed it was bound to be far less productive. His position was vindicated by the record of the planned economies that emerged fully only after their collapse, and it is as a prescient critic of state socialism that he will be remembered.

Unfortunately it was as a theorist of the free market that Hayek achieved influence.[13] His impact on leading politicians was slight, but he contributed to a harmful type of thinking: while illuminating the irrationality of central planning he overlooked that of market processes. Markets are prone to cycles of boom and bust and recurrent collapse. Keynes and others argued the Great Depression was a result of the mistaken belief that the free market is self-stabilizing. As Michael Polanyi's brother, the economist Karl Polanyi, put it, 'The origins of the catastrophe lay in the utopian endeavour of economic liberalism to set up a self-regulating market system.'[14] Even if government policies aggravated economic collapse in the thirties (as Hayek argued), it does not follow that markets can be relied on. There is nothing in market processes that makes them self-adjusting. Hayek's achievement was to show that a successfully planned economy is a

Utopia. He failed to notice that the same is true of the self-regulating market.

Hayek also believed the free market appears spontaneously. Emerging as the unintended consequence of countless human actions, it is not the result of any human design. In the most complete statement of his views, *The Constitution of Liberty*, he praises 'British philosophers' because they rejected the 'French' idea that social institutions embody a rational design: 'They find the origin of institutions,' he writes, 'not in contrivance or design but in the survival of the successful.'[15] As an account of the emergence of the free market this is the opposite of the truth. It is only a slight exaggeration to say that *laissez-faire* came about as a result of central planning. The free market in Britain in the mid-nineteenth century was an artefact of state power. The same was true in the late twentieth century. Reinventing the market meant curbing spontaneously evolved institutions, such as trade unions and (though this was not often recognized) monopolistic corporations. This could be done only by a highly centralized state.

If free markets are normally the result of deliberate construction, spontaneously evolved social institutions are rarely liberal – in Hayek's meaning of the term, at any rate. A political system of the sort Hayek admired came into being in England without anyone planning it; but – as Hume showed in his *History of England* – that was by chance, not as a result of the operation of any divine or natural law. In much the same way, feudal societies came into being without anyone intending it or understanding how it happened, and no one designed the curbs on free markets that were imposed in late Victorian Britain. If there is such a thing as spontaneous social evolution it produces institutions of many kinds.

The error of Hayek's belief that the free market develops spontaneously was shown in Russia during the Yeltsin era. Western governments believed that once state planning was dismantled a market economy would develop automatically. A market economy emerged, but it was dominated by organized crime. Under Putin, Russian anarcho-capitalism was replaced by a new system – still intertwined with crime but seemingly more organized and popularly legitimate than before – that was more efficient than central planning but far removed from the free market. The result of relying on spontaneous processes was a new type of command economy.

Hayek is often compared with Edmund Burke, the Irish-born eighteenth-century parliamentarian who founded English conservatism, and they do have something in common. Like Hayek, Burke believed that tradition encapsulates the wisdom of generations. However, unlike Hayek, Burke based this belief in religious faith: the invisible movement of tradition was providence at work in history. It was difficult to reconcile this idea with the fact of the French Revolution, but provided he was ready to accept the Terror as divine punishment for human wickedness, Burke could maintain his faith. As a secular thinker, Hayek lacked this recourse. Instead he based his belief in tradition on science, and here he was closer to Auguste Comte. Hayek was a sharp critic of Positivism who would have been horrified by the suggestion that he had anything in common with Comte the Positivist ideologue. Yet, like Comte, Hayek turned to science to validate a providentialist view of human development. Though they differed radically about its structure, both believed a universal system was the end-point of history.

Hayek and Comte viewed history as a one-way street, and in this they were at one with Spencer and Marx. All these thinkers underrated the persistent power of nationalism and religion, which have interacted with new technologies to produce a wide variety of economic and political arrangements. Some may be too repressive and unproductive to survive – for example, Soviet-style central planning and the Taliban regime in Afghanistan – but at the start of the twenty-first century the world contains several sorts of regime. China has adopted a mix of nationalism and state capitalism, Iran a type of popular theocracy, America a blend of free markets with protectionism and crony capitalism, Russia an ultra-modern version of authoritarianism, Europe a combination of social democracy and neo-liberal economic integration, and so on. None of these systems is fixed for ever. They are all interacting with one another and changing continuously. But they are developing in different directions, and there is no reason to expect any ultimate convergence.

In many respects Hayek's view of the free market resembles that of Marx. In common with Marx, Hayek viewed the unfettered market not only as the most productive economic system that had ever existed but also as the most revolutionary. Once it has come into being capitalism cannot help spreading, and unless some disaster intervenes it is bound to become universal. However, while Marx understood that the advance of capitalism would overturn bourgeois life, Hayek did not. Hayek believed market societies were based on tradition, writing: 'Paradoxical as it may appear it is probably true that a successful free society will always be in large measure a tradition-bound society.'[16] He failed to notice that free markets work to subvert the bourgeois traditions that underpinned capitalism in the past. Hayek's attempt to link the defence of free markets with a kind of cultural conservatism ran up against the transgressive energy of the untrammelled market. It was a contradiction that neo-conservatives understood, and were determined to do something about.

An American Neo-Conservative in 10 Downing Street

I only know what I believe.   Tony Blair[17]

Neo-conservatism is not the most recent variety of conservatism. It is a new type of politics that can emerge at any point on the political spectrum. In Britain, neo-conservatism's political vehicle was not the Conservative party but the new party that Blair created when he seized the Labour leadership.

The single most important fact in Blair's rise to power was Thatcher's new settlement. Both in economic and political terms it was an established fact, but while this was an index of Thatcher's achievement it was also a source of weakness for the Conservatives. Thatcher often declared that she aimed to destroy socialism in Britain. She never paused to consider what would be the effect on her party if she succeeded. For much of the twentieth century the Conservatives acted as a brake on collectivism. The Conservative party existed to oppose not just socialism but also – and more relevantly – any further advance towards social democracy. By dismantling the Labour settlement Thatcher removed the chief reason for the existence of the Conservative party. Without a clearly defined enemy it lacked an identity. Labour had never been a doctrinaire socialist party – as Labour prime minister Harold Wilson remarked, it had always owed more to Methodism than to Marx – but by identifying New Labour with the market, Blair was able to deprive the Conservatives of the threat that had defined them for generations. As a result they were mired in confusion for nearly a decade.

While Blair's embrace of neo-liberal economic policies was a strategic decision, it soon acquired an ideological rationale. More conventional in his thinking about domestic issues than most politicians and having an even shorter historical memory, Blair embraced without question the neo-liberal belief that only one economic system can deliver prosperity in a late modern context. Modernization became the Blairite mantra, and for Blair it meant something precise: the reorganization of society around the imperatives of the free market. When he was still in opposition Blair curried support from disillusioned Conservatives by representing himself as a One Nation Tory – a progressive conservative who accepted the central role of the market but also understood the importance of social cohesion. Once in power it was clear Blair came not to bury Thatcher but to continue her work.

Blair's One Nation Toryism was like his fabled Third Way, a political marketing tool. The Third Way originated in Bill Clinton's practice of 'triangulation' – a tactic invented in the mid-1990s by Clinton's advisor Dick Morris, which involved Clinton setting himself up as a more pragmatic alternative to both parties in Congress. Adopting the same tactic Blair attacked his own party as much as the Conservatives. His successful campaign to remove Clause Four (which mandated common ownership of the means of production) from the Labour constitution in 1995 was a symbolic act rather than a policy shift. At the same time it was a marker for larger challenges to Labour's social-democratic inheritance. Blair carried on the agenda of privatization that had developed from Thatcher's original programme into core areas of the state such as sections of the justice system and prison service, and inserted market mechanisms into the NHS and the schooling system.

In these respects Blair did no more than consolidate Thatcherism. He did not change British society in the way Thatcher did. His chief impact has been on his own party. New Labour was constructed to bury the past and in this if in nothing else it succeeded. It began as a coup masterminded by a handful of people – Tony Blair, Gordon Brown, Peter Mandelson, Alistair Campbell, Philip Gould and others – who aimed to rebuild the party as an instrument for securing power. New Labour was a purpose-built construction with few links to the political tradition that preceded it. If it displayed any continuity with the past it was with the Social Democratic party that had split from Labour in the eighties, but unlike the Social Democrats New Labour grasped that issues of strategy and organization are more important than questions of policy. New Labour's first priority was to restructure the party as a centralized institution. Power had to be concentrated before anything else could be done. New Labour always had a Leninist aspect, but it was a Leninism that focused on reshaping the image of the party. If New Labour was 'modern' in its acceptance of the free market it was 'post-modern' in its conviction that power is exercised by changing the way society is perceived.

Blair's most prominent talents were his skill in using the techniques of public relations and his sensitivity to the public mood. These traits have led some observers to the view that he is an opportunist with no underlying convictions. It is true there has never been anything like a Blairite ideology, but that does not mean Blair has no beliefs. His career in politics is testimony to the power of neo-conservative ideas, which guided his most fateful decisions. Blair was a neo-liberal by default, but a neo-conservative by conviction.[18]

Neo-conservatism diverges from neo-liberalism at crucial points, and it is specifically neo-conservative beliefs that shaped Blair's view of the world. Unlike neo-liberals, neo-conservatives do not aim to return to an imaginary era of minimum government. They perceive that the social effects of free markets are not all benign and look to government to promote the virtues the free market neglects. Blair has always been a strong advocate of 'law and order', and made this a theme when he served as shadow home secretary under Labour leader John Smith. In part this was a strategic move to wrest the territory from the Conservatives, but it also matched his instincts.

Neo-conservatives may not always be admirers of Victorian values – some (including Blair) have seen themselves as having liberal views on personal morality – but they reject the view that the state can be morally neutral. Government must act to promote the good life, which involves accepting the need for discipline and punishment. It also means promoting religion. Unlike neo-liberals, who are usually secular in outlook, neo-conservatives view religion as a vital source of social cohesion – a view expressed in Blair's support for faith schools.

Above all, neo-conservatives are unwilling to rely on social evolution. Commonly more intelligent than neo-liberals, they understand that while capitalism is a revolutionary force that overturns established social structures and topples regimes this does not happen by itself – state power and sometimes military force are needed to expedite the process. In its enthusiasm for revolutionary change, neo-conservatism has more in common with Jacobinism and Leninism than with neo-liberalism or traditional conservatism. The common view of Blair as a crypto-Tory could not be more mistaken. There is no trace in him of the scepticism about progress voiced by Tories such as Disraeli. Nor is he simply another neo-liberal prophet of the free market. He is an American neo-conservative and has been throughout most of his political life.

It is in international relations that neo-conservatism shaped Blair most deeply. Whatever he may have wished his inheritance to be – British entry into the single European currency, perhaps – he will be remembered for taking the UK into a ruinous war. His part in the Iraq war destroyed him as a politician, and he cannot have wanted this result. It would be a mistake to imagine that he was as committed at the beginning of this ill-conceived venture as he later came to be; he made errors of judgement at every stage. At the same time his support for the war expressed his most basic beliefs.

From one point of view it was a misjudged exercise in *realpolitik*. Like other British prime ministers Blair feared the consequence of opposing US policies and was prey to the conceit that by being America's unswerving ally Britain could help shape its behaviour in the international system. Anthony Eden's attempt to topple Egyptian president Nasser and reassert British control of the Suez Canal in

1956 destroyed his political career and underlined the risks of any British leader opposing American power. Later prime ministers successfully distanced themselves from American policies – most notably Harold Wilson, who wisely declined to send troops to support the Americans in Vietnam – but Blair was insistent that Britain must give the US full support. He feared the impact on the international system if the US acted alone and saw an opportunity for Britain to 'punch above its weight' by acting as the bridge between America and Europe.

In fact, the war left the transatlantic divide wider than at any time since the Second World War, with British opinion alienated from the US, and Britain at the same time more at odds with Europe even than in Thatcher's time. But it was not only a misguided attempt at higher strategy, and there can be no doubt that Bush's decision to overthrow Saddam chimed with Blair's convictions. Saddam was a tyrant who represented a stage in human history whose time had passed. A new international order was under construction with America in the lead, and Blair wanted to be at the forefront of this project. As John Kampfner has written, 'Blair was not dragged into war with Iraq. He was at ease with himself and his own beliefs.'[19]

What were those beliefs? In a span of six years Blair took Britain into war five times. He sanctioned air strikes against Saddam Hussein in 1998, the Kosovo war in 1999, British military intervention in Sierra Leone in 2000, the war in Afghanistan in 2002 and Iraq in 2003. He dispatched further contingents of British troops to Afghanistan in 2006 when US forces were run down in the country. There is a strong strand of continuity in these decisions. Blair believes in the power of force to ensure the triumph of the good. From this point of view the attack on Iraq was a continuation of policies in the Balkans and Afghanistan. In each case war was justified as a form of humanitarian intervention. This may have had some force in the Balkans and Sierra Leone. It was dubious in Afghanistan and duplicitous in Iraq.

Blair justified these military involvements in terms of a 'doctrine of international community', which he presented in a speech at the Economic Club in Chicago in 1999. Blair's new doctrine rested on the belief that state sovereignty could no longer survive in an interdependent world:

We are witnessing the beginnings of a new doctrine of international community. By this I mean the explicit recognition that today more than ever before we are mutually dependent, that national interest is to a significant extent governed by international collaboration and that we need a clear and coherent debate as to the direction the doctrine takes us in each field of international endeavour. Just as within domestic politics, the notion of community – the belief that partnership and cooperation are essential to advance self-interest – is coming into its own; so it needs to find its own international echo.[20]

Blair's speech reflects the unreal intellectual climate of the time. In the nineties it was fashionable to maintain that the world had moved into a 'post-Westphalian' era – so called after the Treaty of Westphalia of 1648, which is often seen as marking the point at which the modern state was recognized in law. This system had ended in the post-Cold War period, it was believed: state sovereignty was no longer at the centre of the international system, which was governed by global institutions. In fact the sovereign state was as strong as it had ever been, and its seeming decline was a by-product of the interval after the end of the Cold War in which the US seemed able to act without restraint from other powers. The interval was destined to be brief. China and India were emerging as great powers whose interests diverge at important points but which are at one in rejecting any system based on American hegemony. In the nineties as in the past several great powers were interacting in a mix of rivalry and cooperation. In many ways this was a re-run of the late nineteenth century with different players.

The idea that the sovereign state is on the way out was nonsense, but it served Blair well. In the first place it matched his view of the world in which human development is seen as a series of stages, each better than the last. This is a Whiggish variant of the belief in providence to which Blair subscribed as part of his Christian worldview. It would be unwise to take too seriously Blair's claim to have been inspired by the Quaker philosopher John Macmurray (1891–1976) – a Christian communitarian thinker who developed from the British Idealist tradition and argued for a positive understanding of freedom as a part of the common good. To a greater extent than most politicians, Blair's view of the world was formed by the conventional beliefs of the day. He never doubted that globalization was creating a worldwide market economy that must eventually be complemented by global democracy. When he talked of the necessity for continuing 'economic reform' – as he often did – he took for granted this meant further privatization and the injection of market mechanisms into public services. The incessant 'modernization' he demanded was, in effect, an ossified version of the ideas of the late eighties. Like Thatcher – with whom he has very little else in common – Blair lacked scepticism. For him the clichés of the hour have always been eternal verities.

As with George W. Bush, however, there is no reason to doubt the reality of Blair's faith. Like Bush, Blair thinks of international relations in terms derived from theology. To be sure this is not the theology of Augustine or Aquinas. It failed to persuade Pope John Paul II when Blair had an audience with him in late February 2003. Medieval Christian thinkers developed a rigorous theory of the conditions that must be satisfied before a war can be considered just, and the pontiff rightly believed they had not been met. The audience must have pained Blair, but it failed to shake his sense of rectitude. It was enough that he felt he was right. The scrupulous casuistry of medieval thinkers regarding the consequences of human action was of no interest. Good intentions are what matter and they are bound in the end to prevail. And yet these same 'good intentions' were promoted through ill-conceived and ideologically motivated policies, whose distance from any prudent assessment of facts he seemed unable to perceive.

The idea that the international system was moving towards global governance expanded the traditional purposes of war. The 'international community' could take military action whenever it was morally right to do so. Not only 'rogue states' that threatened the international system by developing weapons of mass destruction but also states that violated the human rights of their citizens should be the target of armed force. The aim was not just to neutralize threats – even pre-emptively. It was to improve the human condition. War was no longer a last resort against the worst evils but an instrument of human progress. In his speech in Chicago, Blair acknowledged that military action should be taken only when diplomacy had failed, and then only if it had a reasonable prospect of achieving its goals. Nevertheless he dismissed the views of those – many of them in the professional military in the UK and the US – who demanded that an exit strategy be identified before military intervention could be seriously contemplated. For Blair their caution smacked of defeatism. 'Success is the only exit strategy I am prepared to consider,' he declared.[21] Later speeches show Blair accepting that military force alone cannot bring about the radical transformation in the international system to which he is committed. Addressing the World Affairs Council in Los Angeles in August 2006 Blair declared that the struggle against terrorism 'is one about values'. He was reticent in specifying what these values might be; but whatever they were, he had no doubt they spearheaded human advance: 'Our values are worth struggling for. They represent humanity's progress throughout the ages and at each point we have had to fight for them and defend them. As a new age beckons, it is time to fight for them again.'[22] Blair returned to the subject in January 2007, when he opined: 'Terrorism destroys progress. Terrorism can't be defeated by military means alone. But it can't be defeated without it.'[23]

Lying behind Blair's view of international relations is a view of America. Along with his fellow neo-conservatives in Washington Blair regards America as the paradigm of a modern society. Propelled by the momentum of history, it is invincible. In giving his backing to the Bush administration in Iraq, Blair was able to believe that he was aiding the cause of human progress while having the consoling sense of being on the side of the big battalions. Blair's faith in American invincibility was misguided. America's defeat by the Iraqi insurgency was in no way unexpected. The French were driven from Algeria despite prosecuting the war with extreme ruthlessness and being backed by over a million French settlers. In conditions more like those American forces faced in Iraq, the Soviets had also been driven from Afghanistan. The lesson of asymmetric warfare – where the militarily weak use unorthodox tactics against the seemingly overwhelmingly strong – is that the weak have the winning hand.

If Blair failed to heed these lessons, the reason was partly ignorance. A politician who has unusual intuitive gifts in divining the British public mood, he lacked the knowledge necessary to make well-founded judgements in international contexts. His record of success in domestic politics was based on banishing the past. He was led into the Iraq débâcle by the belief that history was on his side. Actually he knew very little history, and what he did know he refused to accept when it undercut his hopes. History was significant only as a record of human advance. To turn to it to chasten current ambitions was unthinkable, even immoral. Like Bush, Blair viewed history as the unfolding of a providential design, and a feature of their view is that the design is visible to the faithful. Others may be blind to the unfolding pattern, and in that case they may have to be guided. In Augustinian terms this is unacceptable, for only God can know the design of history. Here Blair has been the modern man he claims to be: for him a sense of subjective certainty is all that is needed for an action to be right. If deception is needed to realize the providential design it cannot be truly deceitful.

Deception has been integral at every stage of the Iraq war. In Chapter 4 I will consider the process through which war was engineered in America. Here it may be sufficient to consider some of the key episodes of disinformation that enabled British involvement in the war. In the run-up to the invasion Blair always insisted publicly that its goal was not regime change – which he knew to be legally unacceptable as a ground for attacking the country – but the threat posed by Iraq's supposed WMD. A document was circulated titled *Iraq's Programme of Weapons of Mass Destruction: The Assessment of the British Government* (published on 24 September 2002 under the title *Iraq's Weapons of Mass Destruction: The Assessment of the British Government*). The document – which came to be known as the 'dodgy dossier' – claimed to be an authoritative statement based on intelligence concerning Iraq's capabilities and intentions regarding WMD; but it contradicted earlier intelligence assessments. In March 2002, a report to the Joint Intelligence Committee (JIC), which brings together information from all of the UK's intelligence services, concluded that there was 'no evidence that Saddam Hussein posed a significantly greater threat than in 1991 after the Gulf War'. Moreover, while the dossier claimed to be based on intelligence sources, 90 per cent of it was copied from three published articles. In the case of one of them the meaning was changed to imply that Iraq was supporting Islamist terrorist groups such as al-Qaeda – a claim for which there was no basis, and which evidence of enmity and suspicion between the two rendered highly implausible.[24]

Like Bush, Blair has focused on intelligence failures as being among the chief reasons for the difficulty of prosecuting the war. In fact a recurrent feature of the conflict has been that intelligence findings that ran counter to claims made in support of the decision to go to war have been ignored or suppressed. In February 2003 a leaked document from the UK Defence Intelligence Staff (DIS) acknowledged that there had been contact between al-Qaeda and the Iraqi regime in the past but noted that any relationship between them foundered on mistrust. '[Bin Laden's] aims are in ideological conflict with present-day Iraq,' the report concluded.[25] The report contradicted the claim that Saddam cultivated contacts with the group that organized the 9/11 attacks – a claim central to Blair's defence of the attack on Iraq as part of the 'war against terror'. An earlier report, the 'Iraq Options' paper produced by the Overseas and Defence Secretariat of the Cabinet Office on 8 March 2002, surveyed the evidence and concluded unambiguously:

In the judgement of the JIC, there is no recent evidence of Iraq[i] complicity with international terrorism. There is therefore no justification for action against Iraq based on self-defence to combat imminent threats of terrorism as in Afghanistan.[26]

This report and others show that Britain's intelligence agencies were repeatedly tasked to find evidence for links between Saddam and al-Qaeda. Unable to find any such evidence and unwilling to invent it, they reported that none existed. The only effect their reports had was that Blair shifted the case for war to arguments about WMD, where intelligence could be more easily manipulated.

In this instance, as in others, the problem was not defective intelligence. It was that intelligence was disregarded when it did not support the case for war. Blair had no use for intelligence based on facts. He was only interested in 'faith-based intelligence' – as a former arms-control expert who used to work for the American Department of State, Bureau of Intelligence and Research, described the way intelligence is viewed in the Bush administration.[27] One of the administration's key proponents of faith-based intelligence headed the Office of Special Plans – an ad hoc organization set up to screen out inconvenient intelligence, which will be examined in Chapter 5.

Secret planning for the invasion seems to have started in America months or weeks after the 9/11 terrorist attacks late in 2001, and it was clear to Blair that Bush meant to go to war in Iraq from the time he visited Bush at Camp David in April 2002. A memorandum from the foreign secretary Jack Straw, which was sent to Blair on 25 March 2002 in preparation for the visit, noted that while it seemed clear Bush had made up his mind, the case for war was thin – Saddam was not threatening his neighbours, and his WMD capability was less than that of Libya, North Korea or Iran. Despite this advice Blair gave his full backing to Bush when the two met at Camp David. At a meeting held at 10 Downing Street at 9 a.m. on 23 July 2002 whose details were subsequently leaked in the 'Downing Street Memo', Blair was told by 'C' – the head of the Secret Intelligence Service MI6, Sir Richard Dearlove, who had recently had talks in Washington with the head of the CIA, George Tenet – that military action against Saddam was 'seen as inevitable' and 'the intelligence and facts were being fixed around the policy'.[28] Partly in order to placate opinion in the Labour party, Blair persuaded Bush to go to the UN to seek a second resolution authorizing military action. Yet at a meeting in the White House on 31 January 2003, Bush made it clear to Blair that he meant to go to war regardless of the UN's decision, and Blair again promised Bush his full support.[29] He also rejected an offer from Bush that could have spared Britain from full involvement in the war. In March 2003, fearful that Blair's government might fall, Bush gave him the option of British forces not participating in the invasion. Blair dismissed the option and insisted he was fully committed.[30] However, in the House of Commons Blair maintained the pretence that war could still be avoided right up to the crucial vote on 18 March (two days before the war).

Blair's complicity in deception in the run-up to war has led to him being seen as mendacious. This is a misreading. It is not so much that he is economical with the truth as that he lacks the normal understanding of it. For him truth is whatever serves the cause, and when he engages in what is commonly judged to be deception he is only anticipating the new world that he is helping to bring about. His silences serve the same higher purpose. Blair has remained silent regarding the abuses that occurred at Abu Ghraib and he has dismissed well-sourced reports that American planes have used British airports to implement the policy of 'special rendition' in which terrorist suspects are kidnapped and transported to countries where they can be tortured. Blair's stance on these issues must by ordinary standards be judged to be thoroughly dishonest, but it is clear he believes ordinary standards do not apply to him. Deception is justified if it advances human progress – and then it is not deception. Blair's untruths are not true lies. They are prophetic glimpses of the future course of history, and they carry the hazards of all such revelations.

During Blair's decade in office British government changed in character. All administrations aim to present a positive image of themselves, and some have departed from truth in the process. Where Blair was unique was in viewing the shaping of public opinion as government's overriding purpose. The result was that whereas in the past lies were an intermittent feature of government, under his leadership they became integral to its functioning.[31] Writing about the role of lying in Soviet politics, the French political thinker Raymond Aron observed:

In the exact, strict sense of the word, he who consciously says the opposite of the truth is lying: Lenin's companions were lying when they confessed to crimes they had not committed, and Soviet propaganda was lying when it sang of the happiness of the people during the days of collectivization . . .

On the other hand, when the Bolsheviks, the Communists, call the Soviet Union *socialist*, must we say that they are lying? . . . if they recognize the difference between what socialism is today and what it will be when it conforms to its essence, then they are not, in the strictest sense, lying, but rather substituting for reality [something that can be described as] 'pseudo reality': the meaning that they give something in terms of a future they imagine as conforming to the ideology. Despite everything, Sovietism becomes a step along the road to socialism, and hence a step toward the salvation of mankind.[32]

If there is an historical precedent for Blair's methodical disregard for truth it is in the Soviet era, when a generation of western communists represented the USSR as a stage on the way to universal democracy. Believing they were serving an invincible cause, these fellow-travellers were ready to 'lie for the truth' by portraying the Soviet system not as it was in fact but as it would inevitably – so they believed – become. It was absurd to describe the Soviet Union as a democracy. It is no less absurd to suggest that Iraq is an emerging liberal democracy and to refer to the country as the place in which the war against global terrorism is being won. In factual terms Iraq is a failed state, and insofar as there is anything like democracy it is working to produce Iranian-style theocracy. In the same way, facts tell us that the US-led invasion has turned the country into a training ground for terrorists. Blair did more than conceal these facts. He constructed a pseudo-reality that aimed to shape the way we think. As in the Soviet case, the pseudo-reality failed to withstand the test of history. The hideous facts of life in Iraq refute the post-modern dogma that truth is a construction of power. If they have yet to penetrate into Blair's awareness they have entered that of American voters, and as a result he is condemned to live out his days as the redundant servant of a failed administration.

The political environments in which Blair and Bush came to power could hardly be more different. Blair could not mobilize popular religious belief behind him as Bush did, and a neo-conservative intellectual movement supporting his messianic foreign policy began to develop in Britain only towards the end of his period in power. Yet there was a kinship between Bush and Blair. The combination of a shallow but intense religiosity with a militant faith in human progress that defines Bush's world-view also shaped Blair's. Blair and Bush interpreted the history of the past two decades – the only history they knew – as showing that humanity had entered a wholly new era. Like Thatcher at the end of the 1980s, they interpreted the collapse of communism not as a setback for western universalism – which it was – but as a sign of the triumph of 'the West'. Lacking any longer historical perspective, they understood the challenges of the early twenty-first century in terms of the triumphal illusions of the post-Cold War era.

Blair and Bush came at the end of a period of ascending utopianism in western politics. For them human progress was axiomatic; but it was never understood only in the terms of secular thought. Both practised a missionary style of politics, whose goal was nothing less than the salvation of mankind.

4

The Americanization of
the Apocalypse

*We have it in our power to begin the world over again. A
situation, similar to the present, hath not happened since
the days of Noah until now. The birthday of a new world
is at hand.*
                                                    Thomas Paine[1]

The murder of thousands of civilians on 11 September 2001 brought
apocalyptic thinking to the centre of American politics. At the same
time it re-energized beliefs that form part of America's myth. The
Puritans who colonized the country in the seventeenth century viewed
themselves as creating a society that would lack the evils of the Old
World. Established on universal principles it would serve as a model
to all of humankind. For these English colonists, America marked a
new beginning in history.

   In fact there are no such beginnings, and the sense of bringing into
being a new world that has been present in America from the time
the first English settlers arrived to the present day is not new or
uniquely American. It is a current of the millenarian ferment that
passed from medieval chiliasm through the English Revolution.
The sense of universal mission that is such a prominent feature of
American politics is an outflow from this ancient stream.

   The state that emerged from the American war of independence
adapted the traditions of English government to the conditions of a
struggle for national self-determination and rendered them into the
language of universal rights. The American colonists and those who
later turned the country into a self-governing republic imagined that
governments could be created by an appeal to first principles. In

reality both their principles and their belief that history could be started afresh were inheritances from the past.

FROM PURITAN COLONY TO REDEEMER NATION

We Americans are the peculiar, chosen people – the Israel of our time; we bear the ark of the liberties of the world.

Herman Melville[2]

The Puritan colonists who came to New England brought with them many of the prophetic beliefs that had fuelled the English Civil War. For them, the colonization of the New World was itself an apocalyptic event. John Winthrop's famous sermon of 1630 to the English Puritans who founded the Massachusetts Bay Colony, in which he described New England as a 'city on a hill' embodying a new contract with God, was probably delivered in England, before the colonists set off, rather than on board ship as was once thought. Winthrop's sermon was clear that the colony that was about to be established marked a new era in history; but he also warned of the dreadful fate that awaited it if it strayed from virtue:

For we must consider that we shall be as a city on a hill. The eyes of all people are upon us. So that if we shall deal falsely with our God in this work we have undertaken . . . we shall open the mouths of enemies to speak evil of the ways of God . . . We shall shame the ways of many of God's worthy servants, and cause their prayers to be turned into curses upon us until we be consumed out of the good land whither we are going.[3]

Among the colonists, the hope of a new world was combined with fear that the End-Time was near. John Cotton, minister of Boston's First Church, used the section of the Book of Revelation describing the defeat of the Beast as his text for a sermon on the occasion of the execution of Charles I and prophesied the destruction of the Antichrist in 1655. Such beliefs were commonplace in mid-seventeenth-century England, not only in groups such as the Fifth Monarchy Men but among a wide range of religious leaders and sects. As the scholar of American prophetic traditions Paul Boyer has noted, Puritan leaders urged support for the colonizing venture in America on explicitly eschatological grounds, with John Davenport describing it as 'a bulwark against the Kingdom of Antichrist'. Apocalyptic enthusiasm died down in England with the Restoration and the accession of Charles II in 1660, but by then it had found a new home in America. By the start of the eighteenth century Cotton Mather, minister at Boston's First Church and author of a richly apocalyptic history of New England, was describing it as 'the Spot of Earth, which the God of Heavens spied out' as the capital of the millennial kingdom.[4]

Openly apocalyptic movements did not die out. As has been seen in Chapter 1, early nineteenth-century Britain witnessed the mass movement led by Joanna Southcott, while Methodism channelled a powerful millenarian current. Around the same time millenarian ideas were assuming more secular shapes. Radical thinkers such as William Godwin and Thomas Paine reformulated the post-millennialist belief that the world could be transfigured by human action as an Enlightenment faith in progress. Godwin – the anarchist writer mentioned in Chapter 1 who married the early feminist Mary Wollstonecraft – viewed history as a series of stages in the development of human reason, ending in a world that no longer needed government. Godwin's view of history is teleological and clearly indebted to Christianity, but it lacks the expectation of any sudden transformation; the abrupt arrival of a new world, which is the core of millenarian hope, is absent. In contrast Paine – who achieved fame as an ideologue of the American Revolution and was read with admiration by George Washington – showed clear signs of apocalyptic thinking. The declaration in the appendix to the 1776 edition of his book *Common Sense*, which affirmed that the American Revolution allowed the world to be made over again, is a classic statement of apocalyptic belief. Along with many of his friends in revolutionary France – where like Condorcet he was imprisoned by the Jacobins – Paine was a Deist who believed that the existence of a divine being could be demonstrated by the use of reason. Yet this ardent rationalist thought of the American Revolution as a millennial event.

It was chiefly the formative role of apocalyptic religion in America that prevented it from establishing a variant of European civilization in the New World. There have always been some in America who have seen it as renewing Europe's achievements at a higher level. In his biography of Benjamin West, John Galt portrayed the great late eighteenth-century American painter as having revived a European artistic heritage. West's work exceeded anything that had been achieved in Europe, but the decline of the arts in Europe was only 'the gorgeous omen of the glory which they would attain in their passage over America'.[5] There is no sense here of America making a new start. Instead, rather in the way that classical historians viewed history in cyclical terms, European civilization is seen as finding another lease on life on American shores. Had this vision triumphed, America might have produced – like the countries south of the border – a new version of the Old World. Instead it came to see itself as different from Europe, a new civilization founded on universal principles.

Among the ideas that informed the American founders was the political theory of John Locke – a theory of government as a social contract designed to protect natural rights. Unlike nearly all the states that have existed, the United States was founded on the basis of an ideology, and if it is new it is in virtue of this fact. Locke's political theory served Americans well in the war of independence. It has been less useful when applied in foreign policy, where it promotes the belief that freedom is a condition that comes about simply through the removal of tyranny. Despite its universal claims, Locke's thought is a distillation of beliefs and values that make sense only in particular historical conditions. His political philosophy depends at every point on Protestant theology.[6] Human rights are grounded in our duties to God: we may not take our own lives, for example, because God created us and we remain his property. Locke's conception of the state of nature expresses Christian beliefs about the divine creation and ownership of the world. His ideal of limited government was an abstraction derived from the conflicts of seventeenth-century England. Freedom is not, as Locke imagined, a primordial human condition: where it exists it is the result of generations of institution building. Yet in America an idea of natural freedom became the basis of a civil religion that claimed universal authority.

By no means all of America's founders subscribed to this religion.

The authors of the *Federalist Papers*, which appeared in 1787–8 when the ratification of the US Constitution was under discussion, viewed government in a more sceptical light. Thinkers such as James Madison and Alexander Hamilton did not see the regime that was coming into being as an instrument whereby humanity would scale undreamt-of heights. With wise guidance America might surpass other forms of government, but it could not overcome the flaws inherent in all constitutions. The Federalists belong in an American anti-utopian tradition that has persisted through many vicissitudes, but it is a tradition that has never displaced the sense of universal mission with which the American colony was founded.

In claiming a foundation in a universal ideology, the United States belongs with states such as post-revolutionary France and the former Soviet Union, but unlike them it has been remarkably stable. American institutions have changed less over the past centuries than those of practically any other country. In an analysis of American nationalism, the British scholar Anatol Lieven has observed:

Given the general stereotype of the United States as a new, young and ever-changing country, it is important to note that the antiquity of American institutions is one reason why Americans are so loyal to them ... Even the British political system has changed far more fundamentally than the American over the past two hundred years ... Far from being a 'new' or 'young' state, America therefore has some claim to be almost the oldest state in the world.[7]

It is partly the antiquity of America's institutions that explains the abiding American belief in the country's exceptional role in the world. In nearly all other countries the ruling regime has changed again and again. Even Britain has been the site of a succession of political experiments and settlements. In lacking this experience of political transience, America belongs with only a small handful of countries such as Switzerland and Iceland. In a way few other peoples are able to do, Americans can identify themselves as a nation with the institutions by which they are governed. Despite the hiatus of the Civil War and the extension of federal government during the Roosevelt era, the US remained recognizably the same regime for over two hundred years.

The shift that occurred under the Bush administration was made possible by America's exceptional religiosity, which more than any other factor accounts for its difference from most of the rest of the world. As Alexis de Tocqueville (who coined the term[8]) recognized, American exceptionalism is a religious phenomenon. From the time the first colonists from England landed to the time when the country gained its independence America saw itself through the lens of religion. Both the post-millennial thinking that looked forward to a world transformed in part by human action and more chiliastic pre-millennial beliefs that anticipated cataclysmic conflicts shaped the way Americans interpreted their history and viewed the future. Each gave America a unique role in history, and the result was the Americanization of an apocalyptic myth.

The belief in Manifest Destiny that was formulated in the mid-nineteenth century was part of this process. The idea of a messianic saviour, which was at the core of early Christianity, became the idea of a Redeemer Nation – the belief in America as the land of a 'chosen people' to which Melville gave expression. Only a faith in America's redemptive role in history can account for the language used by Woodrow Wilson, when in his 1919 address attacking opponents of American membership of the League of Nations he declared:

I wish that they could feel the moral obligation that rests upon us not to go back on those boys, but to see the thing through, to see it through to the end and make good their redemption of the world. For nothing less depends on this decision, nothing less than the liberation and salvation of the world.[9]

Wilson may be a more complex figure than is sometimes recognized. In domestic contexts he was thoroughly reactionary on issues of racial segregation, and as far as the Americas were concerned the military interventions he favoured – in Mexico, for example – were exercises in classical imperialism rather than missions to export American government. Outside the Americas he recognized that democracy is not always practicable, and as an admirer of Edmund Burke he accepted that its growth could not be forced. Wilson still embodies a core conviction of American liberal internationalism – the belief that national self-determination should be extended throughout the world

– that has had a recurring influence on US policy. The Bush administration's policies in the Middle East were a replay of the programme that Wilson promoted in central and eastern Europe after the First World War. Neither had any understanding of the forces they were unleashing – ethnic nationalism then, radical Islam today. The belief has persisted that the American nation-state – which was achieved only after vast bloodshed – is a recipe for peace and freedom throughout the world.

Wilson embodies one version of a view of America's role in history that has been renewed down to the present. This view has been summarized by two American writers:

... there has been throughout American history, with only the briefest exceptions, a single style of diplomacy, once the United States has turned its attention from the problem of the defence of the Republic and its territorial expansion to distant problems, to the problems of the larger world. That style has been a compound of the American experience of isolation and a moral fervour that is explicitly theological in origin.[10]

Beliefs of this kind have informed America's foreign relations as much in times of isolation as in periods when it was engaged in large-scale intervention abroad. It is wrong to see these two modes as opposites, for in America even isolationism has an evangelical quality. Isolation and global intervention are phases in an American engagement with the world that has always been in some degree faith-based. This faith has altered its shape, at times becoming militant and proselytizing, at others being expressed in an inward-looking nationalism that fears being entangled in the corrupt machinations of the Old World. For much of American history it has been the latter that prevailed. For many Americans the sense of national mission has not translated easily or automatically into active support for overseas military intervention – they had to be persuaded to enter the two world wars, for example – but the belief in a special mission that inspired the Puritan colonists has persisted. As the scholar of American religion Conrad Cherry has commented:

The belief that America has been elected by God for a special destiny in the world has been the focus of American sacred ceremonies, the inaugural addresses of our presidents, the sacred scriptures of the civil religion. It has been so pervasive a motif in the national life that the word 'belief' does not really capture the dynamic role that it has played for the American people.[11]

In according itself an exceptional role in history, America is in no way unusual. Many countries have given themselves a world-redeeming role. There are obvious parallels with the idea of global mission that inspired revolutionary France, and America's revolutionary war was linked in the minds of many of the country's founders with the overthrow of the *ancien régime*. If the American sense of secular mission is not exceptional, neither is the conviction of being a nation chosen by God. The Dutch Afrikaners in South Africa, Protestant communities in Ulster in Northern Ireland and some Zionists have had similar beliefs.[12] So have many Russians. A belief in a God-given national mission was central in the reactionary messianism espoused in the nineteenth century by Slavophils, which I considered in Chapter 2. Where America differs from other nations is in the persistent vitality of messianic belief and the extent to which it continues to shape the public culture.

There have been long periods when the apocalyptic tradition was quiescent. During the interwar era it failed to stir even against the backdrop of a catastrophic Depression. It was not revived when in one of its noblest acts America entered the Second World War – a decision that was eventually taken in stoical recognition of a grim job that had to be done rather than any expectation of a much better world. Nor – despite the paranoia rampant at the time – were such beliefs strong during the early part of the Cold War. Here again the American mood was one of resisting a manifest danger rather than remaking the world. Apocalyptic thinking returned in the later part of the Cold War, but it was not a powerful force. Though he described the Soviet Union as an 'evil empire' and reaffirmed Winthrop's view of America as a 'city on a hill' in his farewell address, Ronald Reagan was not much influenced during his time in office by the Christian Right. Even when the Berlin Wall fell, George Bush Snr responded by speaking of the difficulties that lay ahead. It was only when his son became president that religion began to move into the centre of American politics, and only after 9/11 that it informed policies on a broad front.

George W. Bush's references to some countries as forming an 'axis of evil' may not be as overtly apocalyptic as his under-secretary of defence, Lieutenant-General William Boykin, who declared, '. . . the enemy is a spiritual enemy, he's called the principality of darkness. The enemy is a guy called Satan.'[13] Boykin's speech provoked controversy, but he continued to work on intelligence matters in the Pentagon – despite the fact that he had been centrally involved in extending 'stress and distress' interrogation methods from Guantánamo to Abu Ghraib. There can be little doubt that he represents a view of the world Bush shares. There are many examples of apocalyptic imagery in Bush's speeches. In his October 2001 speech in response to the 9/11 terrorist attacks Bush made numerous biblical references, using phrases from the Revelation of St John and Isaiah. Later speeches on abortion and gay marriage also contained biblical allusions.[14] In 2003, some months after the US invasion of Iraq, Bush told the Palestinian prime minister, Mahmoud Abbas, 'God told me to strike al-Qaeda and I struck them, and then he instructed me to strike at Saddam, which I did.'[15]

The formative influence of fundamentalist thinking on Bush is not confined to foreign policy. A number of the Christian leaders with whom Bush associates belong to the movement known as Christian Reconstructionism, or Dominion Theology. A post-millennial fundamentalist movement holding that a Christian form of government can be achieved in the present age in which every aspect of life will be subject to divine law, the movement has defined its aim as 'world dominion under Christ's lordship, a "world takeover" if you will . . . We are the shapers of world history.'[16] The Dominion movement also believes that following the divine command humankind must 'subdue' the Earth – a task that includes exploiting the world's natural resources and controlling the weather. Bush's opposition to environmentalism has been explained by the fact that much environmental legislation is unpopular in America. But the hostility to environmentalism of American voters is often exaggerated, and a larger reason may be that environmental policies conflict with Bush's religious beliefs. There is no good reason to be concerned with global warming if you believe Armageddon is around the corner.

There were powerful political reasons for Bush to align himself with the forces of fundamentalism. As a number of insider accounts have revealed, there has been an element of cynical manipulation in the Bush administration's relations with the Christian Right.[17] Evangelical votes were crucial in the struggle for control of Congress, and there can be no doubt that for the administration the Christian Right was, until the mid-term elections of 2006, an instrument of political control. But it would be wrong to think Bush has viewed the fundamentalists simply as an ally. There is a true affinity of world-view. By his own account Bush is himself a born-again Christian whose conversion saved him from alcoholism and who begins each day with prayer and bible study, and like other fundamentalists he has suggested that theories of 'intelligent design' should be taught alongside Darwin's theory of natural selection.[18] There is no reason to question the sincerity of Bush's religious convictions, which belong in the American tradition of post-millennialism, or to doubt that they have shaped his view of America and its place in the world. In a talk to conservative journalists in September 2006 Bush told them that he senses that what he called a 'Third Awakening' of religious devotion is underway in America. The 'First Great Awakening' is the term commonly used to describe the intense religiosity that gripped the colonies around 1730–60, while the 'Second Great Awakening' is usually said to have occurred in the period between 1800 and 1830. He went on to say that like 'a lot of people in America' he viewed the 'war on terror' as a 'confrontation between good and evil'.[19]

Bush's view of American opinion should not be accepted at face value. According to a *Newsweek* poll in 2002, 45 per cent of Americans viewed the United States as 'a secular nation', 29 per cent as 'a Christian nation' and only 16 per cent as a 'biblical nation, defined by the Judaeo-Christian tradition'.[20] None the less, America is unique among advanced countries in having a Christian majority and a large fundamentalist minority, and no other western leader could have spoken in such terms. In Britain, Blair's statement that his decision to go to war in Iraq will be judged by God deepened his unpopularity, and any claim that a policy has divine backing exacts a penalty from voters. With the partial exception of Poland, the same is true throughout Europe and all other English-speaking countries: any confession of strong religious belief, especially the claim to have a direct line to divine intentions, is dangerous and damaging to politicians. This is not so in the United States, where changes in society have enhanced the power of religion. The declining role of the old East Coast elites and the increasing ascendancy of the South in American politics; the mass mobilization of evangelical Christians, who were in the past often politically inactive, in support of a militant politics of 'traditional values'; and the increasing role of the Christian Right as a core constituency of the Republican party – without these shifts, which have gathered pace over the past thirty years, the Christian Right could not have achieved the political power it has exercised during the Bush administration. Bush embodies a type of religious belief that goes back to the first Puritan settlers, but without the changes in society of the last few decades he could not have used it to promote a faith-based politics.

Equally it is difficult to see how Bush could have mobilized American opinion behind the war in Iraq without the traumatic events of 9/11. Before the terrorist attacks, Bush's foreign policy reflected a number of influences. The US was already beginning its withdrawal from foreign treaties that were seen as limiting its capacity for unilateral action, but Bush's tone was not stridently assertive. Though they occupied important positions in government, neo-conservatives were not calling the shots. After 9/11 this changed. Apocalyptic myths that had been dormant re-emerged, and it was not difficult for neo-conservatives in the administration to link the 'war on terror' with their geo-political objectives. By 2004 a Homeland Security Planning Scenario Document was describing the terrorist threat facing the United States as being perpetrated by the Universal Adversary. National security was understood in terms of concepts derived from demonology.[21]

This demonological perception of the terrorist threat was a by-product of the alliance between neo-conservatives and the Christian Right. The origins of this alliance are in the end of the Cold War, which left America without a defining enemy. Though neo-conservatives overrated it, Soviet power posed a real threat, and one might think its collapse might permit a less adversarial American stance towards the world. But an enemy was indispensable, and one soon appeared in the shape of Saddam Hussein. In strategic terms the Gulf War of

1990–91 was a success – Saddam was pushed back into Iraq where he could no longer threaten his neighbours or global oil supplies. For neo-conservatives the war was a failure because it left Saddam in power. Throughout the Clinton era they were vociferous in their view that American forces should have marched on Baghdad. When they joined the administration of George W. Bush it was with Iraq on their minds. As Richard A. Clarke, who served as a senior advisor on terrorism under four US presidents, has commented:

> The administration of the second George Bush did begin with Iraq on its agenda. So many of those who had made the decisions in the first Iraq war were back: Cheney, Powell, Wolfowitz. Some of them had made clear in writings and speeches that the United States should unseat Saddam, finish what they had failed to do the first time. In the new administration's discussions of terrorism, Paul Wolfowitz had urged a focus on Iraqi-sponsored terrorism against the US even though there was no such thing.[22]

By allying with the Christian Right, neo-conservatives were able to mobilize millions of Americans in support of renewed military action against Iraq. Many Christian fundamentalists are influenced by the theory of dispensationalism that was developed by John Nelson Darby (1800–1882), a minister in the Church of Ireland who resigned to join a sect called the Brethren, and ended up leader of a group that split off in the 1840s to form the Plymouth Brethren. Believing that God revealed his will in a succession of events, or dispensations, Darby introduced two of the most important ideas of American pre-millennialism – the idea of the Rapture, when believers will ascend into the heavens to meet Christ, and the idea that the final battle between Christ and the hosts of Antichrist will occur on the plain of Armageddon in modern Israel. The latter is a belief held by many of those who are now called Christian Zionists – ardent supporters of Israel who believe its destruction is to be welcomed as a sign of the millennium. Fundamentalists who accepted Darby's prophecies were far from being a marginal group. As Michael Lind has written, 'To dismiss these Americans as members of the lunatic fringe was mistaken. They were the political base of the Bush administration and the contemporary, Southernized Republican party.'[23]

The alliance with the Christian Right has had many advantages for neo-conservatives. It leveraged their influence in the Republican party – for which the Christian Right was increasingly important as a source of funding and votes – and enabled them to transmit their ideas to very large numbers of people. Along with Rupert Murdoch's Fox News it gave neo-conservatives a voice in national politics that could not be ignored. In the 1980s neo-conservatives were a few dozen ideologues, mostly in Washington think tanks. They had some impact in the area of national defence and several joined the Reagan administration, but they were nothing like a dominant force. By allying themselves with Southern fundamentalism they linked themselves with the single most important constituency in American politics. Only around a quarter of American voters are born-again Christians, but over three quarters of them voted for Bush in 2004. Though Bush won only by a hair's breadth, it was the Christian Right that ensured his victory.

While the political ascendancy of the Christian Right reflects recent changes in American society, it also confirms America's unrivalled religiosity. The US is a secular regime, but unlike nearly every other long-established democracy America lacks a secular political tradition. Though the separation of church and state is a pillar of the Constitution, this has not prevented religion exercising enormous power in American political life. Like some other European countries Britain has an established Church; but organized religion has far less political influence than in the supposedly secular United States. The contrast is not only with the post-Christian countries of Europe but also with some Muslim countries. Judged by almost any standard the US is a less secular country than Turkey. In no other highly industrialized country is there widespread popular belief in Satan or a powerful movement contesting Darwinian theory. Nowhere else does a large segment of the population believe that the events of 9/11 were predicted in the Bible, as did a quarter of Americans polled in 2002.[24] There is no other advanced country of which it could be observed that a theological dispute between pre-millennial and post-millennial Christians has 'had profound implications for [American] politics'.[25]

With the 'Southernization' of American politics the Christian Right gained in strength. On George W. Bush's first day in office he restored a gag rule on aid to international organizations that counsel women on abortion, and his withdrawal of federal funding for stem cell research and US aid programmes that involve population control and the use of condoms as the most effective way of countering the spread of AIDS are signs of the Christian Right's power.[26] This power is not unchallenged, and in domestic politics there are limits to the extent to which any administration can advance a fundamentalist agenda. Despite attempts to change it, American law on abortion and gay rights remains similar to that in other democracies. America has not – and will not – turn into a theocracy, and it is conceivable that the Republican strategy of courting the fundamentalist vote could cease to be productive if it locks the party into policy positions – such as favouring restrictions on immigration from Hispanic countries, for example – that alienate other significant constituencies.

None the less the theo-conservative Right remains a force no administration can ignore, and its impact on American society could grow. The blow to America inflicted by Iraq is profound, and the impact on fundamentalists may be a state of mind not unlike that described by the early twentieth-century sociologist Karl Mannheim, when he wrote:

Chiliasm has always accompanied revolutionary outbursts and given them their spirit. When this spirit ebbs and deserts these movements, there remains behind in the world a naked mass-frenzy and a despiritualized fury.[27]

If America is exceptional it is in the power of religion. In the last chapter I will consider what this tells us about the Enlightenment tenet that there is an inherent connection between modernization and secularization. At this point it may be worth underlining the paradoxical quality of American modernity. Throughout most of its history America has seen itself as the prototype of a new civilization that will someday be universal. Yet its unique origins and singular religiosity preclude American life being replicated in any other country.

These contradictions appear in neo-conservatism. In neo-conservative thinking America is the supreme modern regime, which all others are bound to emulate. At the same time it is unique and unparalleled. Neo-conservatism is a movement that could only have arisen in America, mobilizing conflicting beliefs that have recurred throughout the country's history.

THE ORIGINS OF NEO-CONSERVATISM

When we forget, or wilfully choose to ignore, the intracta-
bility of human behaviour, the complexity of human insti-
tutions, and the probability of unanticipated consequences,
we do so at great risk, and often immense human cost.

Jeane Kirkpatrick[28]

The United States is the last militant Enlightenment regime and the only advanced country that is still unshakably Christian. The two facts are not unrelated and help to explain the peculiar qualities of neo-conservatism and its rise to power in America. Despite its name, neo-conservatism is an ideology that originated on the Left. It has been able to gain power in America by allying itself with the Christian Right and with sections of liberal opinion. By allying itself at once with apocalyptic religion and a secular belief in human progress, the neo-conservative movement mobilized two powerful American traditions.

Like several other political labels, 'neo-conservative' was coined as a term of abuse. It seems to have been first used in the 1970s by the American socialist Michael Harrington to describe – and condemn – a small group of former leftists who were adopting stances in foreign policy that had in the past been confined to the Right. As the neo-conservative writer and Catholic theologian Michael Novak has written:

It is worth remembering that the first so-called neocons were a tiny band, indeed, usually quickly named as Irving Kristol and Gertrude Himmelfarb, the two Daniels, Bell and Moynihan, Norman Podhoretz and Midge Decter, and a very few of their intellectual friends. Virtually all of this company had a history as men and women of the left, indeed to the left of the Democratic party, maybe in the most leftward two or three per cent of Americans, in some cases socialist in economics, in others social democratic in politics.[29]

The origins of neo-conservatism on the Left explain some of its persisting qualities. Many of the older generation of neo-conservatives began on the anti-Stalinist far Left – Irving Kristol, the political godfather of the movement, wrote an autobiographical essay called 'Memoirs of a Trotskyist'[30] – and the intellectual style of that sectarian milieu has marked the neo-conservative movement throughout its history. The chief figures who shaped the neo-conservative movement – such as Irving Kristol, the Harvard sociologist Daniel Bell, the editor of *Encounter* magazine Melvin Lasky, the writer and editor of *Public Interest* Nathan Glazer, the political scientist Seymour Martin Lipset and the Democratic politician Patrick Moynihan – did not take their intellectual nourishment from conservative thinkers. It is doubtful if they read much of Edmund Burke, the eighteenth-century parliamentarian who first articulated English conservatism, or of Benjamin Disraeli, the British prime minister whose novels contain an elegant statement of a conservative view of the world. If the present generation of neo-conservatives reads Russell Kirk or Michael Oakeshott – twentieth-century conservative thinkers, the first American and the second British, who aimed to deflate ideology in favour of practice – it is likely with distaste. All these conservative thinkers believed the ideological type of politics that emerged from the French Revolution was a destructive force that had wreaked havoc in the twentieth century. In opposition to this view, neo-conservatives believe that politics is a type of warfare in which ideology is an essential weapon.

It was this conception of politics rather than any specific doctrines that neo-conservatives carried over from their time on the Left. Few of the leading neo-conservative intellectuals were Trotskyists for any length of time, and the chief political lesson that many of them took from Trotsky was the deeply repressive character of the Soviet regime. Here neo-conservatives did no more than reflect the post-war development of the Left. Marxists like Sidney Hook and Trotskyists such as

Max Shachtman developed into anti-communist social democrats not unlike the ex-communists who were among the most intrepid cold warriors in 1950s Europe. Like many others, these thinkers of the Left rejected Marxism during the Cold War. It is too simple to view neo-conservatives as reformulating Trotskyite theories in rightwing terms, but the habits of thought of the far Left have had a formative influence. It is not the content of Leninist theory that has been reproduced but its style of thinking. Trotsky's theory of permanent revolution suggests existing institutions must be demolished in order to create a world without oppression. A type of catastrophic optimism, which animates much of Trotsky's thinking, underpins the neo-conservative policy of exporting democracy. Both endorse the use of violence as a condition of progress and insist the revolution must be global.

In abandoning Trotskyism, neo-conservatives moved closer to the American mainstream, but at the same time they lost Trotsky's broad perspective on world events. The callow and parochial ideologues that hijacked US foreign policy lacked Trotsky's knowledge of history and could only emulate his utopianism and his ruthlessness. Trotsky's delusion that the European working class longed for socialist revolution in the interwar years is matched by the neo-conservative fantasy that the Arab world yearns for American-style democracy. His contempt for the 'Quaker-vegetarian chatter' of those who condemned Bolshevik methods such as hostage taking in the Russian Civil War is mirrored in neo-conservative scorn for those who condemn the use of torture in the 'war on terror'.

Neo-conservative thinking is a mix of crackpot realism and chiliastic fantasy. The changing views of Francis Fukuyama illustrate the difficulties that arise when this mix becomes a basis for foreign policy. A major influence on Fukuyama's thinking was the work of Alexandre Kojeve, a Russian émigré philosopher who settled in Paris. Kojeve wrote his doctoral dissertation on the Russian religious philosopher Vladimir Solovyev (1853–1900), who in 1899 published a book entitled *War, Progress and the End of History* in which he depicted Nietzsche as the precursor of the Antichrist. A version of Solovyev's idea of the end of history appears in Kojeve's work and reappears in Fukuyama's book *The End of History and the Last Man*. Kojeve presented the end of history in terms derived from Hegel, suggesting the terminus was not communism – as Marx had imagined – but a global capitalist system. Kojeve recognized that Soviet communism was another attempt at the utopian project pursued in the Great Terror in revolutionary France, which could not prevail against the overwhelming dynamism of capitalism. The model for the post-historical world that was coming in to being was the US rather than the USSR.

This view of America was embraced by Fukuyama, who was introduced to Kojeve's thought by Alan Bloom. Along with the defence analyst Albert Wohlstetter, Bloom – a disciple of Leo Strauss who popularized a version of Strauss's thought in his best-selling book *The Closing of the American Mind* (1987) and features as the central protagonist of Saul Bellow's novel *Ravelstein* (2000) – forged the neo-conservative network and provided it with the ideas its members took into government. A lifelong friend and admirer of Kojeve, Strauss had for many years sent favoured students to study under him. Bloom was one of them and carried on the Straussian tradition by impressing on Fukuyama the value of Kojeve's work.

More than Strauss, Kojeve shaped the thinking of Fukuyama and neo-conservatives as a whole. With his background in Solovyev and Hegel, Kojeve took for granted an eschatological view of history. So does Fukuyama, who continues to believe that America is the first post-historical society. Fukuyama has denied he ever believed history had ended in any literal sense. It is true he did not commit himself to the view that all sources of large-scale historical conflict were disappearing – a risible notion, though one he often came close to endorsing. He did assert that conflict about the most legitimate type of government had ceased. In the summer of 1989 he wrote:

What we are witnessing is not just the end of the Cold War, or a passing of a particular period of postwar history, but the end of history as such: that is, the end point of mankind's ideological evolution and the universalization of western liberal democracy as the final form of human government.[31]

This pronouncement contains two elements – the claim that history has reached a final consummation and a more specific proposition to the effect that liberal democracy is now the only legitimate mode of government. The idea that history is moving towards an End is a myth that cannot be supported or refuted by rational argument. In contrast, the claim that liberal democracy is now the only legitimate mode of government has the merit of being demonstrably false.

The proposition that 'western liberal democracy' is 'the end point of mankind's ideological evolution' is a confession of eschatological faith. It is curious that this fact has gone unnoticed. It was only to be expected that in the aftermath of the Soviet collapse long-suppressed conflicts would be reactivated. In other words history was set to resume, but in an entertaining inversion of language those who noted this fact were accused of doom-mongering. The truly apocalyptic notion that history had ended was accepted as realism.[32]

In recent years Fukuyama has attacked the Bush administration's foreign policy, criticizing the push to democracy in Iraq and elsewhere on the ground that it attempts to force long-term trends to a premature conclusion. He has condemned this policy as Leninist but it is a judgement that is unfair to Lenin. Certainly Lenin's goals were utopian, but he was supremely realistic in reformulating his policies. He reversed War Communism when it became obvious that it was leading to famine, and signed a humiliating treaty with the Germans at Brest-Litovsk in 1918 in order to allow Russia to exit from the First World War. Lenin displayed a capacity to learn from experience that has never been visible among neo-conservatives, who attacked the Bush administration's conduct of the Iraq war only on grounds of incompetence (and for the most part only when it was clear voters were about to repudiate the war).[33]

While Fukuyama has criticized the attempt to spread democracy by force he has not abandoned the neo-conservative idea that American-style government is the model for the world. His work exemplifies what one scholar describes as Fukuyama's 'passive "Marxist" social teleology' – a description he has endorsed.[34] He still holds to a view of history in which it has an overall goal, and that goal has not changed. The end-point of history continues to be America, which he believes embodies the only type of government that can be legitimate in contemporary conditions.

In fact legitimacy in government depends on many things that often cannot be achieved together, and no one type of regime can be everywhere the best. Security against anarchy and conquest by other states; an acceptable level of subsistence for the majority and the prospect of rising prosperity; institutions that respect and reflect the identities of those who are ruled – these conditions are necessary if any government is to possess legitimacy in modern times. Often liberal democracy meets them better than available alternatives, but there is no universal rule. When they cannot ensure tolerable living standards for the majority, liberal democratic regimes may be rejected – as happened when Russian voters repudiated Yeltsin in favour of Putin. Again, when they run strongly counter to the religious beliefs of the majority, liberal democracies tend to mutate into some kind of popular theocracy – as is happening in much of Iraq. Liberal democracy is far from being universally accepted as the only or most legitimate regime. Human affairs are too complicated and difficult for any one kind of government to be universally practicable or desirable.

An earlier generation of neo-conservative thinkers grasped this truth. In her book, *Dictatorships and Double Standards: Rationalism and Reason in Politics* (1982), Jeane Kirkpatrick – who was appointed US ambassador to the UN during the Reagan administration and was until her death in 2006 a fellow of the neo-conservative American Enterprise Institute – identified the consequences of imposed regime change with great clarity. As Kirkpatrick notes, the global promotion of democracy blends rationalism with utopianism:

Rationalism encourages us to believe that anything that can be conceived can be brought into being. The rationalist perversion in modern politics consists in the determined effort to understand and shape people and societies on the basis of inadequate, oversimplified theories of human behaviour . . . Rationalism not only encourages utopianism, but utopianism is a form of rationalism.

Kirkpatrick goes on to identify the qualities of the rationalist mind in terms that apply to neo-conservatives today. Referring to the 'rationalist spirit of the age', she analyses it as

that spirit that assumes that human nature in the future may be qualitatively different than in the past, that views non-rational factors such as sentiment, habit, and custom as obstacles that can and should be overcome, the spirit that views each situation as a *tabula rasa* on which a plan can be imposed and therefore sees experience in other times and places as having no relevance . . . The rationalist spirit takes no note of the fact that institutions are patterned human behaviour that exist and function through the people of a society, and that radically changing institutions means radically changing the lives of people who may not want their lives changed. Because it assumes that man and society can be brought to a preferred plan, the rationalist orientation tends powerfully to see everything as possible and prospects for progress as unlimited.[35]

Though she did not mention him, Kirkpatrick's critique has much in common with that of Michael Oakeshott. For Oakeshott the central error of rationalism in politics is a belief in principles of government that can be expressed in an ideology and applied anywhere. Rightly, Oakeshott believed such principles are summaries of particular historical experiences, with no universal authority. Oakeshott's idea of tradition takes too little account of the plurality of values in modern societies and his view of politics is too narrowly English to be generally useful. His central insight that freedom is not an ideal that can be exported but a practice that grows up in particular historical circumstances remains sound. It is an insight fatal to missionary politics, neo-conservative or liberal.[36]

Kirkpatrick deployed her critique of political rationalism against American liberals who condemned the US in the 1980s for cultivating close relations with dictatorships in Latin America while favouring détente with the Soviet Union. In her hands it served the neo-conservative agenda, which was to undermine the policies of the Carter administration. The irony is that it rebounds against neo-conservatives today. Policies of regime change are political rationalism of the most primitive kind. They assume that freedom is a condition that can be achieved anywhere, even against the will of the peoples whose lives are turned upside down in the process. It is hard to think of a clearer example of the rationalist perversion of modern politics – as Kirkpatrick recognized when, in her posthumously published *Making War to Keep Peace*, she questioned the decision to invade Iraq and argued that the result had been to create chaos in the country.

Neo-conservatives have never doubted that one type of regime is best – the type of liberal democracy that existed, until quite recently, in the United States. In recent years they have argued that versions of this regime can be exported throughout the world. One of the paradoxes of the neo-conservative movement is that these convictions were not shared by its chief intellectual progenitor. Leo Strauss never assumed that liberal democracy was the best regime or that it could be secured against tyranny. He would have regarded the idea that liberal democracy could become universal with incredulity if not contempt.

Strauss's political outlook was formed in Weimar Germany, a regime whose legitimacy was contested from the outset. In circumstances of this kind, political thinkers tend to be anti-liberal, and Strauss was no exception. Strauss's chief early mentor was the German jurist Carl Schmitt, a thinker who continues to cast a spell over radical intellectuals, though these days his admirers are found mainly on the Left. Schmitt was instrumental in obtaining a Rockefeller grant that enabled Strauss to leave Germany for Paris in 1932. After the Nazis came to power Strauss – who came from an orthodox Jewish background and held a position in the Academy of Jewish Research in Berlin – severed his links with Schmitt, but Schmitt's view of liberal democracy left a lasting imprint on Strauss's thinking.

Schmitt – a devout Catholic – wrote a number of books on politics and religion and the crisis of parliamentary democracy before the Nazis came to power. He joined the Nazi party in 1933, becoming president of the Union of National Socialist Jurists and defending the political murders of the Night of the Long Knives in 1934 as a form of administrative justice. By 1936 he had thrust himself into the forefront of the Nazi campaign of persecution of Jews, and proposed that publications by German Jewish scientists be marked with a special sign. Despite his active complicity, the Nazis did not trust Schmitt, suspecting him of opportunism. He lost his position as chief Nazi jurist but continued as professor of law in Berlin. In 1945 he was captured by American forces and interned for a time. Schmitt's Nazi past did not stand in the way of his reputation after the war. Many leading European intellectuals visited him over the course of his lengthy retirement (he died in 1985 at the age of 96), including Alexandre Kojeve, who declared 'Schmitt is the only man in Germany worth talking to.'[37]

Schmitt's view of government has much in common with that of Hobbes. Law is the creature of the state; constitutional devices cannot ensure the survival of liberal democracy, for constitutions are created and destroyed by political decisions. In Strauss's view, Schmitt – the authoritarian jurist who became a Nazi functionary – demonstrated the futility of liberalism. The statement may sound paradoxical but only so long as it is forgotten that for Strauss Hobbes was the progenitor of liberalism. 'If we call liberalism that political doctrine that regards the rights, as distinguished from the duties, of man and which identifies the function of the state with the protection or the safeguarding of those rights,' he writes in his book *Natural Right and History*, 'then we must say that the founder of liberalism was Hobbes.'[38] For Strauss, liberalism meant the assertion of freedom over virtue, a modern doctrine of natural right that turns politics into a conflict of wills in which anything is as good as anything else so long as someone wants it. The end result of liberalism is nihilism, which undermines liberalism itself.

In linking liberalism with nihilism Strauss was following a path much trodden in Germany. Nietzsche and Heidegger viewed nihilism as the defining modern disorder, which infected liberal politics as well as culture. Nietzsche viewed nihilism as an after-effect of Christianity, which (partly under the influence of Plato) had devalued the world in favour of a non-existent spiritual realm, while Heidegger interpreted nihilism as an attempt to understand 'Being' in a way that obscured its true nature. However it was spelt out, the idea that nihilism is the essential modern malady had an enormous appeal in interwar Germany. Taken up by Oswald Spengler and Moeller van den Bruck, the diarist and novelist Ernst Jünger and the Expressionist poet Gottfried Benn, it fostered the dangerous belief that overcoming nihilism meant leaving liberal values behind.

Strauss's belief that the liberal Weimar regime was destroyed by nihilism invokes a common, but over-simple and in some ways mistaken view of Nazism and, by implication, of the Nazi leader. As a bohemian autodidact of a kind that was common in central Europe in the early twentieth century, Hitler absorbed a popular world-view in which scraps of Social Darwinism were mixed with vulgarized versions of Nietzsche. In this scheme of ideas, survival and power were the only values – a position that might well be seen as nihilistic. Hitler's actions suggest a different view – one closer to the negative eschatology of some pagan traditions, as was noted in Chapter 2. In 1944–5, when it was clear the Allies had won, he continued a hopeless war and was ready to put Germany to the torch rather than surrender. Hitler chose to wreak maximum destruction on the world even at the cost of his life and destroying his country. It was his indifference to patriotism that led some of Hitler's early conservative supporters, who initially turned to him to protect Germany from the threat of communism, to see him as a nihilist who posed a mortal threat to Germany (a view that seems to have informed the July 1944 plot to kill Hitler that was mounted by Claus von Stauffenberg, Adam von Trott and other conservative nationalists). Along with other Nazis Hitler shared in the ideas that were current in interwar Europe – including the belief, accepted by many on the Left, that advancing knowledge enabled the artificial development of a higher human type. It was debased science of this kind, together with apocalyptic beliefs derived partly from pagan and partly (in the case of Hitler's anti-Semitic demonology) from Christian sources, that formed the Nazi world-view. While this was a deeply repugnant mix, it was too incoherent to be straightforwardly nihilistic.

If Strauss's analysis of Nazism was faulty, his larger analysis of liberal democracy is also implausible. No liberal democratic regime – not even the most powerful or long lasting – is secure from the temptations of tyranny, but where these regimes are subverted it is rarely by an excess of scepticism. Liberal democracy has existed for long periods in countries without any consensus on metaphysical beliefs. In Switzerland it has thrived for centuries against a background of religious diversity, while in Britain it has advanced as religious belief has waned. The countries of northern Europe are among the most successful liberal democracies in the world and they are post-Christian. Strauss's analysis of democracy is mostly a diagnosis of Weimar Germany, but mass unemployment, hyperinflation, war reparations and national humiliation destroyed any legitimacy the Weimar regime ever had. As has been seen, the Nazis were able to make use of Christian millenarian traditions and of anti-Semitic Christian demonology, but it was the built-in lack of legitimacy of the Weimar regime rather than a largely imaginary state of mass nihilism that enabled them to come to power.

Despite being based on events that had no American parallels, Strauss's analysis found a receptive audience among American conservatives. Unnerved by mass protest against the Vietnam War they found the argument that liberal democracy needs firm metaphysical foundations reassuring. At the time American democracy was in no danger, but the cultural shifts that flowed from the 1960s engendered a spurious sense of crisis. In some ways Strauss's style of thinking was tailor-made for American use. His claim that political order rests on the acceptance of moral constraints that lie outside the human sphere matched the creedal character of American public life. America has always been hospitable to the belief that its values are God-given, and so long as he was not read too closely Strauss could be seen as suggesting that the United States was the best regime.

Strauss suggested that if America's future could be secured it was by reviving the conception of natural law embodied in classical philosophy. In ancient and medieval thought natural laws contained prescriptions for the good life, which meant achieving the virtues that were appropriate to one's nature. Early modern thinkers such as Hobbes broke with this conception by identifying natural law with self-preservation and the pursuit of power. Later the philosophers of the Enlightenment embraced a type of humanism in which science and technology were supposed to enable humanity to remake the world. For Strauss the end-point of this tradition was Nietzsche's cult of the will, which was not so much a remedy for modern nihilism as its purest expression.

The only real remedy was to recover the classical conception of natural law, which Thomas Aquinas had formulated definitively. In Aquinas, Aristotle's view of the world was reproduced in a Christian context; the classical philosophy of nature was joined with Christian theology. Rightly, Strauss was always deeply sceptical about this synthesis. As he observed: 'The ultimate consequence of the Thomistic view of natural law is that natural law is practically inseparable not only from a natural theology which is, in fact, based on biblical revelation – but even from revealed theology.'[39] Here we reach a crucial feature of Strauss's thought – his insistence on the unbridgeable gulf between reason and revelation. The classical world-view that was reinstated by Aquinas rested on the assumption that reason and revelation could be made to point in the same direction. In rejecting this assumption, Strauss pointed to a breach in the western tradition. Like many after him Aquinas tried to show that faith and reason were complementary. Strauss understood that all such attempts are bound to fail: the rational cosmos of Greek philosophy and the biblical vision of divine creation – Athens and Jerusalem – are irreconcilable. Here Strauss joined hands with other early twentieth-century Jewish fideists – thinkers such as Martin Buber, Franz Rosenzweig and Lev Shestov – who accepted that first and last questions could be answered only by an act of faith. Strauss's own religious beliefs cannot be known (it has been claimed he was in fact an atheist). What is evident is that he did not think reason could supply a remedy for nihilism.

The difficulty with Strauss's belief that we can cure nihilism by returning to a classical view of things is that he never gives any ground – other than the need to escape nihilism – for accepting such a view. The classical view of the world is that it is a rational order, but Strauss was proposing that we accept this view by an act of will. It is a contradictory position, which only shows how difficult it is to overcome the 'modern project'. However much he might have wished otherwise, Strauss was in the end himself a modern thinker who had more in common with Nietzsche than with any ancient or medieval thinker. Aristotle and Aquinas held to a teleological view of the world that modern science has rendered obsolete. Each viewed the cosmos as a system in which everything has a purpose. Since Darwin, this view of the natural world has ceased to be available. Nature is ruled by chance and necessity, and natural laws are regularities rather than prescriptions for the good life. If there is a realm of value beyond the physical world it cannot be reached by human reason.

What does Strauss's view of the limits of reason mean for politics? He denied that liberal democracy could be detached from metaphysical beliefs – without a belief in a moral order not created by human will, modern politics was vulnerable to nihilism. But in denying that these beliefs are rationally defensible he left liberal democracy without any publicly accessible justification. Strauss's solution to this difficulty may be a modern variation of Plato's noble lie: while philosophers may know the truth they also know that truth is deadly to the mass of humankind. It may be that Strauss himself suffered from nihilism while believing the masses could be protected from it by consoling myths – in contemporary America, Lockean myths of natural rights – but he does not explicitly advocate any of this. The idea that he supported deception can be maintained only by using his own, highly subjective technique of interpretation. If he writes in favour of the noble lie he does so cryptically, hiding his true meaning – as many philosophers did in the past, he believed. Notoriously, Strauss maintained that many of the greatest thinkers had a secret philosophy quite different from the one that is overtly presented in their writings. This view has led some critics of Strauss to attack him as a theorist whose teachings lie behind policies of disinformation implemented by neo-conservatives in the Bush administration.[40]

The idea that Strauss's work sanctions deception is questionable. To say that great philosophers write in code is one thing, to maintain that deception is essential in politics another. Strauss always insisted there was a wide gap between philosophy and practice, writing 'the philosopher ceases to be a philosopher when certainty of a solution becomes stronger than his awareness of the problematic character of the solution.'[41] In the spirit of this maxim he wrote very little about contemporary politics, and it is hard to envision him endorsing any modern political project. His forebodings about the future of liberal democracy cannot be squared with the neo-conservative programme of exporting democracy throughout the world, while the ardent neo-conservative faith in progress is at odds with his mistrust of Enlightenment hopes. While Strauss is celebrated as a defender of the current American regime, he could more accurately be described as one of its most merciless critics. Like Schmitt, Strauss was an anti-liberal. In the vernacular discourse of American politics, neo-conservatives are enemies of liberalism in all its forms. But neo-conservatism is itself a fundamentalist version of liberalism, and – as his account of Hobbes and Schmitt shows – Strauss viewed liberalism as a symptom of the failure of the 'modern project'. His work does not support any very specific political stance and is consistent with a variety of political positions.[42] Yet if there is one movement in contemporary politics this profoundly sceptical thinker would have mistrusted and condemned it is neo-conservatism.

While Strauss cannot be held accountable for the behaviour of a political movement that claims his authority, that does not mean his thought had no influence on it. Strauss's claim that philosophical writings often contain a hidden meaning, different from or opposed to their manifest sense, is a licence for undisciplined thinking. He failed to supply any method of interpretation whereby the claim to have identified a hidden meaning could be tested, and judged by accepted standards of scholarship some of his claims are highly implausible. For example, Strauss interprets Plato not as a utopian thinker but as a critic of utopianism who aimed to show that an ideal state is impossible. However, as classical scholars have demonstrated, this interpretation has no basis in the texts.[43]

The trouble with Strauss's theory is that it allows virtually any interpretation to be advanced. There is a parallel here with the claim of the deconstructionist school that texts have no inherent meaning. In both cases rational inquiry is replaced by arbitrary judgement, and while he may have believed he was recovering a classical way of thinking, Strauss's method has more in common with post-modern thought. In practice Strauss interpreted texts by appealing to subjective intuitions whose authority seemed to depend on a claim to possess some kind of special insight. It is a claim to privileged access to the truth that has led some of his followers into calamitous errors. As applied in government, it helped bring about the Iraq war.

THE POSSESSED

Starting from unlimited freedom, I arrived at unlimited despotism. Shigalyov in Dostoyevsky's *The Devils*[44]

Neo-conservatism is a stance in American policy-making as well as a body of ideas. Its origins as a political movement are in the conflicts surrounding American defence policies in the 1970s and 1980s. The neo-conservative network that had such a deep influence on George

W. Bush is a by-product of the Cold War. Many of its errors come from applying habits of thought acquired during that time to the different conditions prevailing today.

The first beginnings of neo-conservatism may be glimpsed in the alarm felt by figures such as Patrick Moynihan and Norman Podhoretz during the Vietnam War. Worried by the lack of patriotism they believed was exhibited by protestors against the war, they objected to the idea that the US was in any sense evil. Flawed, no doubt – but still the best society that had ever existed. The idea that America is the best – perhaps the only truly legitimate – regime in history remains a mainstay of neo-conservative thinking. But neo-conservatism as an identifiable political force emerged later, in an attempt to alter US defence policies.

The key figure in this project was Albert Wohlstetter, like Leo Strauss a professor at the University of Chicago – and far more important in the genesis of neo-conservatism than Strauss. A mathematician who had worked as a defence analyst at the RAND Corporation, Wohlstetter spearheaded a powerful challenge to the policies of arms control and détente that were pursued during the Nixon administration. He identified the importance of the precision weapons that were becoming feasible with new technologies, criticized accepted theories of deterrence and actively supported the defence build-up that gathered speed during the Reagan era.

Wohlstetter was pivotal in the neo-conservative network that developed from the 1970s onwards. Among his protégés are Paul Wolfowitz and Richard Perle (who dedicated a book he co-authored, *An End to Evil*, to Wohlstetter). Wohlstetter introduced Perle to Senator 'Scoop' Jackson, a strongly anti-communist Democrat, who in 1974 co-sponsored legislation that denied normal trade relations with countries that restricted freedom of emigration (as the Soviet Union did in relation to Jews who wished to emigrate to Israel). Assisted by Perle, Jackson also lobbied vigorously against the SALT II arms control treaty. In the mid-seventies Wohlstetter put one of his students, Zalmay Khalilzad, in a think tank he had formed to advise the US government, and assisted by Wohlstetter, Khalilzad soon made useful connections in Washington.[45] By 1984 he was working for Paul Wolfowitz at the State Department, and by the early nineties he was a senior Defense Department official working with Donald Rumsfeld. Khalilzad had long argued that if the US assisted the mujahadeen, Soviet forces could be defeated in Afghanistan, and in the wake of Soviet withdrawal he was among those policy-makers who viewed the Taliban regime as being friendly to American interests. He altered this view after the 9/11 attacks when he was appointed US ambassador to the country, and went on to be US ambassador in Iraq. In 1985 Wohlstetter introduced Perle (then under-secretary for international security in the Reagan administration) to Ahmed Chalabi, a secular Iraqi Shi'ite from a wealthy banking family and a fellow-mathematician who had studied under Wohlstetter at Chicago. Chalabi was a major player in the run-up to the Iraq war as head of the American-backed Iraqi National Congress (INC), touted by neo-conservatives as a potential leader of post-Saddam Iraq and used as a source of intelligence assessments that conflicted with those being produced by the CIA and other American intelligence agencies.

The network that sprang up around Wohlstetter continues to the present day. Many of its members were signatories of the Project for a New American Century (PNAC), a Washington-based think tank established in 1997 to promote the belief that America must act to retain its global primacy. With chairman William Kristol, son of Irving Kristol and editor of the Murdoch-owned *Weekly Standard*, and chief executive Gary Schmitt, a Chicago graduate who had worked as aide to Patrick Moynihan, PNAC advocated large increases in US defence spending to maintain unchallengeable American military pre-eminence. Several members of PNAC served in the Bush administration including Dick Cheney, Zalmay Khalilzad, Donald Rumsfeld, Paul Wolfowitz and I. Lewis 'Scooter' Libby (Cheney's former chief of staff who in March 2007 was convicted on a number of charges arising from the illegal outing of a covert CIA officer, Valerie Plame, whose husband had criticized the Bush administration). The central thesis of PNAC as presented in its report on *Rebuilding America's Defenses*, published in 2000, was not new. The idea that America must maintain its global supremacy was present in earlier documents, including papers published by the then defence secretary Dick Cheney in the early nineties, and continued ideas about American national security developed by Wohlstetter in the early seventies.

The cardinal fact about the defence intellectuals who composed the neo-conservative policy network from the 1970s onwards is that they were opposed to the military doctrines of the time. If there was a figure that embodied everything they rejected in American foreign policy it was Henry Kissinger, whose brand of *realpolitik* they abhorred. Kissinger argued that despite its ideological origins, the Soviet Union had become something like a normal state with interests that need not be always opposed to those of the United States. Against this, the neo-conservatives insisted that because of its totalitarian structure the USSR would always be hostile.

In the view of neo-conservatives, Kissinger's belief that the US could work with the Soviets was wishful thinking, and it was not only Kissinger who suffered from this failing. According to Wohlstetter the CIA had a chronic tendency to misread the Soviet regime. In an article published in 1974 Wohlstetter accused the CIA of systematically underestimating Soviet missile capabilities, thereby allowing the USSR to achieve military superiority.[46] Wohlstetter's article triggered a concerted rightwing attack on the CIA, which in 1976 resulted in the establishment of what came to be known as the B Team. Set up as a rival source of intelligence for the US government (the CIA was Team A), the B Team operated through the President's Foreign Intelligence Advisory Board and was organized into three sections, dealing with Soviet low-altitude air defence capabilities, Soviet intercontinental ballistic missiles (ICBMs) and Soviet strategy. The formation of the B Team was resisted by William Colby, director of the CIA, but when George Bush Snr became CIA chief in 1976 the team was launched with president Gerald Ford's backing. The B Team was composed of hard-line opponents of détente and arms control. Key members were Paul Wolfowitz, Richard Pipes, the Harvard historian of Russia, and Edward Teller, a nuclear physicist sometimes called 'the father of the H-bomb' because of his involvement in the Manhattan Project in which the first nuclear weapons were developed, who was later a powerful advocate of the 'Star Wars' Strategic Defence Initiative (and upon whom the film character of Dr Strangelove is believed to have been based).

The B Team revealed some lasting traits of neo-conservative thinking. It mistrusted empirical research, rejecting analysis of the kind carried out by the CIA and other US intelligence agencies on the ground that available evidence – whether derived from open sources or covertly acquired – was liable to be disinformation and could not be used as a reliable guide to Soviet abilities or intentions. To some extent this was an echo of the paranoid world-view associated with James Jesus Angleton, for a time CIA chief of counter-intelligence. Under the influence of the KGB defector Anatoliy Golitsyn, Angleton came to believe that the Soviet Union had been engaged for many years in a global campaign of strategic deception in which it projected a view of itself as weak. For Angleton – an intricate personality who had edited a literary magazine at Yale that published T. S. Eliot and other contemporary poets – intelligence was a branch of the theory of knowledge. The aim was to find out the truth about Soviet conditions, but given the Soviet record of disinformation the normal rules for assessing evidence had to be suspended. Any attempt to assess Soviet behaviour using standard empirical methods led into a 'wilderness of mirrors' (a phrase he borrowed from Eliot's poem *Gerontion*).[47] In this area nothing could be believed or trusted, for even facts could be planted. Acting on this belief, Angleton instigated damaging mole-hunts in the CIA and made wild accusations against several western leaders (including prime minister Harold Wilson, against whom the British intelligence 'spycatcher' Peter Wright conspired on the basis of Angleton's allegations). Discredited within the CIA, Angleton resigned in December 1974.

Because they disdained empirical inquiry, the B Team had no procedures for checking its assessments, and as a result they were wide of the mark. Dr Anne Cahn, who worked in the US Arms Control and Disarmament Agency from 1977 to 1980 and who on examining the Team assessments found them 'all wrong', has described how the B Team's failure to detect a Soviet non-acoustic anti-submarine system was viewed by members of the Team as evidence that such a system could well exist. In other words, the Team viewed the absence of evidence as evidence in favour of its view. A methodology of this kind contains no means of detecting actual disinformation. The B Team was vulnerable on this count, and its belief in Soviet military superiority was in part a result of its being fooled by CIA black propaganda. There was an enormous Soviet military-industrial complex, but much of it was a rustbelt like the rest of the Soviet economy. The reality revealed after the Soviet collapse was closer to the CIA's estimates than it was to the claims the CIA had concocted for public consumption. The theorists of strategic deception in the B Team were themselves among its dupes.[48]

The disregard of evidence displayed by the B Team reflected a systematic rejection of empiricism, and here we find a link with Strauss. Abram Shulsky and Gary Schmitt have consistently attacked America's intelligence agencies, invoking the method of hermetic interpretation practised by Leo Strauss as a superior alternative to empirical procedures. Shulsky studied under Strauss, and in a paper he co-authored with Schmitt on 'Leo Strauss and the World of Intelligence (By Which We Do Not Mean *Nous*)'[49] he suggested that Strauss's doctrine of the hidden meaning of texts 'alerts one to the possibility that political life may be closely linked to deception. Indeed, it suggests that deception is the norm.' The authors describe Strauss as 'resembling, however faintly, the George Smiley of John Le Carré's novels in his gentleness, his ability to concentrate on detail, his consequent success in looking below the surface and reading between the lines, and his seeming unworldliness'. While noting that he wrote nothing on intelligence matters, they argue that his insight into the ways in which different political systems operate demonstrates the limited usefulness of social science in intelligence work. Strauss rejected the idea that politics could be understood by 'an empirical method that observed behaviour, tallied it, calculated correlations between particular actions and particular features of the context in which they occurred, and so on', on the ground that 'the regime shapes human political action in so fundamental a way that the very souls appear different'. Schmitt and Shulsky go on to maintain that failure to understand this damaged American policy in the Cold War, when 'American intelligence analysts were generally reluctant to believe that they could be deceived about any critical question by the Soviet Union or other Communist states. History has shown this view to be extremely naïve.' In this view, only a method that allows analysts to peer into souls can give the guidance needed for effective policies.[50]

When Schmitt and Shulsky rejected empirical inquiry they confused a critique of scientism with a rejection of evidence. Strauss's attack on the belief that the study of society could be conducted by the methods of natural science was well founded. Differences between cultures, unique historical processes and the intermingling of facts and values will always make the study of society different from any natural science. That does not mean facts can be dispensed with, though. History is not a science but there is a difference between good history and bad that reflects how evidence is used. There is also a difference between a type of thinking that is based on historical knowledge and one that lacks any sense of history. Neo-conservative thinking falls into the latter category, and many of the policy blunders committed under neo-conservative influence are the result of a wilful ignorance of the past.

At the beginning of their paper on Strauss and intelligence, the authors admit that their topic 'must appear at first a very strange one', and the link between 'the tumultuous world of spies and snooping paraphernalia, on the one hand, and the quiet life of scholarship and immersion in ancient texts, on the other' is far from obvious. Certainly it seems unlikely that an eccentric method of textual interpretation could assist intelligence gathering, but something like this method was used at the highest levels of American government. The Bush aide who scoffed at what he called the 'reality-based community' who believe that 'solutions emerge from judicious study of discernible reality', and boasted 'That's not the way the world really works any more. We're an empire now, and when we act we create our own reality,' may have been doing no more than voice the witless trium-phalism that was common among neo-conservatives at one time.[51] But he was also disclosing a view of truth that shaped some of the administration's most ill-advised policies, which Schmitt and Shulsky shared.

It is impossible to give a complete account of the disinformation that surrounds the Iraq war. The whole story may not be known for many years, if ever.[52] What can be done is to illustrate the attitude to truth – at once hieratic and instrumental – that informed some of the most important episodes of deception. Those who engineered the Iraq war believed they knew the truth and in deceiving others were only promoting it. But their belief that they could decipher the hidden meaning of events was a delusion, and they may well have ended by being deceived themselves.

This process may be seen at work in the operations of a body set up under the direction of Abram Shulsky to supply intelligence supporting the decision to go to war in Iraq. Shulsky had been a member of the Senate Intelligence Committee in the early 1980s and served in the Pentagon under Richard Perle in the Reagan administration. In 2002 he was made head of the Office of Special Plans (OSP), a Pentagon unit created by Paul Wolfowitz and Donald Rumsfeld and reporting to Bush's under-secretary for defence Douglas Feith, a protégé of Richard Pipes and Richard Perle. Much of what was done in this Office of Special Plans remains obscure. As George Packer, author of an exhaustive account of the machinations leading up to the war, has written, 'for the Office of Special Plans, secrecy was not only convenient. One could even say that it was metaphysically necessary.'[53] Following Shulsky's hermetic methods, the OSP rejected established procedures for evaluating intelligence and 'stove-piped' their own version of events directly to the White House. Like the B Team the OSP had a definite agenda that featured overriding and discrediting the intelligence provided by the CIA and the Defense Intelligence Agency (DIA). The OSP became the chief source of claims about Saddam's weapons of mass destruction and links with al-Qaeda that were used by Bush to justify the attack on Iraq. Partly because of criticism of its role in the war the unit was renamed in July 2003, when it resumed its original title of Northern Gulf Affairs. (The OSP seems to have been granted another lease on life. In mid-2006 an 'Iranian Directorate' was set up in the Pentagon that is run by a number of OSP veterans including the unit's former director Abram Shulsky. Around the same time the 'Iran desk' at the State Department, which reports to the daughter of the vice-president Elizabeth Cheney, was increased to task force size.[54])

The distinctive features of the OSP were its adherence to a view of the world set in advance of empirical inquiry, its heavy reliance on information provided by Chalabi's INC and its close links with the vice-president, Dick Cheney.[55] The principal result was to leave US policy heavily reliant on unverified intelligence from INC sources. The INC produced Iraqi defectors who made large claims about

Saddam possessing weapons of mass destruction. These claims were disputed by the CIA and conflicted with evidence obtained from UN weapons inspections; but they were used repeatedly by Cheney and president Bush to bolster the case for war until the absence of WMD in Iraq could no longer be denied.

It is often said that Cheney and Bush 'cherry-picked' from the intelligence available to them, using items that supported their beliefs while neglecting others that were not useful. In order to suggest a link between Iraq and 9/11, Cheney referred to a meeting that had taken place in Prague between Mohamed Atta (one of the leading 9/11 hijackers) and Iraqi intelligence. He also claimed that 'intelligence sources' advised that Saddam had attempted to purchase aluminium tubes for the production of nuclear weapons. In making these claims Cheney was not selecting some intelligence while passing over the rest in silence. As the American writer Joan Didion has noted:

The White House had been told by the CIA that no meeting in Prague between Mohamed Atta and Iraqi intelligence had ever occurred. The International Atomic Energy Agency and the US Department of Energy had said that the aluminium tubes in question 'were not directly suitable' for uranium enrichment . . . What the vice-president was doing, then, was not cherry-picking the intelligence but rejecting it, replacing it with whatever self-interested rumour better advanced his narrative.[56]

Along with Bush, the vice-president dismissed known facts because they did not support a decision to go to war that had already been made. When Bush and Cheney rejected intelligence that conflicted with the case for war they were not – in their own eyes or those of their advisors in the OSP – suppressing the truth. Like Mr Blair when he argued for war on a basis of disinformation in Britain, they were advancing what they saw as a higher truth. In their book *Silent War*, Schmitt and Shulsky made clear that 'truth is not the goal' of intelligence operations but instead 'victory'.[57] Actually, for these seers victory was the same as truth – not truth of the ordinary kind, to be sure, but the esoteric truth that is concealed in the deceiving mirror of fact.

The problem with this methodology was that it left its practitioners open to deception of the kind against which they warned. Those in charge at the Office of Special Plans based their belief in the existence of WMD in Iraq on the claims of Iraqi defectors, but in doing so they omitted to consider the possibility that these defectors might have been dispatched to foster the belief (which some of them may have believed to be true) that Saddam had an active weapons programme, when in fact he did not. Insofar as it projected an image that enhanced his power in Iraq and throughout the Arab world it was a belief that served Saddam's interests. At the same time the Iranian regime had a strategic interest in overthrowing the Iraqi dictator. Not only had there been a savagely fought war between the two countries but the Iranians knew that if Saddam was toppled the upshot would be Shia power in what remained of Iraq. Destroying Saddam's regime could make Iran the dominant power in the region. Against this background it would have been prudent to guard against the danger that the INC could be used as a channel for Iranian as well as Iraqi disinformation.[58] The CIA had long warned against the dangers of reliance on Iraqi émigré sources. The theorists who were running the OSP dismissed these warnings. Relying on their capacity to divine the truth, they were confident they could do without empirical verification. As far as they were concerned the defectors only confirmed what their own special methods had already shown to be true. The faith-based methodology of the OSP freed it from the cumbersome procedures of the established American intelligence agencies. It also made the OSP a prime target for strategic deception.

The notion that a type of occult insight into a regime or a person removes the need for factual inquiry is a perilous basis for action. President Bush may have believed that when he met Vladimir Putin in June 2001 he was 'able to get a sense of his soul'.[59] Subsequent events appear to have altered Mr Bush's perception and one might have expected developments in post-Saddam Iraq to dent confidence in faith-based intelligence, but this is far from the case. In *The New York Times* in February 2004 the neo-conservative columnist David Brooks renewed the attack on American intelligence methods, writing, 'For decades, the US intelligence community has propagated the myth that it possesses analytical methods that must be insulated pristinely from the hurly-burly world of politics.' Rather than rely on 'a conference-load of game theorists or risk assessment officers',

Brooks declares, 'When it comes to understanding the world's thugs and menaces . . . I'd trust anyone who has read a Dostoyevsky novel over the past five years.'[60] Once again, an esoteric insight into the soul of the regime is presented as a superior alternative to the laborious analysis of evidence.

The neo-conservative idea that one can understand terrorist violence by reading the novels of Dostoyevsky is entertainingly ironic, since what Dostoyevsky describes is the mentality of neo-conservatives themselves. Neo-conservatives believe much of the world as it currently exists is irredeemably bad. As the neo-conservative analyst Michael Ledeen wrote soon after the 9/11 attacks, the 'war on terror' is all of one piece with the 'global democratic revolution':

We should have no misgivings about our ability to destroy tyrannies. It is what we do best. It comes naturally to us, for we are the only truly revolutionary country in the world, as we have been for more than 200 years. Creative destruction is our middle name . . . In other words, it is time once again to export the democratic revolution. To those who say it cannot be done, we need only point to the 1980s, when we led a global democratic revolution that toppled tyrants from Moscow to Johannesburg.[61]

Here a celebrated dictum of the nineteenth-century Russian anarchist Bakunin – 'The passion for destruction is a creative passion' – is restated in neo-conservative terms. Bakunin's disciple, the divinity student Sergey Nechayev, applied this maxim in his 'Catechism of a Revolutionary' (1868), where he argued that in advancing the revolution the ends justified any means – including blackmail and murder. A year later Nechayev murdered one of his comrades for failing to carry out orders. Bakunin severed relations with Nechayev after this episode but Nechayev had revealed the logic of Bakunin's project. Terror followed from the goal of a total revolution.

Ledeen's project of militarily enforced democracy has a similar logic. Nechayev never doubted his was the cause of the people, and Ledeen takes for granted that the countries that have regime change imposed on them will welcome the overthrow of their governments. If they do not they must be purged of retrograde elements. Only then can there be any assurance that forcible democratization will be accepted for what it is: liberation from tyranny. Torture and terror are acceptable if they assist in the global war against evil.

This neo-conservative catechism is the latest incarnation of the revolutionary mind Dostoyevsky dissected a century and a half ago. In his novel *The Possessed*, Dostoyevsky presents a picture of the Russian revolutionaries of his time and their fellow travellers on the intellectual Left. His portrait of Stepan Trofimovich Verkhovensky, the sheltered aristocratic radical who fills his leisure time by toying with revolution, is a masterpiece of cruel insight. In pursuit of a new world, revolutionaries end up as criminals (as happened in the case of Nechayev, whose involvement in murder was used as the basis for part of the plot of the novel). The dream of Utopia ends in squalid horror.

Dostoyevsky wrote his novel as an attack on the leftwing revolutionaries of mid-nineteenth-century Russia. As a description of the radical movements of the period it may be overdrawn, but as an account of the psychology of the revolutionary mind it has lasting value. As the Polish poet and writer Czesław Miłosz commented, 'The Russian Revolution found its prediction in *The Possessed*, as Lunacharsky openly admitted.' Miłosz goes on to criticize Dostoyevsky, 'the Russian millennialist and messianist',[62] and there can be no doubt that when Dostoyevsky strayed into the politics of his day the results were ridiculous and at times repellent. His belief that a revival of Russian spirituality could save the world was messianic thinking at its worst. Yet, because he was himself a millennialist, Dostoyevsky understood the dangers of revolutionary movements inspired by millenarian beliefs.

Beginning with limited goals, revolutionaries have time and again come to accept violence as an instrument for cleansing the world of evil. The ideologues that have shaped the foreign policies of the Bush administration exemplify this pathology. Like Dostoyevsky's deluded visionaries, neo-conservatives embraced force as a means to Utopia.

5

Armed Missionaries

The most extravagant idea that can be born in the head of a political thinker is to believe that it suffices for people to enter, weapons in hand, among a foreign people and expect to have its laws and constitution embraced. It is in the nature of things that the progress of reason is slow and no one loves armed missionaries; the first lesson of nature and prudence is to repulse them as enemies. One can encourage freedom, never create it by an invading force.

Maximilien Robespierre,
speech to the Jacobin Club, Paris, 1792[1]

To some extent the origins of the Iraq war will always be obscure. The reason is not that it was the product of a conspiracy, as some have come to believe. Many strategic objectives were presented in its justification, some of them seemingly rational. Yet when the history of the war comes to be written it will show that none of the groups that supported it had goals that were achievable. If the Bush administration had an overall strategy it assumed regime change in Iraq would promote American interests while curbing terrorism and furthering democracy in the region; but these are not facets of a single programme that can all be realized together. They are disparate and competing objectives and in acting on the belief that they were one the Bush administration revealed its distance from reality.

Liberal democracy cannot be established in most of the countries of the Middle East. In much of the region the choice is between secular despotism and Islamist rule. In attempting the forcible democratization of the Middle East, the Bush administration assumed the result would be regimes like the United States. It overlooked the likelihood that they would be illiberal democracies. Illiberal democracy rests on the belief that the common good is self-evident. Everyone who is not deluded or corrupt will support the same policies so there will be no need to protect personal freedom or the rights of minorities. It is enough that the popular will, which is identical with the common good, can be fully expressed. In practice the people need guidance, which in Rousseau's theory is provided by the Legislator – a shadowy figure who steers them from behind the scenes. Rousseau's Legislator has something in common with the Grand Ayatollah, whose obscure interventions shape theocratic Iran. The type of regime that exists in that country is an Islamist version of Rousseau's illiberal dream, and when the remaining authoritarian regimes in the Middle East are overthrown it is likely to be this type of democracy that will succeed them. The process is already underway in much of Iraq, where a Shia-dominated popular theocracy along the lines of Iran is slowly emerging. Twenty years from now most of the Middle East looks set to be ruled by Islamist versions of illiberal democracy. In some ways these may be more legitimate regimes than those they replace, and accepting them as such will be necessary if they are to have any prospect of defusing some of the forces behind terrorism. Over time some countries may evolve into something more like the pluralist democracies of Europe (a version of which seemed to be re-emerging in Lebanon until the process was derailed by war). But these countries will not be clones of any western political system, and the idea that a 'new Middle East' is on the horizon that will accept the United States as a model of government is fantasy.

The belief that terror can be eradicated is equally delusive. The US and other countries lecture Islamic countries on the need to 'modernize' – that is, to repeat the pattern of development of western countries. They have overlooked the fact that wherever an attempt has been made to impose a western model of development on non-western countries it has involved mass terror, while twentieth-century Europe was itself a site of unprecedented state murder. Terror has been an integral part of the modern West. Where modern states have existed in the Middle East – as in Iraq under Saddam, which before it was destroyed by thirteen years of economic sanctions and the subsequent

American attack was one of the most highly developed Arab countries – they have also practised terror. Even if liberal democracy could be installed it would not end terrorist violence. Many liberal democracies – the UK, Spain, Italy, Germany, Japan and the US, for example – have faced serious threats. In Russia terrorism has worsened since democratization, while in China it remains under control. Political processes can help cope with terror, but democracy is not a panacea. In conditions of the kind that prevail throughout much of the Middle East terrorist organizations are not isolated factions lacking popular support – in Lebanon, in the aftermath of the latest conflict with Israel, Hezbollah speaks for the majority of the population, while in Palestine Hamas has formed an elected government. Throughout the region terrorism is a by-product of unresolved, in some cases perhaps irresolvable, conflicts.

Among these regional conflicts, that between Palestine and Israel may be the most intractable, but there are large clashes looming between Islamic countries as well. Saudi Arabia and Iran are competitors for hegemony in the Gulf – a rivalry that could acquire a dangerous edge if, as seems likely, both are nuclear powers in a decade or so – and the Shia awakening that has followed the destruction of Saddam will be strongly resisted by Sunni regimes. In many countries political instability will be accentuated by rapid population growth. The population of the Gulf will double in around twenty years – a process that will leave unemployed many millions of young males whose attitudes have been shaped by fundamentalist schooling. In these conditions peace is unachievable. Periods of truce may be secured by patient diplomacy and opening up links with Islamist regimes that have some leverage over the irregular militias that commit terrorist violence. But stability is a remote prospect, and while terrorist violence can be reduced, it looks set to be a chronic condition.

Installing liberal democracy and eliminating terrorism are distinct goals, neither of which can be realized in much of the Middle East. Any advance towards greater stability in the region is made difficult by blurring these objectives and by their conflation with American geo-political interests. In Iraq this confusion has had predictably calamitous results.

Iraq: A Twenty-First Century Utopian Experiment

> *With the doctrine of pre-emptive war, the Bush adminis-*
> *tration went far beyond the utopian credos of America's*
> *founders – or even of Wilson, Roosevelt, and Reagan. It is,*
> *fundamentally, a doctrine of endless war.* David Rieff[2]

Many impulses led to war in Iraq, not all of them conscious or rational. The invasion was meant to secure American energy supplies; at the same time it was intended to remake Iraq as a model of liberal democracy for the rest of the region. The first of these objectives was compromised by the war, while the second was unrealizable. A third – dismantling Saddam's WMD programme – was a pretext.

In an attempt to legitimate an act of aggression the Bush adminis-tration, along with the Blair government, represented the attack on Iraq as a response to a threat posed by a developing weapons pro-gramme, but their argument was incoherent. If there was a weapons programme under development it could be dealt with without war – by intrusive inspection procedures and other methods. If Saddam already possessed biological or chemical weapons there was no reason to think they posed a danger to the United States – as analysis released by the CIA concluded, he was likely to use them against the US only in the context of an American invasion. A predictable effect of the war was to demonstrate to 'rogue states' around the world that they would be better off having the WMD that Saddam lacked – otherwise, like Iraq, they would be vulnerable to American attack. Rather than slowing it down the war accelerated the proliferation of WMD. There was, in fact, no cogent argument for the war in terms of American or global security.

The goals of the war lay elsewhere. Among the geo-political objec-tives advanced by neo-conservatives was the argument that the US must decouple from Saudi Arabia, which they viewed as complicit in terrorism. If it was to disengage in this way the US needed another secure source of oil in the Gulf and another platform for its military bases. Iraq seemed to fit these requirements. By controlling a crucial part of the Gulf's oil reserves, the US could detach itself from an ally it no longer trusted. At the same time it could ensure that it remained the dominant power in the region, with the capacity to limit the incursions of China, India and other energy-hungry states.

This was always an incredible scenario. Oil production in post-war Iraq has never achieved the level it did under Saddam, and the oil price has risen greatly. In the anarchy that prevails throughout much of the country – the Kurdish region, where there are no American forces, remains peaceful – a return to previous levels of production is impossible. Over time, production will fall still further as a result of declining investment and the costs of protecting facilities. As a result of the Iraq war America's oil supplies are more insecure than before. The notion that post-Saddam Iraq would accept the transfer of its oil reserves into American hands was anyhow delusional. Why should a democratic Iraq – if that had been possible – accept the expropriation of its resource base? Even as an exercise in *realpolitik* the war was a utopian venture.

Regime change in Iraq was part of a global resource war that began soon after the Soviet collapse. What is sometimes called the first Gulf War – a title that overlooks the savage conflict between Iraq and Iran that took place some years earlier – was a resource war and nothing else. None of the parties to it pretended that it had anything to do with spreading democracy or curbing terrorism. The objective was solely to secure oil supplies. Throughout the nineties this was a major objective of US policy, underpinning the establishment of military bases in Central Asia and spurring closer relations with Russia.

Throughout the twentieth century geo-politics – the struggle for control of natural resources – was a powerful factor shaping conflicts between states. Securing oil supplies was a major issue in the Second World War, helping to trigger Hitler's invasion of the Soviet Union and the Japanese attack on Pearl Harbor. It continued in the abortive attempt by Britain to seize the Suez Canal in 1956. The British-American overthrow of the secularist Iranian president Mohammed Mossadegh in the CIA-led 'Operation Ajax' in 1953 was mounted with the avowed aim of preventing Iran's coming under increased

Soviet influence. Its chief goal was to reassert western control of the country's oil.

The rivalries of the post-Cold War period have developed against a different background. The balance of power between producers and consumers of energy is shifting, with oil-producing states able to dictate the terms on which they do business with the world. Russia is using its position as a supplier of oil and natural gas to reassert itself in global politics, while Iran has emerged as a contender for hegemony in the Gulf. Underlying these shifts is the fact that global oil reserves are being depleted while global demand is rising. Oil is not running out in any simple sense; but the theory of 'peak oil' suggests that global production may be near its maximum. Peak oil is taken seriously by governments. A report by the US Department of Energy entitled *Peaking of World Oil Production: Impacts, Mitigation and Risk Management*, which was released in February 2005, concludes: 'The world has never faced a problem like this. Without massive mitigation more than a decade before the fact, the problem will be pervasive and will not be temporary. Previous energy transitions (wood to coal and coal to oil) were gradual and evolutionary; oil peaking will be abrupt and revolutionary.'[3] When dwindling oil is combined with accelerating industrialization the result is bound to be intensifying rivalry for control of the world's remaining reserves. The geo-politics of peak oil is shaping the policies of great powers.[4]

The role of oil as the supreme asset was recognized by the Bush administration's most powerful strategist. In a speech at the Institute of Petroleum's autumn lunch in 1999, when he was CEO of Haliburton, Dick Cheney observed:

Producing oil is obviously a self-depleting activity. Every year you've got to find and develop reserves equal to your output just to stand still, just to stay even. This is true for companies in the broader sense as it is for the world . . . So where is the oil going to come from? Oil is unique in that it is so strategic in nature. We are not talking about soapflakes or leisurewear here. Energy is truly fundamental to the world's economy. The Gulf War was a reflection of that reality. The degree of government involvement makes oil a unique commodity . . . Governments and the national oil companies are obviously controlling about 90 per cent of the assets. Oil remains fundamentally a government business. While many regions offer great oil opportunities, the Middle East with two thirds of the world's oil and the lowest cost, is still where the prize ultimately lies.[5]

Cheney's remarks show a clear understanding of peak oil, which was reflected in the first Bush administration's decision to reclassify energy policy under the heading of national security. There can be little doubt that oil was a vital factor in the decision to launch the Iraq war. The US acted to install a regime that would secure America's oil supplies and to signal its determination to control the reserves of the Gulf as a whole.

The adventure ran aground on the impossibility of establishing an effective state in place of the one that was demolished. It has become conventional wisdom to think that disaster could have been avoided by planning for post-war reconstruction. This view is supported by the fact that some planning did take place – in the US State Department's 2002 paper on the future of Iraq, for example – but was disregarded by Bush and Rumsfeld.[6] Yet the belief that the chaos that followed the American invasion could have been averted is groundless. It assumes the goals of the war were achievable when in fact they were not. If there had been anything resembling realistic forethought, the war would never have been launched. Establishing liberal democracy in the country was impossible, while overthrowing the regime meant destroying the state.

None of this is hindsight. The insurgency that followed the initial military success was widely anticipated,[7] while the history of Iraq shows that the risks of majority rule in the country were well understood generations ago. First known as Mesopotamia, the state of Iraq is largely the work of the British diplomat Gertrude Bell, who – along with T. E. Lawrence (Lawrence of Arabia) and Harry St John Philby, the British colonial officer and father of the Soviet spy Kim Philby – constructed it from three provinces of the collapsed Ottoman Empire and established it as a Hashemite kingdom in 1921. With the fall of the Ottomans in 1919, Bell – the first woman to be appointed a political officer in the British colonial service – became secretary to the British high commissioner, Sir Percy Cox, and began building a new state. In 1920 Bell met Seyyid Hasan al-Sadr, the leading figure among Iraq's Shias and great-grandfather of Moqtada al-Sadr, the commander of the Mahdi Army that rebelled against the American occupation in 2004. She recognized that democratic government would mean theocratic rule: 'I do not for a moment doubt that the final authority must be in the hands of the Sunnis, in spite of their numerical inferiority, because otherwise we will have a theocratic state, which is the very devil.' One of her chief goals was to 'keep the Shia divines from taking charge of public affairs', which required rule by the Sunni elite. A British strategic interest was to retain control of the country's northern oilfields. By creating a new kingdom in which the Shias were kept from power and the Kurds denied a separate state these two objectives could be achieved together.

One reason Bell was able to construct the new kingdom was that she was deeply versed in the culture of the region. Fluent in Arabic and Persian, she translated the verses of the Sufi libertine-mystic Hafiz into English. She founded the Baghdad Archaeological Museum, later the National Museum of Antiquities, which after nearly eighty years of conservation of the country's treasures was looted in the aftermath of the American invasion. The looting – which occurred while the Oil Ministry alone among government institutions was under American guard – drew from Donald Rumsfeld the comment, 'Stuff happens.'[8] From the early 1920s onwards Bell was out of sympathy with British policy in the country. In 1926, sidelined by the colonial service and lacking influence over events, she took an overdose of sleeping pills in Baghdad, where she was buried in the British cemetery.[9]

Bell knew the state she had created could never be democratic. In the Shia regions democracy would mean theocracy, in Sunni areas sectarian conflict, and separatism in the Kurdish north. The kingdom Bell created lasted until Nasserite officers murdered the royal family in 1958 two years after the collapse of British power in the region that followed the ill-conceived Franco-British attempt to seize control of the Suez Canal. Saddam's despotism was based on the same realities of sectarian division and Sunni rule that sustained Bell's kingdom. Overthrowing the regime meant destroying the state through which it operated and creating the theocracy Bell had warned against. While it was never as fully totalitarian, Saddam's Iraq was an Enlightenment regime on the lines of Soviet Russia. It was thoroughly secular, the only state in the Gulf not ruled by Islamic Sharia law but by a western-style legal code, and implacably hostile to Islamism – a fact accepted by the US in the 1980s when it supplied Saddam with weaponry and intelligence in the war with Iran.

Iraq has always been a composite state with deep internal divisions. Though it was more repressive, Saddam's regime was built on the same foundations as Bell's kingdom. Saddam held Iraq together while repressing the Shia majority, the Kurds and others. Destroying Saddam's regime emancipated these groups and left the Iraqi state without power or legitimacy. Democracy was impossible, for it required a degree of trust among the communities that make up the underlying society that did not exist. Minorities need to be assured that they will not be permanent losers, or else they will secede to set up a state of their own. The Kurds were bound to follow this path, and the five million Sunnis were sure to resist majority rule by the Shias. The fissures between these groups were too deep for Iraq's rickety structures to survive. Nearly everywhere, states that suddenly become democratic tend to break apart, as happened in the USSR and former Yugoslavia. There was never any reason to think Iraq would be different, and by the time of Saddam's sordid and chaotic execution in December 2006 the Iraqi state had ceased to exist.

Though at every stage it has been joined with a crazed version of *realpolitik*, the neo-conservative project of regime change in Iraq is a classic example of the utopian mind at work. For the neo-conservatives who masterminded the war democracy would come about simply through the overthrow of tyranny. If there were transitional difficulties they could be resolved by applying universal – that is to say, American – principles. Hence the construction of an imaginary structure of federalism that followed. The system that was devised for Iraq expressed a faith in paper constitutions that hardly squares with the history of the United States, which achieved national unity only via the route of civil war.

In practice the Bush administration was clueless. Weeks before the invasion, it had no idea how the country was to be governed. Opinion oscillated between installing a military-style governor on the model of post-war Japan and implementing an immediate transition to democracy. Donald Rumsfeld – a military bureaucrat and American nationalist rather than any kind of neo-conservative – never had any interest in bringing democracy to Iraq, but equally he had never proposed any strategy for governing the country once the Saddam regime had been overthrown. Replacing Saddam by a military governor – as some British officials suggested – was not a realistic option, for it meant setting up what would in effect be a colonial administration whose longer-term viability would be highly dubious and which the US was in any case predisposed to reject. For a powerful faction in the Bush administration, the war had always been a means of imposing American-style democracy on the country. This was notably true of Paul Wolfowitz. James Mann, author of a study of the self-styled 'Vulcans' – the circle of defence strategists who made up George W. Bush's war cabinet – has written that Wolfowitz

became the administration official most closely associated with the invasion of Iraq. In the midst of the invasion Americans working in the war zone came up with the nickname Wolfowitz of Arabia for the deputy secretary of defence; the phrase captures the degree of intensity, passion and even, it sometimes seemed, romantic fervour with which he pursued the goals of overthrowing Saddam Hussein and bringing democracy to the Middle East.[10]

For Wolfowitz, the chief architect of the war, the invasion was a prelude to democratizing the entire region. In the event, the incompetence of Bush's proconsul in Baghdad, Paul Bremer, was so devastating that a sudden move to democracy in Iraq soon came to be accepted as the only way the American administration could pretend to any kind of legitimacy.

In his first communiqués in May 2003 Bremer disbanded the Iraqi Army and sacked Baathist public officials, including university professors and primary school teachers, nurses and doctors. The *Washington Post*'s Pentagon correspondent Thomas E. Ricks has described Bremer's decision:

. . . on May 23, Bremer issued CPA (Coalition Provisional Authority) Order Number 2, Dissolution of Iraqi Entities, formally doing away with several groups: the Iraqi armed forces, which accounted for 385,000 people; the staff of the Ministry of the Interior, which amounted to a surprisingly high

285,000 people because it included police and domestic security forces; and the presidential security units, a force of some 50,000 ... Many of these men were armed.[11]

Disbanding Iraqi forces came after Bremer's Order Number 1 – De-Baathification of Iraqi Society – which had barred senior Baathist party members from public office. Taken together, the two orders – which Ricks reports were strongly opposed by the CIA station chief in Baghdad – left over half a million people unemployed. In a country where families average around six people, this meant over two and a half million – about a tenth of the population – lost their income. Bremer appears to have issued the orders on the advice of Ahmed Chalabi, who aimed to install his allies in the positions left vacant.

The effect of Bremer's orders was to dismantle the Iraqi state. The police and security forces ceased to be national institutions and were captured by sectarian militias, which used them to kidnap, torture and murder. Outside the Green Zone – the high-security area in central Baghdad where the American and British embassies and the coalition-backed Iraq government are located – the country became a zone of anarchy. By the end of 2006 around a hundred people were being killed every day, and according to a UN estimate torture was worse than under Saddam.[12]

The perception fostered by the Bush administration that Iraq has a fledging government that is rebuilding the country has no basis in reality. The American-backed government is a battleground of sectarian forces, while the Iraqi state has disappeared into history's memory hole. If Saddam had been assassinated or had died of natural causes, the regime would most likely have survived. By imposing regime change, the Bush administration created a failed state, with a fragile government heavily dependent on the Shia militias – a fact ignored in Bush's buffoonish criticisms of its policies. The resulting chaos has left the declared goal of the invasion – finding and destroying Saddam's supposed WMD programme – beyond reach. If Saddam possessed any chemical or biological weapons – as he certainly did in the nineties – they have disappeared along with the state of Iraq.

There are some who argue that the failure of American forces to pacify Iraq is due to their being deployed in insufficient numbers.

Certainly the war plan that was drawn up by Donald Rumsfeld went badly wrong in not anticipating the insurgency that followed the collapse of Saddam's forces. Rumsfeld – who throughout his time in the administration was a forceful proponent of a 'revolution in military affairs' involving high levels of reliance on technology and the limited use of ground forces – was loathed by the military for imposing an unworkable strategy for the war and was first to be sacrificed when American voters rejected it. But a larger deployment would have made little difference. Despite having over 400,000 troops in the country in the aftermath of the First World War, Britain was unable to impose its will by military force; when a type of order was created it was by political means. The British invaded Mesopotamia in 1914 partly in order to secure crude oil supplies for their warships, which Winston Churchill as First Lord of the Admiralty had switched from coal to more efficient oil-burning engines. The course of the occupation was far from smooth – between December 1915 and April 1916 the British Mesopotamian Expeditionary Force suffered over 20,000 casualties at the hands of Ottoman forces at Kut-al-Amara, resorting later to razing villages by air strikes (a tactic the British also used in Afghanistan in the 1920s).

The state of Iraq was constructed to achieve a condition of peace that could not be achieved by the use of military force. In contrast, American military operations in Iraq have not been accompanied by any achievable political objectives. By early 2007 over 3,000 Americans had been killed – more than died as a result of 9/11 – and over 20,000 wounded, for the sake of goals that, insofar as they were ever coherently formulated, were unrealizable. American forces have made mistakes and committed some crimes; but blame for American defeat cannot be attached to the soldiers who were sent to discharge an impossible mission. Responsibility lies with the political leaders who conceived the mission and ordered its execution.

It is true that US forces were badly equipped for counter-insurgency warfare of the kind that began after the occupation of Baghdad. In the aftermath of humiliating defeat in Vietnam and Somalia, US military doctrine has been based on 'force protection' and 'shock and awe'. In practice, this means killing any inhabitant of the occupied country that might conceivably pose any threat to US forces and overcoming the enemy through the use of overwhelming firepower. Effective in the early stages of the war when the enemy was Saddam's forces, these strategies are counter-productive when the enemy comprises most of the population, as is now the case. The current conflict is what General Sir Rupert Smith, who commanded the British 1st Armoured Division in the Gulf War, UN peacekeeping forces in Sarajevo and the British Army in Northern Ireland from 1996 to 1998, has called a 'war among the people'.[13] In a conflict of this kind, superior numbers count for little and the heavy use of firepower is useless or counter-productive. Any initial sympathy sections of the population may have had for American occupying forces evaporated after the razing of the city of Fallujah in early 2004. Involving the use of cluster bombs and chemical weapons (a type of white phosphorus, or 'improved napalm'[14]) in 'shake and bake' operations against the city's population, this was an act that can be compared with the destruction by Russian forces of the Chechen capital city of Grozny. In military terms it was a failure – a few days later the insurgents captured the bigger city of Mosul where they were able to seize large quantities of arms – and it demonstrated a disregard for Iraqi lives that fuelled the insurgency. A senior British officer, speaking anonymously in April 2004, commented: 'My view and the view of the British chain of command is that the Americans' use of violence is not proportionate and is over-responsive to the threat they are facing. They don't see the Iraqi people the way we see them. They view them as *Untermenschen*.'[15]

The use of torture at Abu Ghraib followed a familiar pattern. During the year after the fall of Saddam anyone could end up a victim. Thousands of people were swept up from the streets and subjected to systematic abuse. In acting in this way, American forces were following a well-trodden path. Torture was used widely by the Russians in Chechnya, the French in Algeria and by the British in Kenya in the 1950s. Unlike these predecessors, who inflicted extremes of physical pain, however, American interrogators focused on the application of psychological pressure, particularly sexual humiliation. The methods of torture employed in Iraq targeted the culture of their victims, who were assaulted not only as human beings but also as Arabs and Muslims. In using these techniques the US imprinted an indelible image of American depravity on the population and ensured that no American-backed regime can have legitimacy in Iraq.

US military authorities have condemned the abuse that took place at Abu Ghraib. However, while the practice seems to have been resisted by sections of the Army, torture did not occur as a result of accident or indiscipline. From the start of the 'war on terror' the Bush administration flouted international law on the treatment of detainees. It declared members of terrorist organizations to be illegal combatants who are not entitled to the protection of the Geneva Convention. The detainees held in the concentration camp at Guantánamo fall into this category, and so did Taliban and al-Qaeda suspects captured in Afghanistan. Being beyond the reach of international law, they were liable to torture. In Iraq the Bush administration evaded international law by a different route. Security duties at Abu Ghraib and other American detention facilities were outsourced to private contractors not covered by military law or the Geneva Convention. In effect, the Bush administration created a lawless environment in which abuse could be practised with impunity. Torture at Abu Ghraib was not the result of a few officers acting beyond their brief. It was the result of decisions at the highest levels of American leadership.

Since Abu Ghraib, the Bush administration has continued to defend the use of torture, while military judges, the CIA and the US military have continued to resist the practice. In February 2006 the CIA's chief counter-terrorism officer Robert Grenier was fired for opposing torture and 'extraordinary rendition'.[16] It has been reported that the network of secret jails set up by the administration to house prisoners sent there under the special rendition programme (whereby suspects are abducted to countries where they can be tortured without difficulty) may have been shut down because the CIA – unconvinced of the efficacy of torture and fearful that officers who practise it could later be prosecuted – declined to carry out further interrogations. Senior military judges refused to sign a declaration of support for Bush's policies on 'coercive interrogation'.[17] As with the administration's use of unverified intelligence, its decision to employ torture was resisted in all the main institutions of American government, and, as before, the administration carried on with its policies.

Disaster in Iraq was hastened by the willingness to use methods that were inhumane and counter-productive. Some of these errors may have been avoidable, but a pattern of arrogant incompetence was built into the Bush administration. It refused to accept advice from the branches of government where expertise existed, such as the uniformed military, the CIA and the State Department. Instead it relied on the counsel of those in the administration whose views were shaped by a neo-conservative agenda, including the Office of Special Plans. But the picture of post-war Iraq that neo-conservatives disseminated was a tissue of disinformation and wishful thinking, while the willingness to use intolerable means to achieve impossible ends showed the utopian mind at its most deluded.

The ease with which a wildly unreal assessment of conditions in Iraq came to be accepted in America had several sources. Public opinion accepted the war only after a campaign of disinformation. It was persuaded of a link between Saddam Hussein and al-Qaeda when it was known that none existed and informed that Saddam's regime was engaged in an active weapons programme of which there was no reliable evidence. The neo-conservatives who orchestrated the campaign were themselves blinded by illusions, some of them innate to their way of thinking. They believed the methods needed to achieve freedom were the same everywhere: the policies that were required in Iraq were no different from those that had been used to spread freedom in former communist countries. But what is feasible on the banks of the Danube may not be possible on the Euphrates – even supposing peace prevailed in Iraq as it did in most of post-communist Europe – and this ardent neo-conservative belief in a universal model went with a deep indifference to the particular history of the country. If other cultures are stages on the way to a global civilization that already exists in the US, there is no need to understand them since they will soon be part of America. The effect of this adamant universalism is to raise an impassable barrier between America and the rest of humanity that precludes serious involvement in nation building.[18]

In Iraq this cultural default reached surreal extremes. In the shelter of the Green Zone, interns on short-term secondment from Washington – some from neo-conservative think tanks – plotted the future of Iraq insulated from any perception of the absurdity of their plans.

Had the goals of the American administration been achievable at all, it would only be after many decades of occupation. Instead, the impossible was attempted in months. The armed missionaries who dispatched American forces to Iraq expected the instant conversion of the population, only for these forces to be repulsed as enemies. Robespierre's warning to his fellow Jacobins of the perils of Napoleon's programme of exporting revolution by force of arms throughout Europe was vindicated again, two centuries later, in the Middle East.

Iraq is only the most extravagant example of a trend in foreign policy that aimed to renew, in liberal guise, something resembling the European empires of the past. In this view, toppling tyranny in Iraq was not just an American attempt to secure hegemony in the Middle East. It was the start of a new kind of imperialism guided by liberal principles of human rights.

Missionary Liberalism, Liberal Imperialism

The humanitarian, like the missionary, is often an irreducible enemy of the people he seeks to befriend, because he has not imagination enough to sympathize with their proper needs nor humility enough to respect them as if they were his own. Arrogance, fanaticism, meddlesomeness, and imperialism may then masquerade as philanthropy.

George Santayana[19]

The configuration of ideas and movements that led to America's ruinous engagement in Iraq included more than a fusion of the neo-conservative utopians, Armageddonite fundamentalists and Straussian seers that have been examined so far. This exotic and highly toxic blend of beliefs, none of them grounded in any observable or even plausible reality, had one further but equally dangerous ingredient: a type of 'liberal imperialism' based on human rights. Neo-conservatives were able to gain support for regime change in Iraq and potentially other Middle Eastern countries because it could be seen as applying liberal ideals of self-determination and democracy. Liberals insist that the legitimacy of government depends on its respecting the rights of its citizens. If any government fails in this regard, it can be resisted and overthrown – whether by its own citizenry or by an outside force. Human rights override the claims of sovereign states, and where these rights are severely violated other states – acting as the 'international community', in the terminology Blair coined in his speech in Chicago in 1999 – have the right, even the duty, to intervene to protect them.

This view seemed to be supported by humanitarian intervention in the 1990s, which, while failing to prevent some of the worst atrocities, succeeded in imposing a kind of peace in former Yugoslavia. The Balkan war led many liberals to endorse the attack on Iraq as a means of creating a new world order. Even now, some continue to believe the disastrous upshot does not undermine the rightness of military intervention to overthrow tyranny. Intervention of this kind amounts to a liberal version of imperialism, as has been recognized by some of its most influential advocates. Writing in *The New York Times* three months before the invasion of Iraq, Michael Ignatieff announced:

America's empire is not like empires of the past, built on colonies, conquest and the white man's burden ... The 21st century imperium is a new invention in the annals of political science, an empire lite, a global hegemony whose grace notes are free markets, human rights and democracy, enforced by the most awesome power the world has ever known ... Regime change is an imperial task par excellence, since it assumes that the empire's interest has a right to trump the sovereignty of a state. The Bush administration would ask, What moral authority rests with a sovereign who murders and ethnically cleanses his own people, has twice invaded neighbouring countries and usurps his people's wealth to build palaces and lethal weapons?[20]

Ignatieff shows the attractions the new imperialism had for liberals. Who dares deny that tyranny is bad, or question the ideal of a world based on human rights? Has not liberalism always been a universalist creed? After all, the claim that its values are valid for all of humanity is a cardinal principle of liberal philosophy. Does it not follow that liberal states are entitled – indeed obliged – to impose their values throughout the world, even if this requires the use of force? For many liberals the 'war on terror' has been a successor to the Cold War – a struggle in which democracy prevailed over totalitarianism. Yet the differences are substantial. The Cold War was a conflict between states, while the 'war on terror' is one between states and a far more amorphous range of forces. The Cold War was waged between states pledged to rival Enlightenment ideologies, whereas the 'war on terror' is being waged against Islamist forces that claim to reject the Enlightenment. Yet again, the enemy in the Cold War was a communist system that never had popular legitimacy, while Islamist regimes – though very weak in comparison with the former Soviet Union – are gaining mass support. There is, in fact, hardly anything in common between the two conflicts. But like the Cold War the 'war on terror' could be seen as a universal crusade, a vast progressive enterprise in which practically every good cause under the sun could be subsumed, a new force that was

devoted to a politics of human rights and especially women's rights, across the Muslim world; a politics against racism and anti-Semitism, no matter how inconvenient that might seem to the Egyptian media and the House of Saud; a politics against the manias of the ultra-right in Israel, too, no matter how much that might enrage the Likud and its supporters; a politics of secular education, of pluralism, and law across the Muslim world; a politics against obscurantism and superstition; a politics to out-compete the Islamists and Baathi on their left; a politics to fight against poverty and oppression; a politics of authentic solidarity for the Muslim world, instead of the demagogy of cosmic hatred. A politics, in a word, of liberalism, a 'new birth of freedom' – the kind of thing that could be glimpsed, in its early stages, in the liberation of Kabul.[21]

Paul Berman gave vent to this sublime vision in 2003. It contained no inkling that the result of the overthrow of secular despotism in Iraq would be a mix of anarchy and theocracy. The impossibility of liberalism in Afghanistan – which has only ever had something resembling a modern state when Soviet forces imposed, with enormous cruelty, a version of Enlightenment despotism on parts of the country – was too disturbing to contemplate. All the liberal causes that were wrapped up in the 'war on terror' were inherently desirable, and so – it seemed to follow – practically realizable. In their attitudes to regime change, neo-conservatives have been at one with many liberals. Regime change was an instrument of progress, and for the most part liberals have been no more willing than neo-conservatives to confront its human costs and abject failure. Such political opposition to the war as there has been in the US has come from elements of the paleo-conservative Right and sections of the Old Left. In the liberal media only the *New York Review of Books* remained untouched by war fever, while journals such as *The Nation* and *The American Conservative* voiced criticism from the Left and the Right. The public resistance to the war that voters voiced in the mid-term 2006 elections found few echoes among liberals. Most remained silent in the belief that the war showed American power acting as the final guarantor of freedom in the world.

Yet liberal imperialism was an impossible programme of action. Twentieth-century history has been dominated by resistance to western empires since the destruction of the Russian Imperial Fleet by Japan in 1905 – a defeat for European power that inspired anti-colonial movements throughout Asia and which Jawaharlal Nehru, the first prime minister of India, described as one of the decisive events of his life. Britain's failed attempt to assert its control over the Suez Canal, the withdrawal of France from Algeria, the humiliation of France and America in Vietnam and the defeat of Soviet forces in Afghanistan – these are only some examples of the impotence of western occupiers in non-western lands that has been demonstrated again and again over the past century. American defeat in Iraq is only the most recent example of this impotence.

Beyond the impossibility of any large-scale western imperial project at this juncture in history, the notion that America could be the agent of a project of this kind was highly implausible. The US has few of the attributes of an imperial regime. It has a large portfolio of countries over which it has varying degrees of influence – occasionally exercised by the threat of force, more often through a mix of economic sanctions and inducements. America's relations with many of these countries display an imperialist pattern in which resources are extracted through the agency of governments that the US in some degree controls. In Latin America, the US has long acted in imperialist fashion to protect its economic and strategic interests. At present it has a massive military and naval presence in the Persian Gulf, while it is expanding its bases in central Asia and establishing itself in West Africa. Yet the US does not govern any of these regions and its forces have minimal contact with their peoples. Its bases are hermetically sealed bubbles of American life and its embassies fortress-like structures insulated against any incursion from their host societies. Empires come in several shapes and sizes; not all have been organized around the acquisition of territory. What is striking about American imperial relationships is that they include few long-term strategic commitments that can be counted on to survive the vicissitudes of American politics. When any American overseas military involvement becomes too costly in money or casualties it is likely to be abruptly terminated. As a result of this fact, which is taken as axiomatic in Washington and in the countries concerned, long-term alliances with local ruling elites of the kind that enabled empires to endure for centuries are rare. Most of those existing today, such as those in Britain, Germany and Japan, are survivors from the Second World War.

A lasting imperial system rests on the belief that it embodies a long-term commitment. Empires are commonly established by means that include the use of force, but they have been long-lasting – as in the case of the Romans, the Ottomans and the Habsburgs, for example – when force has served long-range political goals. The European colonial powers normally used force in this way, so that it was clear that their presence in the countries they occupied was meant to be permanent. The creation of the Raj involved savage conflicts, and the Indian Mutiny in the mid-nineteenth century posed a serious threat to British rule. Even so, throughout most of the colonial period a few thousand British officers were able to rule the sub-continent without large scale warfare. They did so by making alliances with the country's rulers – by 1919 there were around 500 princely states locally ruled but pledged to the British monarchy. In contrast, American forces view themselves, and are seen by others, as transients – 'tourists with guns', as a National Guardsman in Afghanistan put it[22] – and rarely forge any but the most short-term bonds with local elites or people. As a result they are compelled to rely on the intensive use of firepower, which cannot deliver long-term goals.

America lacks most of the prerequisites of empire and will not acquire them in any future that can be foreseen. How can there be imperialism – liberal or otherwise – when there are no imperialists? The US has some of the burdens of empire – including its financial costs, which are far more disabling than in the era of European colonialism. Unlike nineteenth-century Britain, which was the world's largest exporter of capital, the United States is the world's largest debtor. America's military adventures are paid for with borrowed money – mostly lent by China, whose purchases of American government debt are crucial in underpinning the US economy. This dependency on China cannot be squared with the idea that America has the capacity to act as the global enforcer of liberal values. It is America's foreign creditors who fund this role, and if they come to perceive US foreign policy as threatening or irrational they have the power to veto it. As Emmanuel Todd, the French analyst who in 1975 forecast the Soviet collapse, has noted:

The United States is unable to live on its own economic activity and must be subsidized to maintain its current level of consumption – at present cruising speed that subsidy amounts to $1.4 billion a day (as of April 2003). If its behaviour continues to be disruptive, it is America that ought to fear an embargo.[23]

The US is losing its economic primacy, and its status as the 'last superpower' is bound to follow. Advancing globalization brings with it new great powers and the unexpected re-emergence of powers that seemed to be in irreversible decline. China and Russia may be able to live in peaceful coexistence with the US, but they will never accept American moral tutelage; the notion that they can be conscripted into service in a campaign to convert the world to American-style democracy is laughable. The 'new American century' envisioned by neo-conservatives has lasted less than a decade. In an episode that believers in Hegel's idea of the cunning of reason will appreciate, neo-conservatives – acting as the unwitting servants of history – have turned the United States into a normal great power, one among several and having no special authority. More generally, power is flowing away from the liberal states that were the apparent victors in the Cold War and for the first time since the 1930s the rising powers in the international system are authoritarian states.

Liberal imperialism has also resulted in a retreat from liberal values in the US. The administration continues to insist that the president must be free to determine what counts as torture. Vice-president Dick Cheney, asked on a radio programme whether he was in favour of a 'dunk in the water' for terrorist detainees, replied that he was, declaring that the question was 'a no-brainer for me'.[24] Techniques of 'water-boarding' – a form of torture used by the Khmer Rouge in Cambodia, and whose use against Americans in the Second World War resulted in a Japanese officer being sentenced to fifteen years' hard labour[25] – are not prohibited and can be practised routinely by the US. The same is true of sleep deprivation, a method of torture used in Guantánamo that was employed by the NKVD in the Stalinist Soviet Union to generate confessions in the 'show trials' of the 1930s.[26] Torture techniques involving sensory deprivation, which were used by the Chinese on American POWs in the Korean War, have also been used on José Padilla, an American citizen arrested as an enemy combatant and detained without charges on a naval brig in South Carolina from mid-2002 until January 2006.[27]

By any internationally accepted standard of what constitutes torture, the world's pre-eminent liberal regime has committed itself to the practice as a matter of national policy. Along with this there has been a shift away from the constitutional traditions that curbed American government in the past. The vote by the Senate on 28 September 2006 that allowed the president the authority to determine what counts as torture also suspended *habeas corpus* for people detained as terrorist suspects, denying their right to know the offence with which they are charged and to challenge their detention in court. Henceforth anyone charged with involvement in terrorism – not only foreign nationals but also US citizens – can be detained without charge and held indefinitely. In effect this put the executive above the law while placing the citizenry outside it. Taken together with the Patriot Acts, which permit surveillance of the entire American population, the US has suffered a loss of freedom that has no parallel in any mature democracy.

It is not the first time American government has acted to invade the freedoms of its citizens. The Alien and Sedition Acts that were passed at the end of the eighteenth century, the Espionage and

Sedition Acts of 1917–18 and the 'Red Scare' that followed the First World War, the forcible internment of people of Japanese descent during the Second World War, all greatly expanded executive power. In each case the damage to freedom was not permanent – the laws that enabled it were passed during a period of war, then were repealed or fell into disuse. The Bush administration's expansion of executive powers has been more far-reaching, and because the 'war on terror' can never be won it has no end-point. As the 2006 mid-term elections showed, the US remains a functioning democracy, and it may be that legislation enabling torture and removing *habeas corpus* will be reversed under future administrations. The fact remains that it has ceased to be a regime in which the power of government is limited by the rule of law. The checks and balances of the Constitution have failed to prevent an unprecedented expansion of arbitrary power.

The shift illustrates the delusive qualities of contemporary liberalism. The liberal theories that have been dominant over the past generation seek an escape from the hazards of politics in the supposed certainties of law. American liberal legalism – a school of thought that includes John Rawls, Ronald Dworkin, Bruce Ackerman and many others – aims to replace the murky negotiations of politics by the transparent adjudication of law.[28] In that way, it has been assumed, any threat to rights can be neutralized. In America, achieving this happy condition is the role of the Supreme Court. However, as the Bush administration has demonstrated, liberalism of this legalist variety is another Utopia. The Supreme Court can be politicized by rigging the judicial selection procedure, and if that fails the Court's rulings can be ignored. The defence of constitutional freedoms then falls to legislators, who may – as in September 2006 – fear the electoral consequences of opposing the executive. At this point politics trumps law, as it does in other countries.

Liberals have come to believe that human freedom can be secured by constitutional guarantees. They have failed to grasp the Hobbesian truth, which Leo Strauss applied to the Weimar Republic, that constitutions change with regimes. A regime shift has occurred in the US, which now stands somewhere between the law-governed state it was during most of its history and a species of illiberal democracy. The

US has undergone this change not as a result of its corrosion by relativism – as Strauss believed occurred in Weimar Germany – but through the capture of government by fundamentalism. If the American regime as it has been known in the past ceases to exist, it will be a result of the power of faith.

Contemporary liberals think of rights as universal human attributes that can be respected anywhere, but here they show a characteristic disregard of history. Current understandings of human rights developed along with the modern nation-state. It was the nation-state that emancipated individuals from the communal ties of medieval times and created freedom as it has come to be known in the modern world. This was not done without enormous conflict and severe costs. Large-scale violence was an integral feature of the process. If the US became a modern nation only after a civil war, France did so only after the Napoleonic wars and Germany after two world wars and the Cold War. In Africa and the Balkans the struggle for nationhood has run in parallel with ethnic cleansing, while the welding of China into a nation that is underway today involves the suppression of Muslim minorities and something not far from genocide in Tibet.

Liberal theorists tend to distinguish between ethnic nationalism, which they judge to be bad, and civic varieties they view as good. Repression is not only a feature of ethnic nationalism, however. Nations are created by the exercise of state power in a process that commonly involves the forcible integration or exclusion of groups viewed as alien. The construction of civic regimes in France and the US involved the use of schooling systems as instruments for integration, while war and conscription were used to create solidarity in the face of enemies. Liberal orthodoxy takes for granted that self-governing nation-states are freer than empires, but empires have often been friendlier to minorities – think of the toleration of the Ottomans when Europe was mired in wars of religion, the ethnic hatreds that were released by the fall of the cosmopolitan Habsburgs, or the destruction of the ancient multicultural city of Alexandria by the Egyptian nationalist Nasser. National self-determination marches hand in hand with ethnic cleansing and the uprooting of eclectic societies in which different ways of life have long coexisted in peace. Promoting self-determination universally, as neo-conservatives and liberal interventionists would like, means reproducing these evils on a worldwide scale.

Nation-states are not only the chief institutional vehicle of modern freedom but also, almost universally, of liberal democracy. In 1959 the American political scientist Seymour Martin Lipset reported the 'absurd fact' that all stable, long-standing democracies were monarchies, with the exception of the US, Switzerland and (at the time) Uruguay.[29] The fact is surprising only if one believes – absurdly – that democracy is self-legitimating. The few indisputably multi-national democracies that are thriving at the start of the twenty-first century – such as the UK, Spain and Canada – are monarchies and relics of empire. India is a flourishing multicultural democracy; but it is not multi-national and achieved its present stability only after a brutal partition with Pakistan, while Kashmir remains bitterly disputed. Except where they draw on monarchy for legitimacy, liberal democracies are nearly always nation-states. The attempt to project democracy beyond the national level – in the European Union, for example – has been a failure. The modern ideal of cosmopolitan democracy seems to be best realized in countries with pre-modern institutions.

With few exceptions, liberal democracy has taken root only in nation-states. But nation-states are rarely formed without mass killing, and in many parts of the world they may not be possible. Few of the countries of post-colonial Africa have developed a cohesive national identity, and the Middle East continues to be ruled by states that were dreamt up in the twilight of empire. Failed or semi-failed states exist in the Balkans and the Caucasus. Japan is a nation-state, but while China is determined to become one it remains an empire, and the same is true of Russia. Much of humanity will probably never live in nation-states. In the future as in the past the world will be governed by many kinds of regime.

The objection to universal democracy is not that some peoples are unfit for it. Democratic governments have been established in countries with very different cultures, while nothing prevents the most seemingly secure democracy slipping into tyranny. Any country can achieve democracy and any can lose it. Humankind is not divided between 'the West' – which despite having engendered totalitarianism still identifies itself with freedom – and the rest. Democracy has many advantages, especially in enabling governments to be changed without the use of force, but it is rarely achieved without a cost in violence while freedom may be no better protected in the end.

Where popular sentiment is illiberal, minorities may fare worse under democratic regimes than under some types of despotism. Even majorities may find their freedom curbed – as in the popular theocracy that is emerging in most of Iraq, where women are losing the freedom they had under Saddam. Overthrowing tyranny may bring democracy without advancing liberty. In the same way, democracy can allow the destruction of long-standing limits on government, as under the Bush administration. No constitution can impose freedom where it is not wanted or preserve it where it is no longer valued.

While liberal imperialism of the sort that was prevalent in the run-up to the war was an impossible programme, the Iraq adventure displayed, in a modified form suited to an intrinsically absurd project, some familiar imperialist traits. The geo-political aim of the enterprise was to seize control of the country's oil, and though it has not enabled the increase of production that was expected, this seizure did occur. Beyond this act of appropriation, Iraq has been the scene of monumental fraud, with billions of dollars disappearing into the pockets of American corporations and Washington lobbyists. The corruption following the American invasion has been on a scale that dwarfs the scandals that surrounded the oil-for-food programme during the Saddam regime. Contracts for the reconstruction of Iraq have been preferentially allocated to American firms, with those that have close connections with the Republican party, the Bush administration and USAID – the United States Agency for International Development, which oversees the distribution of contracts – receiving the lion's share. Many of the activities of government have been outsourced along with many of the traditional functions of the military. Tasks such as policing buildings, streets and oil wells, maintaining weapons systems and guarding supply convoys have been contracted out to corporations. UK private-security firms have been reported to have around 48,000 personnel in the country, outnumbering British troops by a factor of six to one.[30] Government has been privatized, an operation that has created many new sources of profit.

Rapacity of the sort that has occurred in Iraq since the invasion is normal. Imperialism is always about profit before anything else, and the rag-tag army of crooks and shysters that followed in the wake of American troops is not greatly different from that which trailed behind the colonial armies of earlier times. Nor is the crony capitalism in which companies with close connections to Washington have divided the spoils of war among themselves in any way unusual. Though its scale may be larger and its style more blatant in American-occupied Iraq, predatory greed is a universal feature of imperial conquest.

But this is still not imperialism in any classical sense. It is not only that the occupying power lacks the capacity to govern. By hiving off many of the functions of the state, Iraq's American occupiers have institutionalized the anarchy they created when they dismantled the state. The structures of the American-backed regime are not institutions of government. They are targets for capture by sectarian organizations and irregular militias, which use them to share out resources and neutralize opponents. In these conditions, creating a Saddam-like strong man to impose order on this chaos – as some 'realists' in Washington have proposed – is impossible. Such a strong man presupposes a type of Arab nationalism – secular, military and bureaucratic – that hardly exists today. Moreover, there is no state left in Iraq through which such a dictator could operate. The secular tyranny that was destroyed cannot be reinvented.

American analysts who grasp these facts sometimes suggest a three-way partition as a solution. But Iraq cannot be split into three states – it has already broken into two, with a Kurdish state now established in the north and the rest of the country savagely contested. Divided not only by their beliefs but also and more importantly by their rival claims on power and resources, the Sunni and Shia communities cannot be cleanly partitioned. The Sunni minority stands to lose everything and will fight to the death. With only around 60 per cent of the population composed of Shias, Iraq faces decades of ethnic cleansing and sectarian mass murder.

The US is powerless in the face of the anarchy its invasion of the country has created. A phased withdrawal of American combat forces might seem to be the solution, and something of the sort was recommended by the Iraq Study Group, which was set up by Congress in March 2006 and reported in December of that year. The group's co-chair was James Baker III, secretary of state in the administration of George Bush Snr and a consummate Washington insider. As an avowed realist in international affairs, Baker acknowledged there is no policy that can now guarantee stability in the country. But the group failed to confront a harder truth: the situation that has been produced by the US invasion of Iraq belongs to the class of problems that will be resolved by forces no one controls – and certainly not by the US. The anarchy that has been created in the country precludes a Vietnam-style American withdrawal. Vietnam had in the North a government that could govern the country, whereas Iraq has no effective government, and while a 'domino effect' failed to materialize in South-East Asia the fragmentation of the Iraqi state could well produce one in the Gulf. Though it may be masked in Washington, the fact of American defeat is evident throughout the region. Saudi Arabia, Syria, Iran and other countries are increasing their use of proxy forces in the country – with US forces now under fire from Sunni militias armed by America's allies – which is becoming the site of a war for hegemony in the region. Escalation into a wider conflict has been the logic of events since the American invasion. The destruction of Iraq will go down in history as the trigger for a Thirty Years War whose outcome cannot be known but which will involve a revolutionary upheaval throughout the Gulf with repercussions in much of the world.

America's adventure in Iraq has very little in common with the empires of the past. The colonial powers aimed to exploit the resources of the countries they conquered over extended periods. The East India Company and Hudson's Bay Company were effectively governments, which endured for centuries and became part of long-standing colonial administrations. When the colonialists departed they left an inheritance not only of exploitation but also of institutions. Whatever its faults, the state of Iraq was one of these institutions.

The Iraq war served an economic system that forbids long-term commitments. In the casino capitalism that prevails in the early twenty-first century, investment has been replaced by gambling, and it will surely not be long before the war is written off as just another bad bet. Even the wealth that has been extracted in the occupation has a spectral quality. If there is a symbol that captures America in Iraq, it is not the colonial institutions of former times. It is Enron, which vanished leaving nothing behind.

WHY THE 'WAR ON TERROR' CANNOT BE WON

Starting at least as early as the 1950s, the literature on counter-insurgency is so enormous that, had it been put aboard the Titanic, it would have sunk that ship without any help from the iceberg. However, the outstanding fact is that almost all of it has been written by the losers.

Martin van Creveld[31]

In September 2006, a classified report pooling the knowledge of sixteen American intelligence agencies was leaked, and sections of it subsequently published, which pointed to the 'centrality' of the US invasion of Iraq in fomenting Islamist terrorism throughout the world.[32] This judgement came as no surprise to the analysts who predicted such a result well before the war began. They expected that the invasion would assist recruitment and provide a training ground for terrorists; some also anticipated that an Iraqi insurgency against American occupation would be impossible to defeat. If the war was launched despite these warnings it was because the politicians who engineered it were able to convince public opinion that it was part of the 'war on terror'. The assault on Iraq was described by sections of the Pentagon as a move in a 'Long War' – a multi-generational conflict in which pre-emptive attack and regime change are used to defeat terrorism throughout the world. More recent American strategic thinking has noted the crucial role of non-military strategies in combating terrorism. Yet the belief persists that countering terrorism involves defeating a 'global insurgency', which is only a more sophisticated way of talking about how to fight a 'global war on terror'.[33]

The very idea of such a war is questionable. Terrorism is an umbrella term that covers many types of unconventional warfare, which have different causes and remedies. To lump these together into a single global threat indicates a lack of understanding. Again, terrorism is a prime candidate for unqualified moral judgements. For those who think of counter-terrorism as a crusade for an 'end to evil',[34] analysing terror without condemning it is outrageous. But amoral analysis of the sort conducted by military strategists may be more useful, and in the end more moral.

Where the term is used accurately, 'global terrorism' refers to a small – though growing – portion of the unconventional warfare that is occurring at any one time throughout the world. Much that is today described as terrorism was viewed in the past as insurrection or civil conflict and recognized to be a part of struggles that are local in nature. Techniques such as the bombing of government buildings and the assassination of public officials are the stock in trade of national liberation struggles and were employed in places as diverse as Palestine and Malaya under British rule, French Algeria and Vietnam during American occupation. Terrorist techniques are used because they are cheap and highly effective. They are normally employed on a large scale over extended periods only in circumstances of severe conflict when other methods have failed. In other words, terrorism is often a rational strategy.

It has become part of western discourse to link terrorism with Arab culture and an Islamic cult of martyrdom. However, Islam is a religion not a culture, and most of the people who live in the 'Islamic world' are not Arabs. Terrorism in Indonesia cannot be explained by cultural attitudes attributed – in a manner that when applied to other groups would rightly be condemned as racist – to Arabs. Suicide terrorism is not a pathology that afflicts any particular culture nor has it any close connections with religion.

Much terrorism is like other types of warfare. Nearly always, wars are fought within or across cultural boundaries. The first two world wars began as intra-European conflicts, the Sino-Japanese war was fought between countries that both belong in the Confucian cultural world, while the Iran–Iraq war was intra-Islamic. The Balkan wars of the 1990s were fought along ethnic–national not religious–cultural lines, with Christians and Muslims often allies. The idea that wars are conflicts of civilizations – which emerged in the course of an

American dispute about multiculturalism rather than as an attempt to understand international relations – is not supported by facts.[35]

When applied to unconventional warfare, talk of a clash of civilizations is meaningless. It was the Tamil Tigers, a Marxist-Leninist group operating in a Hindu culture in Sri Lanka, that devised the technique of suicide bombing (including the vest that was later adopted by Palestinians), and until the war in Iraq the Tigers committed more such bombings than any other movement. Aircraft hijacking was pioneered by the secular Palestinian Liberation Organization with the help of ultra-leftist groups such as the Red Army Faction. A Japanese Red Army member carried out the first suicide attack in Israel in 1972.

Suicide bombing is a technique that has been adopted by people of various cultures and beliefs to achieve political aims. In the first rigorous empirical study of the subject, *Dying to Win: The Strategic Logic of Suicide Terrorism*,[36] Robert Pape analysed all known cases between 1980 and 2004 and found that over 95 per cent of all incidents had clear political objectives. Whether in Chechnya or Sri Lanka, Kashmir or Gaza, the goal was to expel an occupying force. The ethnic and religious backgrounds of those who committed the bombings were highly diverse. In Lebanon, Hezbollah mounted a campaign against French, American and Israeli targets between 1982 and 1986 that included forty-one suicide attacks (including the attack in 1983 which killed over a hundred Marines and resulted in the abrupt withdrawal of American forces by president Reagan). Of these, only eight were committed by Islamic fundamentalists, twenty-seven by members of secular leftist political groups such as the Lebanese Communist party, and three by Christians. All the people involved were born in Lebanon, but otherwise they were very different. These Hezbollah suicide bombers did not fit into any recognizable profile of social marginality (one of the Christians was a female high-school teacher with a college degree, for example). The single common factor linking them was their adherence to a set of political goals. The decisive conditions in producing long-term, large-scale terrorist violence are not cultural or religious, but political. Where these conditions exist, anyone can become a terrorist.

Terrorism does not always serve a rational strategy, as has been seen. Apocalyptic beliefs played a central role in state terror from the

Jacobins through the Bolsheviks and the Nazis. America's indigenous terrorist movements are driven by similar myths: the rightwing militias that produced the Oklahoma bomber Timothy McVeigh were inspired by a neo-Nazi ideology that anticipated catastrophe and violent renewal in the US, while the Army of God, a Christian fundamentalist terrorist group that murders doctors who practise abortion, views the American state as Satanic. In Japan, the Aum movement, which planted sarin gas on the subway in Tokyo and attempted to obtain supplies of ebola virus for use in further attacks, also subscribed to an apocalyptic world-view – though it recruited among professional people (particularly scientists) rather than the marginal groups that join American rightwing militias. Terrorists of these kinds have more in common with cult members than with the soldiers and strategists of Hezbollah or the Tamil Tigers.

Al-Qaeda's terrorism has both strategic and apocalyptic dimensions.[37] Having morphed into new shapes since the 9/11 attacks, today it is more a loose web of affinity groups than an organized global network. There has been a shift of operational control from the centre to regional and local command centres, and at the same time networks have become increasingly internet-based. Founded towards the end of the Cold War during the Soviet–Afghan conflict in which it was used as a western proxy, al-Qaeda has become a decentralized, mostly virtual entity whose goals are less clearly defined than in the past. This is partly a response to western military action. While the destruction of the Taliban regime disabled most of the units that existed at that time, new ones have sprung up since the invasion of Iraq. Al-Qaeda's original objectives were clear – the withdrawal of US forces from Saudi Arabia and the destruction of the House of Saud – but it has now become a vehicle for inchoate anger. This new phase has been seen in the violent jihad that produced terrorist attacks in the UK, Spain and the Netherlands, which were not only a rejection of western policies but also of western societies.[38]

Al-Qaeda is the only terrorist network that has a global reach, and in this as in other respects it is a by-product of globalization. Radical Islam is often interpreted as a backlash against modernity, but it is striking how closely the lives of the 9/11 hijackers matched a stereotype of modern anomie. Living a semi-nomadic existence, they were not members of any community, and it is difficult to resist the impression that they turned to terrorism more to secure a meaning in their lives than to advance any concrete objective. By taking up terror they ceased to be drifters and became warriors. Most of the hijackers were not long-time practitioners of Islam but became born-again Muslims in Europe. The Islam they represent does not exist in traditional cultures. It is a version of fundamentalism that could only have developed through contact with the West. It is globalization that underpins the utopian vision of a worldwide community of believers. As Olivier Roy, the French scholar who has developed a rigorous sociological analysis of global Islam, has observed, it is 'the growing de-territorialization of Islam which leads to the political reformulation of an imaginary *ummah*'.[39]

Al-Qaeda has been compared with the anarchist terrorists of the late nineteenth century, and there are points of resemblance. Since the destruction of the Taliban regime, al-Qaeda has operated without state sponsorship, and its focus is on destroying existing states rather than founding new ones. Al-Qaeda differs from anarchist terrorism partly in the cruelty of its methods – whereas anarchists mainly targeted state officials, al-Qaeda specializes in attacking civilians – and in the fact that it is acquiring a mass base. Whereas anarchist terrorism was the work of a tiny sect that never had popular support, al-Qaeda now appeals to large numbers of disaffected Muslims, many living in western countries. In these circumstances, further attacks of the kinds seen in New York and Washington, Bali, Madrid, Ankara, London and other cities will not be easily prevented.

The danger of Islamist terrorism is real, but declaring war on the world is not a sensible way of dealing with it. Except in a few countries – such as Saudi Arabia, Israel and Iraq – terrorists pose a security problem rather than a strategic threat. There is no clear enemy against which war can be directed or any point at which victory can be announced. As has often been noted, disabling terrorists is a type of police work that requires support from their host communities. It is not facilitated by futile wars in Islamic lands or by discriminatory policies targetting Muslims in western countries. While concentrated military action may sometimes be effective – as in the destruction of training bases in Afghanistan – conventional military operations are usually counter-productive. Enhanced security measures and continuous political engagement are the only strategies that have ever brought terrorism under control.

A strategy of this kind succeeded in Northern Ireland.[40] Though the IRA and the splinter groups around it were engaged in an insurgency, the terrorism they committed was not treated as an act of war. They were treated as criminals, and after an initial period in which mistakes were made – including mass internment of terrorist suspects – the overriding aim of policy was to detach the terrorists from their underlying communities and divert terrorist leaders into political channels. The strategy was continued throughout serious attacks – including the assassination of several key British figures and an attempt to decapitate the British government by bombing the Conservative party conference in Brighton in 1984 – and it worked. Terrorist violence is now much reduced in Northern Ireland and on the British mainland.

An obstacle to coping with the terrorist threat is the belief that it is unlike anything in the past. Al-Qaeda is different from previous terrorist movements in operating throughout the world, but the emergence of global terrorism does not reflect a quantum leap in international relations of the kind postulated by some American theorists. Philip Bobbitt has argued that global terrorism mirrors the decline of the Westphalian system, which is being replaced by a US-led order in which state sovereignty no longer exists. In this new system the chief task of states will no longer be to reflect the values of their citizens. They will be 'market states' serving the global economy. Establishing this new system will involve a series of epochal conflicts that include several 'wars against terror'. During this period the US – which supposedly embodies the new type of state that the rest of the world is struggling to achieve – will face the necessity of initiating 'preclusive' attacks on rogue regimes that refuse to accept the terms of the new global order.[41]

Though it is more rigorously developed, Bobbitt's analysis has much in common with Fukuyama's. Both believe an historical process is underway in which a version of the American system of government is spreading throughout much of the world. Unlike Fukuyama, who believed the end of history would be peaceful, Bobbitt perceives that it will be a time of large-scale wars; but like Fukuyama he is convinced a major shift is human affairs is underway. As the French writer Bernard-Henri Lévy has noted, 'We have underestimated the importance and centrality of the Fukuyama way of thinking in contemporary American ideology.'[42]

With few exceptions, American analysts have interpreted the large shifts in international relations of the past two decades as signs that the old world of ethnic and religious divisions and great-power conflicts is coming to an end. It is a belief that reflects the survival of faith-based habits of thinking rather than any clear view of the facts. The true shift that is underway is the reverse: all the old conflicts have returned but with new protagonists and a diminished role for the US. The only step-change is in new technologies that give these conflicts a new scale. In operational terms the obsolescence of state sovereignty means the unlimited sovereignty of a single state – the US, which in recent years has treated its laws as having universal jurisdiction – but the conditions in which the US could exercise this authority no longer exist (if they ever did). Accelerated by the Iraq war, the decline in American power that is an integral part of globalization has left it heavily dependent on other states. The US relies on other countries for access to natural resources, finance for its mounting debt and diplomatic aid to deal with international crises. The only unilateral power it retains is the power to bomb, the limits of which have been demonstrated in Iraq.

Instead of other countries following the US in becoming market-states, they are emulating the US in asserting their sovereignty. The US was never a market-state – the imperatives of the market have nearly always taken second place to those of national security and national identity. China, India and Russia are now behaving as the US has done in using global markets to advance their power in the world while American power is in steep decline. The result is a world that is becoming steadily more pluralistic, though not necessarily any safer. The system of sovereign states has entered another phase in which new powers are challenging the status quo and competing among themselves, a process that has happened many times before.[43]

Nor – with one vital exception – does the terrorist threat mark a step-change in history. While the 9/11 attacks were not unprecedented

– there were earlier attacks on US embassies in Africa, for example – they were on a larger scale and the work of a network that is global to an unprecedented degree. Despite these differences, 9/11 was a further development of earlier types of unconventional warfare rather than a qualitative change in the nature of conflict. Aided by the internet, which enables violent jihadists who have never met to form virtual cells, al-Qaeda is extending its influence and reach. At the same time, developments in weaponry are improving the arsenal available to groups such as Hamas and Hezbollah. But Islamist terrorism implements no coherent strategy and cannot command the resources of any great power. It is still far from being anything like a mortal threat to civilized life of the kinds that were confronted and defeated in the twentieth century.

This situation will change if terrorist groups gain access to the means of mass destruction. Not only al-Qaeda but also cults such as Aum have demonstrated an interest in biological warfare. Information technology enables types of cyber-war to be waged that can disrupt the infrastructure of modern societies – power stations and airports, for example – with the potential of causing large-scale casualties. The most catastrophic risk comes from nuclear terrorism. Using 'suitcase bombs' or 'dirty bombs' (conventional explosives salted with radioactive waste), terrorists could kill hundreds of thousands of people and paralyse social and economic life. No doubt the materials needed for such devices are heavily guarded, but if any of the world's nuclear states were destabilized the danger of these materials falling into terrorist hands would be high. In Pakistan – a semi-failed state in which fundamentalist forces are heavily entrenched – that risk may already be present. The murder of Alexander Litvinenko, a former Russian intelligence officer who died in London in November 2006 weeks after receiving a lethal dose of radiation, suggests that nuclear terrorism may already be a reality.

The risk of proliferation has been accelerated by American policies. North Korea acquired nuclear capability as a result of a transfer of know-how from Pakistan – a country whose role in the 'war on terror' insulated it from effective pressure to stop leakage of this kind. The risks have been increased by the Bush administration pulling out of arms control agreements and by a change in US nuclear doctrine that allows the pre-emptive use of nuclear weapons against countries believed to have WMD programmes.[44] Above all, after Iraq everyone knows that the only way to be safe against American attack is to possess the WMD capability Saddam lacked. According to an announcement by the International Atomic Energy Agency in November 2006, six Islamic countries have indicated they wish to acquire nuclear technology. All of them – Algeria, Egypt, Morocco, Tunisia, the United Arab Emirates and Turkey – insist they want it for peaceful purposes, but a nuclear arms race may already have begun. Other countries that may be interested include Nigeria and Jordan. It is not beyond the realm of realistic possibility that the state of Iraq – if it still exists – might at some time in the future acquire a nuclear capability of the kind pre-emptive military action by the US was meant to prevent.

There seem to be some in the US who see an attack on Iran as a means of deterring proliferation, but, as in the case of Iraq, the effect would be to increase it. A large swathe of the Middle East and Asia, which at present contains three theatres of war – in Iraq, Palestine and Afghanistan – would become a zone of armed conflict,[45] while the lesson of Iraq – that the only way to be safe from American attack is to possess nuclear weapons – would be reinforced. At the same time an attack could well fail to halt Iran's nuclear programme. Though it is ethnically diverse, Iran is unlike most other countries in the region in being a fairly cohesive state. The home of an ancient and rich Persian civilization, it currently practises a type of democracy – in effect a more stable version of the system that is developing in Iraq – that gives its present leadership a degree of legitimacy. An American air assault could increase the legitimacy of this leadership, which has already gained in popularity from the nuclear programme. Even if a more liberal version of democracy were to develop, there is no guarantee that Iran would renounce nuclear ambitions. Worse, a bombing campaign could fail to destroy the nuclear programme while weakening the country's government to the point where it would no longer be able to control whatever nuclear facilities actually exist in the country. Worse still, an American attack could trigger upheaval in many Islamic states, including Pakistan – which is already a nuclear power and could easily become another failed state.

From a standpoint of global security few things are more important than preventing the leakage of nuclear technology beyond the control of states. Mutual assured destruction (MAD) forestalled the use of nuclear weapons for over half a century. Deterrence of this kind may not give complete security against a nuclear state headed by an apocalyptic prophet; but since some among its leadership will want to go on living, it affords some protection. When the enemy is an elusive network whose branches can be based anywhere in the world deterrence breaks down completely. Agents of mass destruction cannot be threatened with annihilation if their identity is unknown. The American arms control analyst Fred Ikle has written, 'Military history offers no lessons that tell nations how to cope with a continuing global dispersion of cataclysmic means for destruction.'[46] A crucial part of the task is preventing state collapse. States have failed throughout history – we need only think of the centuries of anarchy that followed the fall of the Roman Empire or the era of Warring States in ancient China. It will not always be possible to prevent states failing in future. To encourage that failure is folly – especially at a time when the development of technology makes anarchy more threatening than ever before. Yet that is what overthrowing governments while lacking the ability to put anything in their place means in practice.

The 'war on terror' is a symptom of a mentality that anticipates an unprecedented change in human affairs – the end of history, the passing of the sovereign state, universal acceptance of democracy and the defeat of evil. This is the central myth of apocalyptic religion framed in political terms, and the common factor underlying the failed utopian projects of the past decade. The promise of an imminent transformation was not a cynical ploy attached to policies adopted on other grounds by leaders who did not themselves believe in it. Bush and Blair genuinely believed such a change was impending or could be brought about, as did the neo-conservatives and liberal interventionists who supported them in Iraq. Apocalypse failed to arrive, and history went on as before but with an added dash of blood.

6

Post-Apocalypse

... the privilege of Absurdity, to which no living creature
is subject, but man only.   Thomas Hobbes, *Leviathan*[1]

The faith in Utopia, which killed so many in the centuries following
the French Revolution, is dead. Like other faiths it may be resurrected
in circumstances that cannot be foreseen; but it is unlikely to trouble
us much further in the next few decades. The cycle in which world
politics was dominated by secular versions of apocalyptic myth has
come to an end, and, in an historic reversal, old-time religion has
re-emerged at the heart of global conflict.

Iraq was the first utopian experiment of the new century and
may be the last. Unending carnage in the country continues to be
described in the secular language of the post-Enlightenment era, with
western countries talking of defending human rights and Islamists
using many of the ideas of western radical thought. Yet it has ceased
to be a contest in which secular ideologies are at stake and has become
instead a many-sided war of religion entwined with an ongoing
resource war.

The political ideologies of the last two hundred years were vehicles
for a myth of salvation in history that is Christianity's most dubious
gift to humanity. The faith-based violence to which this myth gave
rise is a congenital western disorder. The early Christian belief in an
End-Time that would bring about a new type of human life was
transmitted via the medieval millenarians to become secular utopianism and, in another incarnation, the belief in progress. The age of
utopias ended in Fallujah, a city razed by rival fundamentalists. The

secular era is not in the future, as liberal humanists believe. It is in the past, which we have yet to understand.

AFTER SECULARISM

What presents itself as the 'secularization' of theological concepts will have to be understood, in the last analysis, as an adaptation of traditional theology to the intellectual climate produced by modern philosophy or science both natural and political. Leo Strauss[2]

The modern world began with wars of religion. During the Thirty Years War, Europe was devastated by armed struggle between Catholics and Protestants, with around a third of the population in parts of Germany perishing as a result. Much of early modern thought is a response to these conflicts. The need to restrain the violence of faith is central in the writings of Thomas Hobbes and Benedict Spinoza – early Enlightenment thinkers who speak to us about the nature of present conflicts more clearly than most of those who came later.

The central theme of Hobbes's thought is the condition of humanity in a state of nature, where government is lacking. As he put it in the famous thirteenth chapter of *Leviathan*, a state of nature lacks 'commodious living' – there are 'no arts; no letters; no society; and which is worst of all, continual fear, and danger of violent death'. Without the power of government, humans are compelled to engage in a 'war of all against all' in which each is the enemy of every other. Hobbes's insight into the realities of life when government breaks down is unflinching. It is his account of how humanity might escape this condition that is far-fetched. Hobbes was much concerned with taming fanaticism, which he recognized as the deadly enemy of civilization, but he hated fanatical belief too much to understand it and so failed to uncover its roots in the need for meaning. While he recognized the power of the passions, he believed reason could enable humanity to escape the state of nature – not for ever, but at least for a time. Believing he had fathomed the causes of human conflict,

Hobbes imagined that if his writings fell into the hands of an intelligent ruler a new form of government could be established that was concerned only to maintain peace. By obeying such a government, humanity could be delivered from its natural condition. Though he is seen as an ultra-realist, Hobbes actually looked to politics for a kind of salvation.

Hobbes's understanding of the dangers of anarchy resonates powerfully today. Liberal thinkers still see the unchecked power of the state as the chief danger to human freedom. Hobbes knew better: freedom's worst enemy is anarchy, which is at its most destructive when it is a battleground of rival faiths. The sectarian death squads roaming Baghdad show that fundamentalism is itself a type of anarchy in which each prophet claims divine authority to rule. In well-governed societies, the power of faith is curbed. The state and the churches temper the claims of revelation and enforce peace. Where this kind is impossible, tyranny is better than being ruled by warring prophets. Hobbes is a more reliable guide to the present than the liberal thinkers who followed. Yet his view of human beings was too simple, and overly rationalistic. Assuming that humans dread violent death more than anything, he left out the most intractable sources of conflict. It is not always because human beings act irrationally that they fail to achieve peace. Sometimes it is because they do not want peace. They may want the victory of the One True Faith – whether a traditional religion or a secular successor such as communism, democracy or universal human rights. Or – like the young people who joined far-Left terrorist groups in the 1970s, another generation of which is now joining Islamist networks – they may find in war a purpose that is lacking in peace. Nothing is more human than the readiness to kill and die in order to secure a meaning in life.

A deeper understanding of the disorders of faith can be found in the thought of Benedict Spinoza.[3] Like Hobbes, Spinoza knew that religion can be destructive, and he was clear that freedom to practise it must yield to the needs of peace; but he understood, better than Hobbes, the role of religion in human life. Religions are not literally true, as their followers believe. They are myths that preserve in symbolic or metaphorical form truths that might otherwise be lost, and the mass of humankind will never be able to do without them. The term myth comes from the Greek word *mythos*, which means story, and the dominant western myths have been narratives in which history becomes a story of sin and redemption. Spinoza is rare among western thinkers in rejecting any such view of salvation as an historical event. Despite the fact that he seems to have been an atheist for most of his life, Hobbes never questioned the Christian belief that humans can transcend their natural condition. Indeed, this belief underpins his faith in government. In contrast, though he was attracted to a mystical version of rationalism, Spinoza understood that humans are an integral part of the natural world, and so he never turned to the state for salvation. Anarchy could be overcome as evolving patterns of social cooperation crystallized into civil institutions; but the order in society that resulted would regularly break down, and when this happened no social contract could restore order. Spinoza had a vision of salvation – a neo-Stoic ideal in which a few individuals could understand and accept their place in the scheme of things – but it had nothing to do with politics. While it is much preferable to anarchy, government cannot abolish the evils of the human condition. At any time the state is only one of the forces that shape human behaviour, and its power is never absolute. At present, fundamentalist religion and organized crime, ethnic-national allegiances and market forces all have the ability to elude the control of government, sometimes to overthrow or capture it. States are at the mercy of events as much as any other human institution, and over the longer course of history all of them fail. As Spinoza recognized, there is no reason to think the cycle of order and anarchy will ever end.[4]

Secular thinkers find this view of human affairs dispiriting, and most have retreated to some version of the Christian view in which history is a narrative of redemption. The most common of these narratives are theories of progress, in which the growth of knowledge enables humanity to advance and improve its condition. Actually, humanity cannot advance or retreat, for humanity cannot act: there is no collective entity with intentions or purposes, only ephemeral struggling animals each with its own passions and illusions. The growth of scientific knowledge cannot alter this fact. Believers in progress – whether social democrats or neo-conservatives, Marxists, anarchists or technocratic Positivists – think of ethics and politics as being like science, with each step forward enabling further advances in future. Improvement in society is cumulative, they believe, so that the elimination of one evil can be followed by the removal of others in an open-ended process. But human affairs show no sign of being additive in this way: what is gained can always be lost, sometimes – as with the return of torture as an accepted technique in war and government – in the blink of an eye. Human knowledge tends to increase, but humans do not become any more civilized as a result. They remain prone to every kind of barbarism, and while the growth of knowledge allows them to improve their material conditions, it also increases the savagery of their conflicts.

If the political religions of the last century renewed Christian beliefs, secular humanism today is no different. Darwinist thinkers such as Richard Dawkins and Daniel Dennett are militant opponents of Christianity.[5] Yet their atheism and humanism are versions of Christian concepts. As a defender of Darwinism, Dawkins is committed to the view that humans are like other animal species in being 'gene machines' ruled by the laws of natural selection. He asserts nevertheless that humans, uniquely, can defy these natural laws: 'We, alone on earth, can rebel against the tyranny of the selfish replicators.' In affirming human uniqueness in this way, Dawkins relies on a Christian world-view. The same is true of Dennett, who has spent much of his career labouring to show how scientific materialism can be reconciled with a form of free will – a project that would scarcely occur to someone from a culture not moulded by Christianity.

Pre-Christian philosophers such as the Epicureans speculated about free will. But it only became a central issue in western philosophy with the rise of Christianity and has never been prominent in non-western philosophies that do not separate humans so radically from other animals. When secular thinkers ponder free will and consciousness they nearly always confine themselves to humans, but why assume these attributes are uniquely human? In taking for granted a categorical difference between humans and other animals these rationalists show their view of the world has been formed by faith. The comedy of militant unbelief is in the fact that the humanist creed it embodies is a by-product of Christianity.

Showing the origins of humanist beliefs in Christianity does not prove they are mistaken, but it is not only humanist beliefs that are derived from Christianity. It is the whole framework of thought, and when the claim that humans are radically different from other animals is wrenched from its theological roots it is not just indefensible but virtually incomprehensible. Modern humanists think they are natural-ists, who view all forms of life – including the human animal – as part of the material universe; but a genuinely naturalistic philosophy would not start by assuming humans have attributes other animals do not. Its point of departure would be that the evolutionary laws that govern other animals also govern humans. What ground – other than revealed religion – could there be for believing anything else?

Contemporary atheism is a Christian heresy that differs from earlier heresies chiefly in its intellectual crudity.[6] This is nowhere clearer than in its view of religion itself. Marx held to a reductive view in which religion was a by-product of oppression; but he was clear it expressed the deepest human aspirations – it was not only the opiate of the masses but also 'the heart of a heartless world'. The French Positivists wanted to replace Christianity by a ridiculous Religion of Humanity; but they understood that religion answered to universal human needs. Only a very credulous philosopher could believe that showing religion is an illusion will make it disappear. That assumes the human mind is an organ attuned to truth – a quasi-Platonic conception that is closer to religion than science and inconsistent with Darwinism. Yet such seems to be the view of contemporary unbelievers.

The chief significance of evangelical atheism is in demonstrating the unreality of secularization. Talk of secularism is meaningful when it refers to the weakness of traditional religious belief or the lack of power of churches and other religious bodies. That is what is meant when we say Britain is a more secular country than the United States, and in this sense secularism is an achievable condition. But if it means a type of society in which religion is absent, secularism is a kind of contradiction, for it is defined by what it excludes. Post-Christian secular societies are formed by the beliefs they reject, whereas a society that had truly left Christianity behind would lack the concepts that shaped secular thought.

Like other ideas, secularity has a history. Pre-Christian Europe lacked the distinction between the secular and the sacred in much the same way that other polytheist cultures do. The world itself was sacred, and there could be no question of confining religion to a private sphere – the very idea of religion as a set of practices distinct from the rest of life was lacking. A domain separate from the sacred was recognized only when Augustine distinguished between the City of Man and the City of God. In this sense secular thinking is a legacy of Christianity and has no meaning except in a context of monotheism. In East Asia, polytheism has lived side by side with mystical philosophies in much the same way that the two coexisted in pre-Christian Europe, and the clash between science and religion that has polarized western societies has not taken place. It is no accident that Darwinism has not triggered culture-war in China or Japan.

As used by many of its contemporary advocates secularism is not so much a view of the world as a political doctrine. In this sense a secular state is one that banishes religion from public life while leaving people free to believe what they like. Secularism of this kind is consistent with religious belief, but it is mainly defended nowadays by rationalists who lament the renewed strength of religion in politics. They seem to have forgotten the political religions of the twentieth century and cannot have reflected on the fact that in the United States, a model secular regime, religion and politics are intertwined more closely than in any other advanced country. The unreality of this secularist stance does not come only from an ignorance of history. Those who demand that religion be exorcized from politics think this can be achieved by excluding traditional faiths from public institutions; but secular creeds are formed from religious concepts, and suppressing religion does not mean it ceases to control thinking and behaviour. Like repressed sexual desire, faith returns, often in grotesque forms, to govern the lives of those who deny it.

It would be comforting to think that the perversion of politics by repressed religion occurs only in totalitarian regimes. Yet democracies have displayed very similar tendencies. Even more than despotic regimes, liberal states have tended to see the violence they have inflicted as morally admirable. Tzvetan Todorov, the French historian who grew up in Stalinist Bulgaria and has written illuminatingly on the Nazi and Soviet concentration camps, has noted this tendency in the context of the bombing of Hiroshima and Nagasaki:

Atomic bombs killed fewer people than the famine in the Ukraine, fewer than the Nazis slaughtered in the Ukraine and Poland. But what the bombs and the slaughters have in common is that their perpetrators all thought they were but a means to achieve a good. However, the bombs have another feature: they are a source of pride to those who made and dropped them . . . whereas totalitarian crimes, even if they were considered by their perpetrators to be useful and even praiseworthy political acts, were kept secret . . . Both the Soviet and the Nazi leadership knew that the world would damn them if it knew exactly what they had done. They were not wrong, because as soon as their crimes were revealed they were treated as the emblems of absolute evil. Things are quite different in the case of the atomic bombs, and for that very reason, even if the crime is less grave, the moral mistake of the people who killed in the name of democracy is greater.[7]

The loss of life inflicted in Hiroshima and Nagasaki was not the largest in the Second World War – more civilians were killed in the fire bombing of Tokyo than in either of the cities on which atomic bombs were dropped, for example – but it illustrates Todorov's point. Liberal democracies are not only willing to commit acts that when perpetrated by despotic regimes are condemned as signs of barbarism – they are ready to praise these acts as heroic. It may be that such attacks on civilian populations can be justified if they shortened the war and contributed to the destruction of abhorrent regimes. Historians differ on their effects; the issue remains open. But if an attack of this kind can be defended it is only as a hideous necessity, not a triumphant display of higher virtue.

Liberalism is often described as a sceptical creed. The description hardly does justice to the missionary zeal with which it has been promoted. Liberalism is a lineal descendant from Christianity and shares the militancy of its parent faith. The ferocity with which liberal societies have treated their enemies cannot be accounted for in terms of self-defence alone. Liberal societies are worth defending, for they embody a type of civilized life in which rival beliefs can coexist in peace. When they become missionary regimes this achievement is put at risk. In waging war to promote their values actually existing liberal societies are corrupted. This is what happened when torture, whose prohibition was the result of an Enlightenment campaign that began in the eighteenth century, was used at the start of the twenty-first as a weapon in an Enlightenment crusade for universal democracy. Preserving the hard-won restraints of civilization is less exciting than throwing them away in order to realize impossible dreams. Barbarism has a certain charm, particularly when it comes clothed in virtue.

Living in an Intractable World: The Lost Tradition of Realism

> *The business of so conducting ourselves to avoid the worst dangers of this environment will consist of the constant application of palliatives. It will not be a matter of taking a single dramatic step of sweeping difficulties aside, but of the constant surmounting of new crises and facing of fresh difficulties.*
> Hedley Bull[8]

During the past twenty years western governments, led by America, have tried to export a version of liberal values to the world. These policies have been distinguished by the nebulous grandeur of their goals, but the overall aim was a mutation in the nature of war and power, which would come about as a result of the universal adoption of democracy. The attempt to remake the international system has had effects similar to those of previous Utopias. The disaster that continues to unfold in Iraq is the result of an entire way of thinking, and it is this that must be abandoned.

New thought is needed, but it must renew an old tradition. The pursuit of Utopia must be replaced by an attempt to cope with reality. We cannot return to the writings of the realist thinkers of the past with the hope that they will resolve all our dilemmas.[9] The root of realist thinking is Machiavelli's insight that governments exist, and must achieve all of their goals in a world of ceaseless conflict that is never far from a state of war. Despite the distance between Renaissance Italy and the present, this continues to be true; but the implications of Machiavelli's insight change according to circumstances, and even in their time the realist theories of recent generations were seriously flawed. Yet it is from realism more than from any other school that we can learn how to think about current conflicts.

Realism is the only way of thinking about issues of tyranny and freedom, war and peace that can truly claim not to be based on faith and, despite its reputation for amorality, the only one that is ethically serious. This is, no doubt, why it is viewed with suspicion. Realism requires a discipline of thought that may be too austere for a culture that prizes psychological comfort above anything else, and it is a reasonable question whether western liberal societies are capable of the moral effort that is involved in setting aside hopes of world-transformation. Cultures that have not been shaped by Christianity and its secular surrogates have always harboured a tradition of realist thought, which is likely to be as strong in future as it has been in the past. In China, Sun Tzu's *Art of War* is a bible of realist strategy, and Taoist and Legalist philosophies contain powerful currents of realist thinking, while in India, Kautilya's writings on war and diplomacy have a similar place. Machiavelli's writings were a scandal because they subverted the claims of Christian morality. They have not had the same explosive force in non-Christian cultures, where realist thinking comes more easily. In post-Christian liberal democracies it has been political and intellectual elites, more than the majority of voters, that have favoured war as an instrument for improving the world; but public opinion still finds realist thinking distasteful. Can the task of staving off perennial evils satisfy a generation weaned on unrealizable dreams? Perhaps it prefers the romance of a meaningless quest to coping with difficulties that can never be finally overcome. But this has not always been so, and only a couple of generations ago realist thinking enabled western governments to prevail in conflicts far more dangerous than any they have yet had to face in the present century.

It was realism rather than secular faith that allowed liberal democracies to defeat Nazism and contain communism. The long secret telegram that George F. Kennan sent to Washington in 1946, which shaped the policy that averted nuclear disaster during the Cold War while preventing the expansion of Soviet power, did not seek to work up a frenzy of rectitude. It urged that the Soviet system be studied 'with the same courage, detachment, objectivity and the same determination not to be emotionally provoked or unseated by it' as a doctor studies an unruly and unreasonable patient. It did not take for granted that the Soviet elites were ruled by ideology, or always reasonable. Instead it warned against being infected by their irrationality: 'The greatest danger that can befall us . . . is that we shall allow ourselves to become like those with whom we are coping.'[10] Though the dangers are different, Kennan's style of thinking is urgently needed today. Dealing with terrorism and proliferation is not a job for missionaries or crusaders. The heady certainty of faith, which sees every crisis as a heaven-sent opportunity to save humanity, is ill-suited to dealing with dangers that can never be defused. In times of danger, stoical determination and intellectual detachment are more useful qualities, and at its best realism embodied them.

Realist thinking is not error-proof. There are many examples of realist policies failing in their goals, or causing immense suffering while achieving nothing – the bombing of Cambodia during the period when Henry Kissinger was American secretary of state is an obvious example of the latter. A realist approach to international affairs does not ensure success, and there is a kind of crackpot *realpolitik* that is extremely unrealistic. Albert Wohlstetter's picture of the Soviet Union was far removed from actual conditions, as was his disciple Paul Wolfowitz's view of Iraq. Wohlstetter's strategic calculus may seem a world away from Wolfowitz's delusional programme to install liberal democracy in Iraq. Yet the idea that decisions about war and peace can be reduced to a game-theoretic calculus is a symbiosis of rationalism and magic – in other words, a superstition.

Realists do not accept that international relations, any more than human life in general, consist of soluble problems. There are situations in which whatever is done contains wrong – for example, the situation that has been created by American intervention in Iraq. Certainly we can avoid multiplying these situations: we may have to deal out mass death to defeat Hitler but we need not wade in blood to democratize the world. Realism is an Occam's Razor that works to minimize radical choices among evils. It cannot enable us to escape these choices, for they go with being human.

In the past, realist thinkers wanted to replace talk of morality in politics with the analysis of power and interest, which were supposed to be defined in rigorously factual terms. States were supposed to be entities devoted to maximizing their power, and their relations with one another were theorized in terms borrowed from natural science. Developing a discipline of this kind is a type of scientism – the mistaken application of scientific method to areas of experience where universal laws do not exist – and helped discredit realist thinking. There is a good deal of regularity in the behaviour of states that can be identified by a study of history, but these regularities cannot be formulated as universal laws. Again, all the ideas we use to understand politics – such as legitimacy, tyranny and the concept of violence – contain values as an essential part of their meaning. Thinking about international relations cannot avoid being a moral enterprise.

Realists take for granted a number of facts about how the world works. However much empty chatter there may be about the end of the Westphalian era, sovereign states remain the central actors in world affairs. Transnational institutions such as the UN are devices for moderating the rivalries of sovereign powers, not embryonic forms of global governance. In this sense the world of states is a realm of anarchy and will remain so. Of course, states accept many restraints, including those imposed by international treaties, such as the Geneva Convention, that lay down norms of civilized behaviour, and to some extent mutually beneficial trade and civil traditions can replace destructive conflict with competition and cooperation. But such conventions and practices are fragile, and over the long run war is as common as peace.

Realists should reject teleological views of history. The belief that humanity is moving towards a condition in which there will be no more conflict over the nature of government is not only delusive but also dangerous. Basing policies on an assumption that a mysterious process of evolution is taking mankind to a promised land leads to a state of mind that is unprepared for intractable conflict. At its most extreme, historical teleology is embodied in programmes that aim to accelerate this process of evolution, such as the neo-conservative 'global democratic revolution' that for a time deformed American foreign policy. But 'passive teleology' that rejects any attempt to force the pace of evolution is also an unsafe basis for policy. There is nothing in the process of modernization that points to a time when all or most states will be variants of a single type. Modern states come in many varieties – good and bad, intolerable and indifferent. Hitler's Germany was no less modern than social-democratic Sweden, and the popular theocracy that rules Iran is as much a modern system of government as that of contemporary Switzerland. As the world becomes more modern it does not become more uniform. Modern states use the power of knowledge to serve their different ends and are as prone to conflict as any others.

If realists reject any belief in ultimate convergence in history, one reason is that they resist the lure of harmony in ethics. Moral conflicts, sometimes of a kind that cannot be fully resolved, are permanent features in the relations of states. Many moral philosophies take for granted that the requirements of morality, or at least of some part of it, such as the demands of justice, must all be compatible. At least in principle, it is assumed no dictate of morality can collide with any other. This belief underlies all varieties of utopianism, and a version of it underpins the theories of human rights that have been used to justify pre-emptive war. As Isaiah Berlin observed, this belief in moral harmony does not rest on experience; when it is accepted by Enlightenment thinkers it expresses an idea of perfection that is owed to religion. Among Enlightenment thinkers, Berlin writes,

we find the same common assumption: that the answers to all the great questions must of necessity agree with one another; for they must correspond with reality, and reality is a harmonious whole. If this were not so, there is chaos at the heart of things: which is unthinkable. Liberty, equality, property, knowledge, security, practical wisdom, purity of character, sincerity, kindness, rational self-love, all these ideals . . . cannot (if they are truly desirable) conflict with one another; if they appear to do so it must be due to some misunderstanding of their properties. No truly good thing can ever be finally incompatible with any other; indeed they virtually entail one another: men cannot be wise unless they are free, or free unless they are just, happy and so forth.

Here we conspicuously abandon the voice of experience – which records very obvious conflicts of ultimate ideals – and encounter a doctrine that stems from older theological roots – from the belief that unless all the positive virtues are harmonious with one another, or at least not incompatible, the notion of the Perfect Entity – whether it be called nature or God or Ultimate Reality – is not conceivable.[11]

Liberalism has been as utopian as other philosophies in positing a kind of ultimate harmony as an achievable goal. The vision of a world where human rights are universally respected belongs in the same category as Fourier's idea of 'anti-lions' and 'anti-whales' that exist only to serve humans. It is a daydream, which obscures the conflicts among rights and the many sources of human violence.

Realists accept that states are bound to rank what they take to be their vital interests over more universal considerations. They cannot avoid trying to sustain themselves as legitimate institutions. This involves giving priority to their citizens – protecting them from insecurity and conquest, securing a decent subsistence for them and embodying their values and identities. Because they must first serve the interests of those they rule, states cannot adopt an impartial perspective of the kind often thought to be essential to morality; but that does not mean their policies cannot be judged morally. In its ethical aspect a realist foreign policy might be described as one that aims to hold the worst evils at bay. Tyranny and anarchy, war and civil war are threats to what Hobbes called commodious living. No power will ever exist that can rid the world of these evils; but states can refrain from adding to their sum for the sake of inchoate ideals that will never be achieved. A state that acts to suppress torture in its own institutions is more civilized than one that practises it in the pursuit of universal human rights, and more likely to succeed in its goals.

A commitment to civilized restraints on the use of force is a necessary part of realism. Contrary to the thinking of post-modernists who believe all human values are cultural constructions and reject the idea of human nature, there are some values that reflect universal human needs. But these needs are many and discordant, and universal values can be embodied in different ways. If many types of government have been accepted as legitimate, it is not because humanity has yet to accept the local pieties of Atlantic democracy. It is because there is no one right way of settling conflicts among universal values. The prevention of great evils may involve rationally unresolvable dilemmas, as when reasonable people differ on the aerial bombing of civilian populations in the struggle to defend civilization against Nazism. Rationalist philosophers will ask the meaning of civilization, as if in the absence of a definition it could not be defended, while liberal humanists will say that the necessary restraints are provided by human rights. But the problem is not that we do not agree on moral issues, or fail to enforce human rights – it is that there are moral dilemmas, some of which occur fairly regularly, for which there is no solution. Liberal thinkers view human rights as embodying a kind of universal moral minimum that should be secured before any other goals are pursued. A worthy notion, but it passes over the fact that the components of the minimum are often at odds with one another. Toppling a tyrant may result in anarchy, but propping up tyranny can worsen the abuse of power. Freedom of religion is good, but where it leads to sectarian strife it is self-destroying. A private realm protected from intrusion is part of civilized life, but some incursion into privacy may be unavoidable if other freedoms are to be secure. It is better to accept these conflicts and deal with them than deny them, as liberals do when they look to theories of human rights to resolve dilemmas of war and security.

The cardinal need is to change the prevailing view of human beings, which sees them as inherently good creatures unaccountably burdened with a history of violence and oppression. Here we reach the nub of realism and its chief stumbling-point for prevailing opinion: its assertion of the innate defects of human beings. Nearly all pre-modern thinkers took it as given that human nature is fixed and flawed, and in this as in some other ways they were close to the truth of the matter. No theory of politics can be credible that assumes that human impulses are naturally benign, peaceable or reasonable. As Jonathan Swift acknowledged when he placed the only Utopia he could imagine in the kingdom of horses, the pursuit of harmony envisions a form of life that humans cannot live.

Realism need not be a conservative stance. The slow development of institutions, which was favoured by Burke and other conservative thinkers, is very often impracticable. Revolution cannot always be prevented, and may not be undesirable. In any case the sudden destruction of societies and ways of life, which recurs throughout history, has today become normal. Nostalgia for the supposed organic unity of previous societies, to which conservatives are often prone, is a type of utopianism. Nor does realism have anything to do with moral fundamentalism of the kind that promotes the 'right to life', 'traditional values', and similar nonsense. It is nevertheless true that realists share with the conservative philosophies that once existed the perception that no change in human institutions can resolve the contradictions of human needs. Human beings may want freedom, but usually only when other needs have been met, and not always then. Tyrants are not only feared, they are often loved. States do not act only to protect their interests; they are also vehicles for myths, fantasies and mass psychosis. Neo-conservatives and liberal internationalists are fond of saying freedom is contagious, but tyranny can also be contagious. During much of the last century dictators were worshipped. It would be a bold prophet who forecast that this could not happen again.

While realists have accepted that the world of states will remain an arena of conflict, most have worked within schools of social science that rest on principles of rational choice. This Enlightenment tradition can help explain behaviour such as suicide bombing, but it has definite limits. Theories of rational choice assume human beings have reasonable goals – if people seem to behave irrationally it is because they are frustrated. The implication of this benignly reductive analysis is that if the causes of frustration could be removed, harmony would follow. But not all reasonable objectives are compatible, and rational choices can lead to horribly destructive conflicts. Such is often the case in asymmetric warfare. Though the insurgents usually win, occupying powers also have interests that compel them to fight. Both parties may have reason to engage in a mutually damaging conflict.

Above all, human beings have needs that cannot be satisfied by any rational means. The Aum cult that tried to obtain the ebola virus had few achievable goals. Its activities were shaped by classical chiliastic fantasies: the end of the world followed by a post-apocalyptic paradise. A portion of the terrorist violence of al-Qaeda follows a similar pattern. It is no use seeking the causes of this brand of terrorism in unresolved political conflicts. The disorder that is at work is a derangement of the need for meaning like that which energized millenarian movements and totalitarian regimes. This is a disease that may afflict marginal groups more than others, but it may also be endemic in late modern societies. As the means of mass destruction become more accessible to small groups and individuals, anomic terrorism may come to pose a larger threat than the use of terrorist techniques in asymmetric warfare.

The complex phenomenon of terrorism implies a shift in realist thinking away from an exclusive focus on states. States remain pivotal, but they are no longer the sole or always the most important arena for war. Classical warfare – sometimes called Clausewitzian war after the early nineteenth-century Prussian military strategist Carl von Clausewitz – was armed conflict between forces controlled by states. It inflicted huge casualties in the twentieth century as it expanded to include the targeting of civilian populations. Though many assume this kind of warfare lies in the past, armed conflicts between great powers could still recur. Classical warfare remains a major evil, but even when it is total it can be ended by agreement – diplomats can meet, negotiate a settlement and declare peace. No such agreement can be reached with global terrorist networks, which may be internally divided and lack negotiable goals. Armed conflict now involves highly dispersed groups and even entire societies acting beyond the control of any government. If realist thinking is to be productive it must accept that warfare has ceased to be the prerogative of states and become the privilege of Everyman.

Realist thinking cannot avoid the threats posed by environmental crisis. Peaking oil reserves and global warming are the other face of globalization – the worldwide spread of the mode of industrial production based on fossil fuels that has enabled the economic and population growth of the past two centuries. This process is not far from reaching its limits, which are not so much political as ecological. Industrial expansion has triggered a shift in global climate that is larger, faster and more irreversible than anyone imagined, while the non-renewable fuels that power industry are becoming scarcer as demand for them continues to rise.[12] These facts have implications for war and peace, some of which I have touched on in earlier chapters. Yet the military-strategic implications of ecological crisis have rarely been examined, and the subject remains taboo. When a

Pentagon group issued a report on 'An Abrupt Climate Change Scenario and Its Implications for US National Security' in October 2003, its analysis and proposals were uncongenial to the Bush administration and it was shelved.

The report considered the geo-political consequences of abrupt climate change, and identified food shortages due to decreases in net global agricultural production, decreased availability and quality of fresh water in key regions and disrupted access to energy supplies. The overall effect of these changes would be 'a significant drop in the human carrying capacity of the Earth's environment' – in other words, a reduction in the human population the planet can support. The report went on:

> As global and local carrying capacities are reduced, tensions could mount around the world, leading to two fundamental strategies: defensive and offensive. Nations with the resources to do so may build virtual fortresses around their countries, preserving resources for themselves. Less fortunate nations, especially those with ancient enmities with their neighbours, may initiate struggles for access to food, clean water, or energy. Unlikely alliances could be formed, as defence priorities shift and the goal is resources for survival rather than religion, ideology or national honour.[13]

The Pentagon report was pioneering in accepting that abrupt climate change could lead to a drop in the planet's capacity to support human life. Its account of the types of conflict that could follow is plausible, though it may have underestimated their intensity. The analysis assumed they would be rational-strategic conflicts with religion playing no part in them, but much of the planet's remaining patrimony of oil lies in Muslim lands, and conflict over resources could be intensified by antagonisms surrounding the 'war on terror'. The risk is that resource war will be mixed with wars of religion and the otherwise far-fetched theory of clashing civilizations become self-fulfilling.

Unless they can find alternatives to oil, industrial states will be locked in conflict for the foreseeable future. The process of diversifying out of oil will be a good deal harder than most environmentalists believe. If world oil production is near its peak – as seems likely – the shift to other types of energy is an urgent necessity; but there may be no easily available alternatives that will support the world's present human population. It has become conventional wisdom that the basic environmental problem is not human numbers but their per capita resource uses – in other words, the way humans live. In fact, humanity has probably already overshot the carrying capacity of the planet. Current human numbers depend on petroleum-based agriculture, which hastens global warming. Population growth is not always highest in developing countries – it is around twice as fast in the United States as in China, for example – but it is much too high overall for a worldwide switch to alternative technologies to be practicable. A mix of solar power, wind farms and organic farming cannot support six to nine billion people.

If there is a way through the bottleneck, it involves making the most of high-tech fixes. The best prospects may lie with the technologies to which Greens are most hostile, such as nuclear power and GM crops, which despite their hazards do not require further destruction of the biosphere.[14] The alternative is not a low-tech Utopia, as many Greens like to think. As James Lovelock has written, it is 'global decline into a chaotic world ruled by brutal war lords on a devastated Earth.'[15]

Many of those who grasp the scale of the crisis continue to believe it can be overcome by changes in human behaviour. Jared Diamond has presented a powerful argument that contemporary societies could self-destruct by disregarding environmental limits. He suggests that catastrophe can be averted by enhanced cooperation, and cites the Dutch system of polders – areas of land that have been reclaimed from the sea in the Netherlands – as a model that can be adopted throughout the world. Diamond writes:

Our whole world has become one polder ... When distant Somalia collapsed, in went American troops; when the former Yugoslavia and Soviet Union collapsed, out went streams of refugees over all of Europe and the rest of the world; and when changed conditions of society, settlement and lifestyle spread new diseases in Africa and Asia, those diseases moved over the globe. The whole world today is a self-contained and isolated unit.[16]

Diamond is right that the world is more interdependent than in the past, but that is no reason for thinking that it is going to become more cooperative. The Pentagon report suggests a likelier scenario. Where states remain strong and effective, they will act to secure the resources under their control. Where states are weak or collapsed, the struggle will devolve to other groups. The overall result is intensified conflict rather than global cooperation. The Kyoto Treaty illustrates the difficulty. The treaty may have been inherently flawed inasmuch as the targets it set did not apply to emerging countries, but its basic weakness was that it contained no mechanism of enforcement. States could sign up or not as they pleased, and the US and a number of others refused. There is no way round this difficulty. In an anarchical world, global environmental problems are politically insoluble.

Environmental crisis is a fate humans can temper but not overcome. Its origins are in the power to grow knowledge that distinguishes humans from other animals. The advance of knowledge has enabled humans to multiply their numbers, extend their lifespans and create wealth on a scale that has no precedent. But global warming and energy shortage are results of advancing industrialism, which is also a by-product of scientific progress. The proliferation of means of mass destruction, not only to states but also to forces states do not control, is another of its effects. Today the worry is that nuclear materials may slip into terrorist hands, but tomorrow the fear may be of biological weapons doing so. Genetic science enables humans to intervene in the creation of life, but it will surely be used to wreak mass death as well. It cannot be long before genetically selective devices are feasible that can act as tools of genocide, and when this happens there may be no means of preventing them being diffused across the world. Future threats to security may not come mainly from terrorism as conventionally understood. Instead they may come in outbreaks of disease whose origins are never known. The paradigm of future terror may be an inexplicable breakdown in the structures of everyday life.

The increase of knowledge magnifies human power while it creates insoluble dilemmas. We need to accept that the gravest human disorders cannot be remedied, only treated day by day. But can we live with this fact? Ditching the myths of historical teleology and ultimate harmony is highly desirable, but it is also extremely difficult. The western belief that salvation can be found in history has renewed itself again and again. The migration of utopianism from Left to Right testifies to its vitality. An irrational faith in the future is encrypted into contemporary life, and a shift to realism may be a utopian ideal.

THE END, AGAIN

Apocalypse is a part of the modern Absurd.

Frank Kermode[17]

The dominant western myths have been historical narratives, and it has become fashionable to view narrative as a basic human need. Humans are tellers of tales, we have come to think, who cannot be happy unless they can see the world as a story. Over the past two centuries the dominant story line has been one of human progress, but it has also included a tale of a world besieged by dark forces and destined for destruction. The two plots were interwoven – as when Marx and his followers believed that humanity advanced through a series of catastrophic revolutions and the Nazis that demonic powers were conspiring against the *Volk* and its ascension to a state of semi-divine immortal harmony. In a different idiom, liberal humanists have talked of humanity advancing, inch by inch, in a gradual process of improvement. In all these accounts history is told as a coherent narrative, and nothing is more threatening than the idea that it is a meandering flux without purpose or direction.

The belief that history has an underlying plot is central to the millenarian movements, secular and religious, that have been examined in this book. All who belong to these movements believe they are acting out a script that is already partly written. In versions of apocalyptic belief that are avowedly religious, the author of the script is God, with the Devil and assorted demons writing their own lines but finally submitting to the authority of the divine narrator. In secular apocalyptic, the author is that equally elusive figure humanity, battling the forces of ignorance and superstition. Either way, the demand for meaning is met by narratives in which each individual life is part of an all-encompassing story.

The dangers of the need for an overarching human narrative are clear. To feel oneself the target of a global conspiracy as the Nazis did may not seem a positive state of mind, but it banishes the lack of meaning, which is a worse threat. Paranoia is often a protest against insignificance, and collective delusions of persecution bolster a fragile sense of agency. The problem is that this benefit is purchased at a high price: a price measured in the lives of others who are forced to act out a role in a script they have not read, still less written. Those who are crushed or broken in order to create a higher humanity, who are killed or mutilated in acts of spectacular terror or ravaged in wars for universal freedom may have ideas about their place in the world altogether different from those they are assigned in the dramas that are being enacted. If universal narratives create meaning for those who live by them, they also destroy it in the lives of others.

The sense of having a part in such a narrative is delusive, of course. John of Leyden believed God had called him to rule over the New Jerusalem. Lenin was sure he was expediting the laws of history. Hitler was certain the corrupt world of liberal democracy was doomed. True believers in the free market interpreted the collapse of communism as a sign of an inexorable trend, and neo-conservatives greeted the few years of American supremacy that seemed to follow as a new epoch in history. All of these prophets imagined they had grasped the plot of history and were completing a preordained pattern. In fact, their rise to power was accidental, and only the non-arrival of the Millennium was preordained. Millenarian movements come about as the result of a combination of random events, and when they fall from grace it is as a result of features of human life whose permanence they deny. The history of these movements is scarcely tragic, for those who belong to them rarely perceive the fateful contingencies by which their lives are ruled. They are actors in a theatre of the absurd whose lines are given by chance.

Seeing one's life as an episode in a universal narrative is a fantasy, and while it is supported by powerful western traditions it has not always been regarded as a good thing. Many of the world's mystics have aimed to achieve a state of contemplation in which the succession of happenings from which we construct the story of our lives is absent. Plato and his disciples prized an eventless eternity over any process of change, and here they were close to Hindu and Buddhist thinkers.

In a different tradition, Taoists taught that freedom lies in freeing oneself from personal narratives by identifying with cosmic processes of death and renewal. Within Christianity, the temptation to construct a narrative from the accidents of history has been extremely strong. But in the orthodoxy that was created by Augustine the temptation has been curbed by the idea that meaning is to be found in a timeless realm, whose intimations may appear at any moment.

Freedom from narrative is not a condition of which only mystics dream. Poets and epicureans have cultivated a condition of spontaneity in which they could enjoy each moment for its own sake. Spending one's life looking to the future means inhabiting a world fashioned from memory. Yet memory has also been used as a means of freeing oneself from narrative. Marcel Proust writes of the sensation he experienced when drinking tea mixed with crumbs of *petites madeleines*, the small cakes given him by his mother, that it 'had immediately made the vicissitudes of life unimportant to me, its disasters innocuous, its brevity illusory, acting in the same way that love acts, by filling me with a precious essence: or rather this essence was not in me, it was me. I had ceased to feel I was mediocre, contingent, mortal.'[18] Here Proust turned to the past in a search for a way out of time. It was a search that could only be partly successful, since memories that carry intimations of immortality cannot be summoned at will.

The need for narrative can be a burden, and if we want to be rid of it we should seek the company of mystics, poets and pleasure-lovers rather than utopian dreamers. Though they look to the future these dreamers nearly always recall an idealized period of innocence – Marx's primitive communism, or the lost world of bourgeois virtue cherished by neo-conservatives. As the writer and psychoanalyst Adam Phillips has written, 'Clearly, apocalyptic thinking is nostalgia at its very worst.'[19] The effect of seeking refuge in an imaginary future harmony is to bind us to the conflicts of the past.

Myths are not true or false in the way scientific theories are true or false, but they can be more or less truthful in reflecting the enduring realities of human life. Most of the myths by which humans have lived have not been historical narratives of the sort that govern Christian and post-Christian cultures. The promise of liberation from time in Plato and eastern religions is also a myth, but one that dispels the hope of a final triumph of good of the kind that has had such a baleful impact on the modern West.

Secular myths reproduce the narrative form of Christian apocalyptic, and if there is a way of tempering the violence of faith it must begin by questioning these myths. In secular thought science has come to be viewed as a vehicle of revelation, a repository of truth rather than a system of symbols that serves the human need to understand and control. Post-modern philosophies that view science as just one belief-system among many are too silly to be worth refuting at length – the utility of scientific knowledge is a brute fact that is shown in the increase of human power. Science is an instrument for forming reliable beliefs about the world. Religions are also human instruments, but they have other goals. The ideal goal of scientific inquiry may be an end-point at which human beliefs mirror the world in an all-embracing theory, and in science this ideal may be useful (even if it is also illusive). But why should religions aim for consensus? While true beliefs may be useful in our everyday dealings, doubts are more to the point in the life of the spirit. Religions are not claims to knowledge but ways of living with what cannot be known.

The collision between science and religion comes from the mistake that both have to do with belief. It is only in some strands of Christianity and Islam that belief has been placed at the heart of religion. In other traditions, religion has to do with the acceptance of mystery rather than catechisms or creeds. Science and religion serve different needs, which though they pull in different directions are equally human. In the contemporary world science has authority because of the power it confers. That is why fundamentalists ape its claims to literal truth – as in the cartoon science of creationism. Yet creationism is hardly more ridiculous than Social Darwinism, dialectical materialism or the theory that as societies become more modern they become more free or peaceful. These secular creeds are more unreasonable than any traditional faith, if only because they make a more elaborate show of being rational.

The most necessary task of the present time is to accept the irreducible reality of religion. In the Enlightenment philosophies that shaped the last two centuries, religion was a secondary or derivative aspect of human life that will disappear, or cease to be important, when its causes are removed. Once poverty is eradicated and education universal, social inequality has been overcome and political repression is a thing of the past, religion will have no more importance than a personal hobby. Underlying this article of Enlightenment faith is a denial of the fact that the need for religion is generically human. It is true that religions are hugely diverse and serve many social functions – most obviously, as welfare institutions. At times they have also served the needs of power. But beyond these socio-political purposes, religions express human needs that no change in society can remove – for example the need to accept what cannot be remedied and find meaning in the chances of life. Human beings will no more cease to be religious than they will stop being sexual, playful or violent.

If religion is a primary human need it should not be suppressed or relegated to a netherworld of private life. It ought to be fully integrated into the public realm, but that does not mean establishing any one religion as public doctrine. Late modern societies harbour a diversity of world-views. There is little agreement on the worth of human life, the uses of sexuality, the claims of non-human animals or the value of the natural environment. Rather than tending towards a secular monoculture, the late modern period is unalterably hybrid and plural. There is no prospect of a morally homogeneous society, still less a homogenized world. In the future, as in the past, there will be authoritarian states and liberal republics, theocratic democracies and secular tyrannies, empires, city-states and many mixed regimes. No one type of government or economy will be accepted everywhere, nor will any single version of civilization be embraced by all of humanity.

It is time the diversity of religions was accepted and the attempt to build a secular monolith abandoned. Accepting that we have moved into a post-secular era does not mean religions can be freed of the restraints that are necessary for civilized coexistence. A central task of government is to work out and enforce a framework whereby they can live together. A framework of this kind cannot be the same for every society, or fixed for ever. It embodies a type of toleration whose goal is not truth but peace. When the goal of tolerance is truth it is a strategy that aims for harmony. It would be better to accept that harmony will never be reached. Better yet, give up the demand for harmony and welcome the varieties of human experience. The *modus vivendi* between religions that has flourished intermittently in the past might then be renewed.[20]

The chief intellectual obstacle to coexistence among religions is a lack not of mutual understanding, but of self-knowledge. Matthew Arnold's once-famous *Dover Beach* (1867) speaks of the 'melancholy, long, withdrawing roar' of Christianity – as if that meant the end of religion. The Victorian poet underestimated the urgency of the demand for myth. The Utopias of the past two centuries were deformed versions of the myths they denied, and if the last of them has perished in the deserts of Iraq it need not be mourned. The hope of Utopia spilt blood on a scale that traditional creeds cannot match, and the world is well rid of it.

The danger that goes with the death of secular hope is the rebirth of something like the faith-based wars of an older past. A renewal of apocalyptic belief is underway, which is unlikely to be confined to familiar sorts of fundamentalism. Along with evangelical revivals, there is likely to be a profusion of designer religions, mixing science and science fiction, racketeering and psychobabble, which will spread like internet viruses. Most will be harmless, but doomsday cults like those that led to the mass suicide in Jonestown and the attacks on the Tokyo subway may proliferate as ecological crisis deepens.

If the scientific consensus is accurate, the Earth may soon be different from the way it has been for millions of years, certainly since the appearance of humans. In one sense this is a genuinely apocalyptic prospect: while humans are unlikely to become extinct, the world in which they evolved is vanishing. In another sense the prospect is not apocalyptic at all. In wrecking the planetary environment humans are only doing what they have done innumerable times before on a local level. The global heating that is underway is one of several fevers the Earth has suffered, and survived, during its history. Though humans have triggered this episode, they lack the power to stop it. It may mean disaster for them and other species, but in planetary terms it is normal. This is likely to be too much reality for most people to bear, and as climate change runs its course we can expect a rash of cults in which it is interpreted as a human narrative of catastrophe and redemption. Apocalypse is, after all, an anthropocentric myth.

Happily, humanity has other myths, which can help it see more clearly. In the Genesis story humans were banished from paradise after eating from the Tree of Knowledge and had to survive by their labours ever after. There is no promise here of any return to a state of primordial innocence. Once the fruit has been eaten there is no going back. The same truth is preserved in the Greek story of Prometheus, and in many other traditions. These ancient legends are better guides to the present than modern myths of progress and Utopia.

The myth of the End has caused untold suffering and is now as dangerous as it has ever been. In becoming a site for projects of world-transformation political life became a battleground. The secular religions of the last two centuries, which imagined that the cycle of anarchy and tyranny could be ended, succeeded only in making it more violent. At its best, politics is not a vehicle for universal projects but the art of responding to the flux of circumstances. This requires no grand vision of human advance, only the courage to cope with recurring evils. The opaque state of war into which we have stumbled is one such evil.

The modern age has been a time of superstition no less than the medieval era, in some ways more so. Transcendental religions have many flaws and in the case of Christianity gave birth to savage violence, but at its best religion has been an attempt to deal with mystery rather than the hope that mystery will be unveiled. In the clash of fundamentalisms this civilizing perception has been lost. Wars as ferocious as those of early modern times are being fought against a background of increased knowledge and power. Interacting with the struggle for natural resources, the violence of faith looks set to shape the coming century.

Notes

EPIGRAPH

1. Joseph de Maistre, *St Petersburg Dialogues, or Conversations on the Temporal Government of Providence*, translated by Richard A. Lebrun, Montreal and Kingston, London and Buffalo, McGill-Queen's University Press, 1993, p. 145.

I THE DEATH OF UTOPIA

1. E. M. Cioran, *History and Utopia*, London, Quartet Books, 1996, p. 81.
2. Norman Cohn, *The Pursuit of the Millennium: Revolutionary Millenarians and Mystical Anarchists of the Middle Ages*, London, Secker and Warburg, 1957; completely revised edition, London, Paladin, 1970. Cohn's interpretation of medieval millenarianism has been criticized by David Nirenberg, *Communities of Violence: Persecution of Minorities in the Middle Ages*, Princeton NJ, Princeton University Press, 1996, pp. 3–4.
3. R. H. Crossman (ed.), *The God that Failed*, New York and Chichester, Sussex, Columbia University Press, 2001; first published by Hamish Hamilton, London, 1950. The book contained essays by Arthur Koestler, Ignazio Silone, Richard Wright, André Gide, Louis Fischer and Stephen Spender.
4. See the brilliant study by Jonathan Spence, *God's Chinese Son: The Taiping Heavenly Kingdom of Hong Xiuquan*, London, HarperCollins, 1996, p. xix.
5. ibid., p. xxi.
6. See Michael Barkun, *Disaster and Millennium*, New Haven, Yale University Press, 1974, for a study of millenarian movements as responses to a breakdown in normal patterns of perception.
7. The literature on Christian origins is vast and highly controversial. However, a profoundly learned and authoritative picture of Jesus as a

Jewish charismatic teacher can be found in Geza Vermes, *Jesus the Jew: A Historian's Reading of the Gospels*, London, William Collins, 1973, republished by the Fortress Press, Philadelphia, 1981. For an examination of Jesus' birth, see Vermes, *The Nativity: History and Legend*, London, Penguin, 2006. A. N. Wilson presents a view of Jesus similar to that of Vermes in his excellent book, *Jesus*, London, Pimlico, 2003. The central role of eschatological beliefs in the teaching of Jesus is shown in Norman Cohn, *Cosmos, Chaos and World to Come: The Ancient Roots of Apocalyptic Faith*, 2nd edn, New Haven and London, Yale University Press, 1995, Chapter 11.

8. Albert Schweitzer, *The Quest for the Historical Jesus*, New York, Dover, 2006, p. 369. This passage from Schweitzer is cited by Philip Rieff in his brilliant posthumously published *Charisma: The Gift of Grace, and How it Has Been Taken Away from Us*, New York, Pantheon Books, 2007, p. 69.

9. For the possibility that Zoroaster may have believed the outcome of the struggle between light and dark to be uncertain, see R. C. Zaehner, *The Teachings of the Magi*, Oxford, Oxford University Press, 1976.

10. Hans Jonas, *The Gnostic Religion*, 2nd edn, Boston, Beacon Press, 1963, Chapter 13, pp. 320–40. For other authoritative views of Gnosticism, see Kurt Rudolph, *Gnosis: The Nature and History of Gnosticism*, San Francisco: HarperCollins, 1987; and Elaine Pagels, *The Gnostic Gospels*, New York, Random House, 1989.

11. For an overview of the heresy of the Free Spirit, see Cohn, *The Pursuit of the Millennium*, especially Chapters 8 and 9. Cohn's account of the Free Spirit has been criticized in Robert E. Lerner, *The Heresy of the Free Spirit in the Later Middle Ages*, Notre Dame, University of Notre Dame Press, 1991.

12. Cohn, *The Pursuit of the Millennium*, p. 13.

13. F. Dostoyevsky, 'The Dream of a Ridiculous Man', in *A Gentle Creature and Other Stories*, trans. Alan Myers, Oxford, Oxford University Press World's Classics, 1995, p. 125.

14. I. Berlin, 'The Apotheosis of the Romantic Will', in *The Crooked Timber of Humanity: Chapters in the History of Ideas*, London, John Murray, 1990, pp. 211–12.

15. David Hume, 'The Idea of a Perfect Commonwealth', in Henry D. Aitken (ed.), *Hume's Moral and Political Philosophy*, London and New York, Macmillan, 1948, p. 374.

16. See Gustavo Goritti, *The Shining Path: A History of the Millenarian War in Peru*, Chapel Hill NC, University of North Carolina Press, 1999.

17. Ernest Lee Tuveson, *Redeemer Nation: The Idea of America's Millennial Role*, Chicago and London, University of Chicago Press, 1968, pp. 6–7.
18. Christopher Hill, *The World Turned Upside Down*, London, Temple Smith, 1972, p. 77.
19. Cohn, *The Pursuit of the Millennium*, p. 150.
20. David S. Katz and Richard H. Popkin, *Messianic Revolution: Radical Religious Politics to the End of the Second Millennium*, London, Allen Lane, 1999, p. 71.
21. For a profound analysis of the Russian Revolution as the continuation of a western tradition of religious revolt that included the English Civil War, see Martin Malia, *History's Locomotives: Revolution and the Making of the Modern World*, ed. Terence Emmons, New Jersey, Yale University Press, 2006, especially Chapters 6 and 11.
22. E. J. Hobsbawm, *Primitive Rebels: Studies in Archaic Forms of Social Movement in the 19th and 20th Centuries*, Manchester, Manchester University Press, 1959.
23. E. P. Thompson, *The Making of the English Working Class*, rev. edn, London, Penguin, 1968, p. 52.
24. ibid., pp. 419, 423–4.
25. Carl L. Becker, *The Heavenly City of the Eighteenth-Century Philosophers*, New Haven and London, Yale University Press, 1932, p. 123.
26. For a systematic exploration of millenarianism and utopianism, see Ernest Lee Tuveson, *Millennium and Utopia*, New York, Harper and Row, 1964.
27. S. N. Eisenstadt, in his *Fundamentalism, Sectarianism and Revolution: The Jacobin Dimension of Modernity*, Cambridge, Cambridge University Press, 2000, has presented an illuminating interpretation of modern politics in which Jacobinism is central.
28. Michael Burleigh, *Earthly Powers: Religion and Politics in Europe from the French Revolution to the Great War*, HarperCollins, London, 2005, p. 101.
29. See Paul Wood, 'Hunting "Satan" in Falluja hell', BBC News, 23 November 2004.
30. Claes G. Ryn explores the affinities of neo-conservatism with Jacobinism, in *America the Virtuous: The Crisis of Democracy and the Quest for Empire*, Somerset NJ, Transaction Publishers, 2003.
31. George W. Bush, Presidential remarks, National Cathedral, 14 September 2002.

2 ENLIGHTENMENT AND TERROR IN THE TWENTIETH CENTURY

1. Edmund Stillman and William Pfaff, *The Politics of Hysteria: The Sources of Twentieth-Century Conflict*, London, Victor Gollancz, 1964, p. 29.

2. On genocide in the Belgian Congo, see Adam Hochschild, *King Leopolds Ghost*, New York, Houghton Mifflin, 1998.

3. For Arendt's analysis of totalitarianism, see her *The Origins of Totalitarianism* (1951), new edition published by Harcourt, New York, 1973. Arendt's view of Eichmann is presented in *Eichmann in Jerusalem: A Report on the Banality of Evil*, New York, Penguin, 1963.

4. For Eichmann's role in the Holocaust, see David Cesarani, *Adolf Eichmann: His Life and Crimes*, London, Heinemann, 2004.

5. Bertrand Russell, *The Practice and Theory of Bolshevism*, London, Unwin Books, 1920, p. 55.

6. Leon Trotsky, 'Literature and Revolution', http://www.marxists.org/archive/trotsky/1924/lit_revo/index.htm

7. For a discussion of Enlightenment thinking in contemporary transhumanism, see Bryan Appleyard, *How to Live Forever or Die Trying: On the New Immortality*, London and New York, Simon and Schuster, 2007, Chapter 8.

8. For an authoritative account of the assault on science in the USSR and Soviet experiments on human subjects, see Vadim J. Birstein, *The Perversion of Knowledge: The True Story of Soviet Science*, Cambridge MA, Westview Press, 2001, pp. 127–31.

9. For a discussion of Ivanov's role, see Kirill Rossiianov, 'Beyond Species: Ilya Ivanov and his Experiments on Cross-Breeding Humans with Anthropoid Apes', *Science in Context*, Cambridge, Cambridge University Press, 2002, Issue 15, pp. 277–316.

10. I am not sure who coined the expression 'the Enlightenment project', but it came into currency with Alasdair MacIntyre's seminal study, *After Virtue: A Study in Moral Theory*, London, Duckworth, 1981, where it is defined and discussed in Chapters 4–6.

11. See *Journey of Our Time: The Journal of the Marquis de Custine*, London, Weidenfeld and Nicolson, 2001.

12. See Karl Wittfogel, *Oriental Despotism: A Comparative Study of Total Power*, New York, Random House, 1981.

13. A. Nekrich and M. Heller, *Utopia in Power: A History of the Soviet Union from 1917 to the Present*, London, Hutchison, 1986, p. 10.

14. N. Berdyaev, *The Origin of Communism*, London, Geoffrey Bles: The Centenary Press, 1937, p. 228.

15. On Lunacharsky and the Russian messianist tradition, see David G. Rowley, 'Redeemer Empire: Russian Millenarianism', *The American Historical Review*, vol. 104, no. 5, 1999.

16. Lenin's statement is quoted by Thomas P. Hughes, *American Genesis: A Study of Invention and Technological Enthusiasm 1870–1970*, Chicago, Chicago University Press, 2004, p. 251.

17. V. I. Lenin, *A Contribution to the History of the Question of Dictatorship*, www.marxists.org/archive/lenin/works/1920/oct/20.htm

18. Karl Marx and Friedrich Engels, *Address of the Central Committee to the Communist League*, www.marxists.org/marx/works/1847/communist-league/1850-ad1.htm

19. L. Trotsky, *Their Morals and Ours*, www.marxists.org/archive/trotsky/works/1938/morals/morals.htm

20. L. Trotsky, *Hue and Cry Over Kronstadt*, www.marxists.org/archive/trotsky/1938/01/kronstadt.htm

21. See George Leggett, *The Cheka: Lenin's Political Police*, Oxford, Oxford University Press, 1981, p. 178.

22. See Anne Applebaum, *Gulag: A History of the Soviet Camps*, London and New York, Allen Lane, 2003, p. 17.

23. For the relative sizes of Tsarist and Soviet security apparatuses, see John J. Dziak, *Chekisty: A History of the KGB*, New York, Ivy Books, 1988, pp. 35–6. For numbers of executions in late Tsarist and early Soviet times, see ibid., pp. 191–3.

24. On links between German South-West Africa and the Nazis, see Applebaum, *Gulag*, pp. 18–20.

25. Lesley Chamberlain, *The Philosophy Steamer: Lenin and the Exile of the Intelligentsia*, London, Atlantic Books, 2006, pp. 1–2, 4.

26. Dziak, *Chekisty*, p. 3.

27. Harold Laski and Edmund Wilson are cited in Nekrich and Heller, *Utopia in Power*, p. 257.

28. On the human cost of the Great Leap Forward, see Jung Chang and Jon Halliday, *Mao: The Unknown Story*, London, Jonathan Cape, 2005, Chapter 40, especially pp. 456–7. See also Jasper Becker, *Hungry Ghosts: China's Secret Famine*, London, John Murray, 1996, pp. 266–74.

29. For Mao's campaign against sparrows, see Chang and Halliday, *Mao*, p. 449.

30. Christopher Clark, *Iron Kingdom: The Rise and Downfall of Prussia*,

1600–1947, London, Allen Lane, 2006, presents a comprehensive history of the Prussian state.

31. Nekrich and Heller, *Utopia in Power*, p. 661.

32. eszek Koakowski, *Main Currents of Marxism*, London and New York, W. W. Norton, 2005, p. 962.

33. K. R. Popper, *The Open Society and Its Enemies*, London, Routledge and Kegan Paul, 1945, Volume 1, Chapter 9.

34. Varlam Shalamov, 'Lend-Lease', in *Kolyma Tales*, trans. John Glad, London and New York, Penguin, 1994, pp. 281–2. For a systematic account of Kolyma, see Robert Conquest, *Kolyma: The Arctic Death Camps*, Oxford and New York, Oxford University Press, 1979.

35. Robert Conquest, *The Great Terror: A Reassessment*, Oxford and New York, Oxford University Press, 1990.

36. For an account of the Soviet ecological disaster, see Murray Fesbach and Alfred Friendly Jr, *Ecocide in the USSR: Health and Nature Under Siege*, London, Aurum Press, 1992.

37. Lewis Namier, *Vanished Supremacies*, London, Hamish Hamilton, 1958.

38. See Isaiah Berlin, 'The Counter-Enlightenment', in Henry Hardy and Roger Hausheer (eds.) *The Proper Study of Mankind*, London, Chatto and Windus, 1997, pp. 243–68.

39. See Theodor Adorno and Max Horkheimer, *Dialectic of Enlightenment*, trans. John Cumming, London, Verso, 1979.

40. I discuss the political risks of Romanticism in my *Two Faces of Liberalism*, Cambridge and New York, Polity Press and the New Press, 2000, pp. 119–22.

41. For a more extended discussion of Nietzsche's critique of the Enlightenment, see my *Enlightenment's Wake: Politics and Culture at the Close of the Modern Age*, London, Routledge Classics, 2007, pp. 161–6.

42. Karl Kraus, *Half-Truths & One-and-a-Half Truths*, ed. Harry Zohn, Montreal, Engendra Press, 1976, p. 107.

43. For a discussion of Voltaire's political relativism, see my *Voltaire and Enlightenment*, London, Phoenix, 1998, pp. 36–47.

44. I have examined the Positivists in greater detail in *Al Qaeda and What it Means to be Modern*, 2nd edn, London, Faber and Faber, 2007, Chapter 3.

45. See Michael Burleigh, *Earthly Powers: Religion and Politics in Europe from the French Revolution to the Great War*, London, HarperCollins, 2005, pp. 226–7.

46. Richard Popkin, 'The Philosophical Bases of Modern Racism', in Richard A. Wilson and James E. Force (eds.), *The High Road to Pyrrhonism*, Indianapolis and Cambridge, Hackett Publishing Company, 1980, p. 85.

47. Immanuel Kant, 'Of National Characteristics, So Far as They Depend upon the Distinct Feeling of the Beautiful and Sublime', http://www.public.asu.edu/~jacquies/kant-observations.htm

48. See John Stuart Mill, *On Liberty and Other Essays*, ed. John Gray, Oxford and New York, Oxford University Press, 1998, p. 80.

49. Popkin, 'Philosophical Bases of Modern Racism', p. 89.

50. See Michael Coren, *The Invisible Man: The Life and Liberties of H. G. Wells*, London, Bloomsbury, 1993, p. 66, for this quote from Wells's *Anticipations* (1901).

51. John Toland, *Adolf Hitler*, New York, Doubleday, 1976, p. 702.

52. Richard J. Evans, *The Third Reich in Power*, London and New York, Allen Lane, 2005, pp. 506–7.

53. See Pierre Drieu La Rochelle, *Chronique Politique, 1934–1942*, Paris, Gallimard, 1943.

54. Evans, *The Third Reich in Power*, p. 534.

55. Norman Cohn, *Warrant for Genocide: The Myth of the Jewish World Conspiracy and the Protocols of the Elders of Zion*, London, Serif, 1996, p. xii. For an account of the medieval Christian demonization of witches and heretics, see Cohn's *Europe's Inner Demons: The Demonization of Christians in Medieval Christendom*, London, Pimlico, 2005.

56. Michael Burleigh, *The Third Reich: A New History*, London, Pan Books, 2000, p. 7.

57. For the comparisons of Hitler and John of Leyden by Klemperer and Reck-Malleczewen, see Burleigh, *The Third Reich*, pp. 4–5.

58. F. A. Voigt, *Unto Caesar*, London, Constable, 1938, pp. 49–50. I owe my acquaintance with Voigt's work to a conversation with Norman Cohn.

59. See James R. Rhodes, *The Hitler Movement: A Modern Millenarian Revolution*, Stanford, Hoover Institution Press, 1980, pp. 29–30.

60. Joseph Goebbels, *Michael: Ein deutsches Schicksal in Tagebuchblättern*, 6th edn, Munich, Franz Eher Nachf, 1935, pp. 96–7. The passage is cited in Rhodes, *The Hitler Movement*, p. 115.

61. Dmitri Merezhkovsky, *The Secret of the West*, trans. John Cournos, London, Jonathan Cape, 1931.

62. Aurel Kolnai, *The War Against the West*, London, Victor Gollancz, 1938.

63. Eric Voegelin, *The New Science of Politics*, Chicago and London, University of Chicago Press, 1952, pp. 113, 125–6.

64. Olivier Roy, *Globalised Islam: The Search for a New Ummah*, London, Hurst, 2004, p. 44.

65. For the role of Shariati and the influence of Heidegger on his thought, see Janet Afary and Kevin B. Anderson, *Foucault and the Iranian Revolution: Gender and the Seductions of Islamism*, Chicago, Chicago University Press, 2005.

66. On al-Qaeda and Mahdism, see Timothy R. Furnish, 'Bin Ladin: The Man who would be Mahdi', *The Middle East Review*, vol. IX, no. 2, spring 2002.

67. Kaveh L. Afrasiabi, 'Shiism as Mahdism: Reflections on a Doctrine of Hope', www.payvand.com/news/03/nov/1126.html

68. Ahmed Rashid, *Taliban: Militant Islam, Oil, and Fundamentalism in Central Asia*, New Haven, Yale University Press, 2000, pp. 176–7. Rashid's comment is cited by Robert Dreyfuss in his excellent *Devil's Game: How the United States Helped Unleash Fundamentalist Islam*, New York, Metropolitan Books, 2005, p. 326.

69. I discuss the modern character of radical Islam and its relations with globalization in *Al Qaeda and What it Means to be Modern*.

70. Ian Buruma and Avishai Margalit claim that liberal democracy is 'the idea of the West' in *Occidentalism: A Short History of Anti-Westernism*, London, Atlantic Books, 2004.

3 UTOPIA ENTERS THE MAINSTREAM

1. Reinhold Niebuhr, *Faith and History*, New York, Scribner's, 1949. Cited in Edmund Stillman and William Pfaff, *The Politics of Hysteria*, London, Victor Gollancz, 1964, p. 10.

2. Thatcher's remark is cited by Jason Burke in 'The history man: a profile of Francis Fukuyama', *Observer*, 27 June 2004.

3. For an account of how *laissez-faire* was engineered in early Victorian England, see my *False Dawn: The Delusions of Global Capitalism*, London and New York, Granta Books, 1999, pp. 7–17.

4. Hoskyns' paper was presented at a private dinner in late 1977. So far as I know it has not been published. It is archived at the Margaret Thatcher Foundation.

5. Hugo Young, *One of Us: A Biography of Margaret Thatcher*, London, Pan Books, 1993, p. 113.

6. For a brilliantly perceptive account of the rise and dominance of Thatcherism, see Simon Jenkins, *Thatcher and Sons: A Revolution in Three Acts*, London, Allen Lane, 2006.

7. Jacob Viner, *The Role of Providence in the Social Order: An Essay in*

Intellectual History, Philadelphia, American Philosophical Society, 1972, p. 81.

8. Smith's thought has been the subject of a number of valuable recent studies. See especially Charles L. Griswold Jr, *Adam Smith and the Virtues of Enlightenment*, Cambridge, Cambridge University Press, 1999, and Emma Rothschild, *Economic Sentiments: Adam Smith, Condorcet and the Enlightenment*, Cambridge MA, Harvard University Press, 2001.

9. Griswold Jr, *Adam Smith and the Virtues of Enlightenment*, p. 302.

10. Viner, *The Role of Providence in the Social Order*, pp. 78–9.

11. For an examination of the role of economics as a contemporary religion, see Robert H. Nelson, *Economics as Religion: From Samuelson to Chicago and Beyond*, University Park PA, Pennsylvania State University Press, 2001.

12. I discuss some common misunderstandings of Spencer's thought in *Liberalisms: Essays in Political Philosophy*, London and New York, Routledge, 1989, Chapter 6, pp. 89–102.

13. I have given a critical assessment of Hayek as a liberal theorist in my *Hayek on Liberty*, 3rd edn, London and New York, Routledge, 1998, pp. 146–61.

14. Karl Polanyi, *The Great Transformation*, Boston, Beacon Press, 1944, p. 140.

15. F. A. Hayek, *The Constitution of Liberty*, London, Routledge, 1960, p. 57.

16. ibid., p. 61.

17. Blair's statement was made to the Labour party conference in September 2004 as part of a defence of his role in the Iraq war. See *Guardian*, 29 September 2004.

18. For samples of neo-conservative thinking, see Irwin Stelzer (ed.), *Neoconservatism*, London, Atlantic Books, 2005, which contains a contribution by Tony Blair; and Irving Kristol, *Neoconservatism: The Autobiography of an Idea*, New York, Free Press, 1995.

19. John Kampfner, *Blair's Wars*, London and New York, Free Press, 2004, p. 173.

20. Tony Blair, prime minister's speeches, http://www.number-10.gov.uk/output/Page1297.asp

21. ibid.

22. Tony Blair, speech to the World Affairs Council in Los Angeles, 1 August 2006.

23. Tony Blair, 'Defence – Our Nation's Future', 12 January 2007, http://www.pm.gov.uk/output/Page10735.asp

24. See Dilip Hiro, *Secrets and Lies: The True Story of the Iraq War*, London, Politico's, 2005, pp. 62–6, 131–3. See also Brian Jones, 'What they didn't tell US about WMD', *New Statesman*, 11 December 2006.

25. BBC News World Edition, 5 February 2003, 'Leaked report rejects Iraqi al-Qaeda link', http://news.bbc.co.uk/1/hi/uk/2727471.stm

26. The quote from the 'Iraq Options' paper is cited by Henry Porter, 'It's clear. The case for war was cooked up', *Observer*, 5 November 2006.

27. Gary Leupp, 'Faith-based intelligence', *Counterpunch*, 26 July 2003.

28. A full version of the memo together with other leaked documents (including Jack Straw's memo to Blair of 25 March 2002) can be seen at www.downingstreetmemo.com

29. For an account of the meeting at which Bush and Blair agreed to go to war whatever the UN decided, see Philippe Sands, *Lawless World: Making and Breaking Global Rules*, 2nd edn, London, Penguin, 2006.

30. Bush's offer to Blair is detailed in Bob Woodward, *Plan of Attack*, New York, Simon and Schuster, 2004. The conversation between Bush and Blair was published in an excerpt from Woodward's book on www.washington post.com on 24 April 2004, under the title 'Blair steady in support'.

31. For a penetrating account of political lying in the Blair era, see Peter Oborne, *The Rise of Political Lying*, London and New York, Free Press, 2005.

32. Raymond Aron, Foreword to Alain Besançon, *The Soviet Syndrome*, trans. Patricia Ranum, New York, Harcourt Brace Jovanovich, 1978, pp. xvii–xviii.

4 THE AMERICANIZATION OF THE APOCALYPSE

1. Thomas Paine, *Common Sense*, Appendix to the Third Edition, www.ushistory.org/paine/commonsense/sense6.htm

2. Herman Melville, *White Jacket*, London and New York, Oxford University Press World's Classics, 1924, p. 142.

3. See http://history.hanover.edu/texts/winthmod.html

4. See Paul Boyer, *When Time Shall Be No More: Prophecy and Belief in Modern American Culture*, Cambridge MA, Harvard University Press, 1992, pp. 68–70.

5. John Galt, *The Life and Studies of Benjamin West*, London, 1819, p. 92; cited by Ernest Lee Tuveson, *Redeemer Nation: The Idea of America's Millennial Role*, Chicago and London, University of Chicago Press, 1968, pp. 95–6.

6. For the theological context and content of Locke's thought, see John Dunn's pioneering *The Political Thought of John Locke*, Cambridge, Cambridge University Press, 1969 and 1982.

7. Anatol Lieven, *America Right or Wrong: An Anatomy of American Nationalism*, London, HarperCollins, 2004, p. 51.

8. For a discussion of de Tocqueville on American exceptionalism, see Hugh Brogan's definitive biography, *Alexis de Tocqueville*, London, Profile, 2006, p. 270.

9. Woodrow Wilson speaking at Pueblo, 25 September 1919, www.americanrhetoric.com/speeches/wilsonleagueofnations.htm

10. Edmund Stillman and William Pfaff, *Power and Impotence: The Futility of American Foreign Policy*, London, Victor Gollancz, 1966, p. 15.

11. Conrad Cherry (ed.), *God's New Israel: Religious Interpretations of American Destiny*, Chapel Hill NC, University of North Carolina Press, 1998, p. 11. I am indebted to Kevin Phillips's *American Theocracy: The Peril and Politics of Radical Religion, Oil and Borrowed Money in the 21st Century*, New York, Viking, 2006, where Cherry's statement is cited on p. 129.

12. For a discussion of the role of ideas of divine covenant in modern nationalism, see Anthony Smith, *Chosen Peoples: Sacred Sources of National Identity*, Oxford and New York, Oxford University Press, 2002.

13. See Lisa Myers and NBC team, 'Top Terrorist Hunter's Divisive Views', *NBC Nightly News*, 15 October 2003. For an analysis of Boykin's role in the Bush administration and fundamentalist support for the war, see Paul Vallely, 'The fifth crusade: George Bush and the Christianisation of the war in Iraq', in *Re-Imagining Security*, London, British Council, 2004, pp. 42–68.

14. Bush's use of biblical phrases in the speeches has been analysed by the American theologian Bruce Lincoln in *Holy Terrors: Thinking About Religion After 9/11*, Chicago, University of Chicago Press, 2006.

15. *Haaretz*, 26 June 2003.

16. Statement cited in Boyer, *When Time Shall Be No More*, p. 305.

17. See David Kuo, *Tempted by Faith: An Insider Story of Political Seduction*, New York, Free Press, 2006.

18. 'Bush: Intelligent Design should be taught', *SF Gate*, 2 August 2005.

19. 'Bush tells group he sees a "Third Awakening" ', *Washington Post*, 13 September 2006.

20. For further details of the *Newsweek* poll, see Michael Lind, *Made in Texas: George W. Bush and the Southern Takeover of American Politics*, New York, Basic Books, 2003, p. 108.

21. The Homeland Security document can be viewed at www.global security.org/security/library/report/2004/hsc-planning-scenarios-jul04 .htm

22. Richard A. Clarke, *Against All Enemies: Inside America's War on Terror*, New York and London, Free Press/Simon and Schuster, 2004, p. 264.

23. Lind, *Made in Texas*, p. 144.

24. Time/CNN poll, *Time*, July 2002. Cited in Phillips, *American Theocracy*, p. 96.

25. Lind, *Made in Texas*, p. 112.

26. For an account of the far-reaching character of Bush's push to faith-based government, see Gary Wills, 'A country ruled by faith', *New York Review of Books*, vol. 53, no. 16, November 2006.

27. Karl Mannheim, *Ideology and Utopia*, London, Routledge, 1960, p. 192.

28. Jeane J. Kirkpatrick, *Dictatorships and Double Standards: Rationalism and Reason in Politics*, New York, American Enterprise Institute/Simon and Schuster, 1982, p. 18.

29. Michael Novak, 'Neocon: some memories', www.michaelnovak.net

30. See Irving Kristol, 'Memoirs of a Trotskyist', *New York Times Magazine*, 23 January 1977, reprinted in Irving Kristol, *Reflections of a Neoconservative: Looking Back, Looking Forward*, New York, Basic Books, 1986.

31. Francis Fukuyama, 'The End of History?', *National Interest*, summer 1989. Fukuyama developed the views presented in this article in *The End of History and the Last Man*, New York, Free Press, 1992.

32. Criticizing Fukuyama's original article in October 1989, I wrote: 'Ours is an era in which political ideology, liberal as much as Marxist, has a dwindling leverage on events, and more ancient, more primordial forces, nationalist and religious, fundamentalist and soon, perhaps, Malthusian, are contesting with each other . . . If the Soviet Union does indeed fall apart, that beneficent catastrophe will not inaugurate a new era of post-historical harmony, but instead a return to the classical terrain of history, a terrain of great-power rivalries, secret diplomacies, and irredentist claims and wars.' See John Gray, 'The End of History – or of Liberalism?', in *National Review*, 27 October 1989, pp. 33–5. This article is reprinted in my *Post-Liberalism: Studies in Political Thought*, London and New York, Routledge, 1993, pp. 245–50.

33. See 'Neo-cons turn on Bush for incompetence over Iraq war', *Guardian*, 4 November 2006, and David Rose, 'Neo Culpa', *Vanity Fair*, 3 November 2006.

34. See Francis Fukuyama, *After the Neocons: America at the Crossroads*, London, Profile, 2006, p. 55. The scholar who identified Fukuyama's 'passive "Marxist" social teleology' is Ken Jowitt, author of the interesting Study, *New World Disorder: The Leninist Extinction*, Berkeley and Oxford, University of California Press, 1992.

35. Kirkpatrick, *Dictatorships and Double Standards*, pp. 11, 17–18.

36. See M. Oakeshott, *Rationalism in Politics and Other Essays*, ed. Tim Fuller, Indianapolis, Liberty Press, 1991. I have criticized Oakeshott's philosophy in my 'Reply to Critics' in John Horton and Glen Newey (eds.), *The Political Theory of John Gray*, London, Routledge, 2006.

37. For a discussion of Kojeve and Schmitt, see Mark Lilla, *The Reckless Mind: Intellectuals in Politics*, New York, New York Review of Books, 2003.

38. Leo Strauss, *Natural Right and History*, Chicago and London, University of Chicago Press, 1953, pp. 181–2.

39. ibid., p. 164.

40. For the claim that Strauss's thought condoned deception in politics, see Shadia B. Drury, *Leo Strauss and the American Right*, London, Palgrave Macmillan, 1999.

41. Leo Strauss, *What is Political Philosophy?*, New York, Free Press, 1959, pp. 115–16.

42. For a careful discussion of Strauss and neo-conservatism, see Stephen B. Smith, *Reading Leo Strauss: Politics, Philosophy, Judaism*, Chicago, University of Chicago Press, 2006.

43. See, for example, M. F. Burnyeat, 'Sphinx without a secret', *New York Review of Books*, 30 May 1985.

44. F. Dostoyevsky, *The Devils*, London, Penguin, 2004, p. 404.

45. For an account of Khalilzad's early days as a student in Chicago, see Anne Norton's excellent *Leo Strauss and the Politics of American Empire*, New Haven and London, Yale University Press, 2004, pp. 185–6.

46. Albert Wohlstetter, 'Is there a strategic arms race?', *Foreign Policy*, no. 15, summer 1974, pp. 3–20.

47. For Angleton's life and career, see Tom Mangold, *Cold Warrior: James Jesus Angleton, the CIA's Master Spy Hunter*, London and New York, Simon and Schuster, 1991.

48. For an authoritative analysis of the methods and errors of the B Team, see Anne H. Cahn, *Killing Détente: The Right Attacks the CIA*, University Park PA, Pennsylvania State University Press, 1998. See also her article, 'Team B: the trillion dollar experiment', *Bulletin of Atomic Scientists*, vol. 49, no. 3, April 1993.

49. Gary Schmitt and Abram Shulsky, 'Leo Strauss and the World of

Intelligence (By Which We Do Not Mean *Nous*)', in Kenneth L. Deutsch and John A. Murley (eds.), *Leo Strauss, the Straussians and the American Regime*, New York, Rowman and Littlefield, 1999, p. 410 *et seq.*

50. Schmitt and Shulsky developed their view of intelligence methods more systematically in *Silent Warfare: Understanding the World of Intelligence*, 3rd edn, Washington DC, Brassey's, 2002.

51. For the remarks of the Bush aide, see Ron Suskind, 'Without a doubt', *New York Times*, 17 October 2004.

52. Bob Woodward has provided an account of the deception and delusion surrounding the war in the White House in his brilliant exposé, *State of Denial: Bush at War, Part III*, New York, Simon and Schuster, 2006.

53. George Packer, *The Assassins' Gate: America in Iraq*, New York, Farrar, Straus and Giroux, 2005, p. 105.

54. For a report on the 'Iranian Directorate', see Laura Rozen, 'US moves to weaken Iran', *Los Angeles Times*, 19 May 2006.

55. For a well-sourced account of the formation and operations of the OSP, see Seymour M. Hersh, *Chain of Command*, London and New York, Allen Lane and HarperCollins, 2004, pp. 207–24.

56. Joan Didion, 'Cheney: the fatal touch', *New York Review of Books*, 5 October 2006, p. 54.

57. Schmitt and Shulsky, *Silent Warfare*, p. 176.

58. For a report suggesting intelligence analysts feared émigré claims of Iraqi WMD may have been disinformation, see Bob Drogin, 'US suspects it received false arms tips', *Los Angeles Times*, 28 August 2003.

59. 'Bush and Putin: best of friends', BBC News, 16 June 2001.

60. David Brooks, 'The CIA: method or madness?', *New York Times*, 3 February 2004.

61. Michael Ledeen, 'Creative destruction', *National Review Online*, 20 September 2001.

62. Czesław Miłosz, 'Dostoyevsky', in *To Begin Where I Am: Selected Essays*, New York, Farrar, Straus and Giroux, 2002, pp. 281–2.

5 ARMED MISSIONARIES

1. Robespierre's speech can be read at
http://faculty.washington.edu/jonas/Text/ParisRomeProgram/Readings
For a superb account of Robespierre and his part in the Terror, see Ruth Scurr, *Fatal Purity: Robespierre and the French Revolution*, London, Chatto and Windus, 2006.

2. David Rieff, *At the Point of a Gun: Democratic Dreams and Armed Intervention*, London and New York, Simon and Schuster, 2005, p. 180.

3. Robert L. Hirsch *et al.*, *Peaking of World Oil Production: Impacts, Mitigation and Risk Management*, p. 64. The report can be viewed at http://www.projectcensored.org/newsflash/The_Hirsch_Report_Proj_Cens.pdf

4. There is a growing literature on the geo-politics of oil. The best studies of which I am aware are Michael T. Klare, *Blood and Oil: The Dangers and Consequences of America's Growing Petroleum Dependency*, London, Penguin, 2004.

5. The full text of Cheney's speech can be read in the *Energy Bulletin* at http://www.energybulletin.net/559.html

6. For an account of the State Department's paper and its fate, see M. W. Shervington, 'Lessons of Iraq: Invasion and Occupation', *Small Wars Journal*, vol. 5, July 2006, pp. 15–29. The journal can be accessed at www.smallwarsjournal.com

7. Ten days before the US-led invasion, I wrote that the Bush administration's 'view of the aftermath of the war is muddy in the extreme ... There is a risk that the Iraqi state, a rickety structure cobbled up by departing British civil servants, will fracture and fragment in Yugoslav or even Chechen fashion.' See 'America is no longer invincible', *New Statesman*, 10 March 2003, reprinted as 'On the Eve of War: American Power and Impotence', in John Gray, *Heresies: Against Progress and Other Illusions*, London, Granta Books, 2004, p. 140.

8. See *The Nation*, 14 April 2003, for Rumsfeld's comment.

9. For an authoritative account of Bell's life and career, see Georgina Howell, *Gertrude Bell: Queen of the Desert, Shaper of Nations*, New York, Farrar, Straus and Giroux, 2007.

10. James Mann, *Rise of the Vulcans: The History of Bush's War Cabinet*, New York, Viking, 2004, p. 367.

11. Thomas E. Ricks, *Fiasco: The American Military Adventure in Iraq*, London, Penguin, 2006, p. 162.

12. The *Lancet* analysis is summarized in '655,000 Iraqis killed since invasion', *Guardian*, 11 October 2006. A more detailed summary can be found on the website of the Johns Hopkins Bloomberg School of Public Health, which carried out the survey, at http://www.jhsph.edu/public healthnews/press_releases/2006/burnham_iraq_2006.html

For details of the UN report on torture in post-Saddam Iraq, see 'New terror stalks Iraq's republic of fear', *Independent*, 24 September 2006.

13. See Rupert Smith, *The Utility of Force: The Art of War in the Modern World*, London, Allen Lane, 2005.

14. The American use of chemical weapons in Fallujah has been confirmed in the US Army's *Field Artillery Magazine*, March/April 2005. See 'US Army article on Fallujah white phosphorus use', *Scoop*, 11 November 2005, http://www.scoop.co.nz/stories/HL0511/S00173.htm

15. 'US tactics condemned by British officers', *Daily Telegraph*, 10 April 2004.

16. 'CIA chief sacked for opposing torture', *Sunday Times*, 12 February 2006.

17. For a report and analysis of the opposition of American military judges to the Bush administration's authorization of torture, see Sidney Blumenthal, 'The torture battle royal', *Guardian*, 21 September 2006.

18. For a discussion of the cultural aspects of American foreign policy, see George Walden, *God Won't Save America: Psychosis of a Nation*, London, Gibson Square, 2006.

19. George Santayana, *The Birth of Reason and Other Essays*, New York, Columbia University Press, 1968, p. 87.

20. Michael Ignatieff, 'The burden', *New York Times Magazine*, 5 January 2003.

21. Paul Berman, *Terror and Liberalism*, New York and London, Norton, 2004, pp. 189–90.

22. The remark is quoted by Robert Kaplan in *Imperial Grunts: The American Military on the Ground*, New York, Random House, 2005, p. 205.

23. Emmanuel Todd, *After the Empire: The Breakdown of the American Order*, London, Constable, 2003, p. 197.

24. 'Cheney condemned for backing water torture', *Guardian*, 28 October 2006.

25. See Walter Pincus, 'Waterboarding historically controversial', *Washington Post*, 5 October 2006.

26. On the use of sleep deprivation in Stalinist Russia and Guantánamo Bay, see Vladimir Bukovsky, 'Torture's long shadow', *Washington Post*, 18 December 2005. As the article relates, Bukovsky was himself tortured when he was a Soviet dissident. For sleep deprivation in Guantánamo, see also 'The real victims of sleep deprivation', BBC News, 8 January 2004.

27. See Deborah Sontag, 'A videotape offers a window into a terror suspect's isolation', *New York Times*, 4 December 2006.

28. I have analysed liberal legalism more fully in *Two Faces of Liberalism*, Cambridge, Polity Press, 2000.

29. See S. M. Lipset and J. M. Lakin, *The Democratic Century*, Norman OK, University of Oklahoma Press, 2004.

30. 'Security firms abusing Iraqis', BBC World News, 30 October 2006.

31. Martin van Creveld, *The Changing Face of War: Lessons of Combat, from the Marne to Iraq*, New York, Ballantine Books, 2006, p. 229.

32. See 'Campaign in Iraq has increased terror threat, says American intelligence report', *Guardian*, 25 September 2006.

33. For Donald Rumsfeld's conception of the Long War, see 'Rumsfeld offers strategy for current war: Pentagon to release 20-year plan today', *Washington Post*, 3 February 2006. The US Army and Marine Corps' *Counter-insurgency Field Manual*, published in December 2006, contains a more sophisticated analysis. See www.military.com, 16 December 2006, 'New counter-insurgency manual'.

34. See, for example, David Frum and Richard Perle, *An End to Evil: How to Win the War on Terror*, New York, Random House, 2003.

35. Samuel P. Huntington presented the theory of 'clashing civilizations' in his *The Clash of Civilizations and the Remaking of World Order*, New York and London, Simon and Schuster, 1996. I have assessed it at greater length in 'Global utopias and clashing civilisations', *International Affairs*, vol. 74, no. 1, January 1998, pp. 149–63.

36. Robert A. Pape, *Dying to Win: The Strategic Logic of Suicide Terrorism*, New York, Random House, 2005.

37. I consider the evolution of al-Qaeda in the new Introduction to my *Al Qaeda and What it Means to be Modern*, 2nd edn, London, Faber, 2007.

38. For a superb narrative and analysis of the development of al-Qaeda, see Lawrence Wright, *The Looming Tower: Al-Qaeda and the Road to 9/11*, New York, Knopf, 2006.

39. Olivier Roy, *Globalised Islam: The Search for a New Ummah*, London, Hurst, 2004, p. 44.

40. Martin van Creveld gives an account of British strategy in Northern Ireland in *The Changing Face of War*, pp. 229–36.

41. See Philip Bobbitt, *The Shield of Achilles: War, Peace and the Course of History*, London, Allen Lane, 2002.

42. Bernard-Henri Lévy, *American Vertigo: On the Road from Newport to Guantánamo*, London, Gibson Square, 2006, p.328.

43. For a realistic assessment of the international system, see the late Paul Hirst's brilliant short book, *War and Power in the 21st Century*, Cambridge, Polity Press, 2001.

44. For a report of the changes in US nuclear doctrine, see William Arkin, 'Not just a last resort', *Washington Post*, 15 May 2005.

45. See Paul Rogers, 'Iran: Consequences of a War', Briefing Paper, Oxford

Research Group, 2006, http://www.oxfordresearchgroup.org.uk/publications/
briefing_papers/iranconsequences.php

46. Fred Charles Ikle, *Annihilation from Within: The Ultimate Threat to
Nations*, New York, Columbia University Press, 2006, p. xiii.

6 POST-APOCALYPSE

1. Thomas Hobbes, *Leviathan*, London, J. M. Dent, 1914, Chapter 5,
p. 20.

2. Leo Strauss, *Natural Right and History*, Chicago and London, University
of Chicago Press, 1953, p. 317.

3. For an analysis of Spinoza as a decisive thinker of the early modern
Enlightenment, see Jonathan I. Israel, *Radical Enlightenment: Philosophy
and the Making of Modernity, 1650–1750*, Oxford, Oxford University
Press, 2001.

4. I discuss Spinoza in my 'Reply to Critics' in John Horton and Glen
Newey (eds.), *The Political Theory of John Gray*, London, Routledge,
2006. For an illuminating recent interpretation of Spinoza's philosophy,
see Stuart Hampshire, *Spinoza and Spinozism*, Oxford, Clarendon Press,
2005.

5. See Richard Dawkins, *The God Delusion*, London, Bantam, 2006, and
Daniel C. Dennett, *Breaking the Spell: Religion as a Natural Phenomenon*,
London, Allen Lane, 2006.

6. I leave aside atheism in Islamic cultures, though the same analysis applies.

7. Tzvetan Todorov, *Hope and Memory: Lessons from the Twentieth
Century*, Princeton NJ, Princeton University Press, 2003, pp. 236–7.

8. Hedley Bull, *The Control of the Arms Race*, London, Weidenfeld and
Nicolson, 1961, p. 212.

9. For canonical statements of the realist position, see Hans J. Morgenthau,
Scientific Man versus Power Politics, Chicago, University of Chicago Press,
1974; Reinhold Niebuhr, *Moral Man and Immoral Society*, London, Con-
tinuum, 2005; Hedley Bull, *The Anarchical Society: A Study of Order in
World Politics*, London, Palgrave Macmillan, 2002; and Martin Wright,
Power Politics, London, Continuum, 1995.

10. A text of Kennan's telegram setting out the policy of containment
can be read at http://www.learner.org/channel/workshops/primarysources/
coldwar/docs/tele.html

11. Isaiah Berlin, *Political Ideas in the Romantic Age*, Princeton NJ, Princeton University Press, 2006, pp. 54–5.

12. For authoritative analyses of the scale and speed of climate shift, see James Lovelock, *The Revenge of Gaia*, London, Allen Lane, 2006; Fred Pearce, *The Last Generation: How Nature Will Take Her Revenge for Climate Change*, London, Transworld Publishers, 2006; and Jim Hansen, 'The threat to the planet', *New York Review of Books*, vol. 53, no. 12, 13 July 2006. A seminal discussion of global oil peaking can be found in C. J. Campbell, *The Coming Oil Crisis*, Brentwood, Essex, Multi-Science Publishing Company, 1997. An authoritative analysis of the peaking of oil reserves in Saudi Arabia can be found in Matthew R. Simmons, *Twilight in the Desert: The Coming Saudi Oil Shock and the Global Economy*, London, Wiley, 2005.

13. The report, authored by Peter Schwartz and Doug Randall, can be downloaded at http://www.environmentaldefense.org/documents/3566_AbruptClimateChange.pdf

14. For an argument in favour of zero-emission fossil fuels as a sustainable alternative, see Mark Jaccard, *Sustainable Fossil Fuels: The Unusual Suspect in the Search for Clean and Enduring Energy*, Cambridge, Cambridge University Press, 2005.

15. See Lovelock, *The Revenge of Gaia*, p. 154.

16. Jared Diamond, *Collapse: How Societies Choose to Fail or Survive*, London, Allen Lane, 2005, p. 521.

17. Frank Kermode, *The Sense of an Ending: Studies in the Theory of Fiction*, New York and Oxford, Oxford University Press, 1967, p. 123.

18. Marcel Proust, *The Way by Swann's*, London, Allen Lane, 2002, p. 47.

19. Adam Phillips, *Side Effects*, London, Hamish Hamilton, 2006, p. 99.

20. I develop the idea of *modus vivendi* more fully in *Two Faces of Liberalism*, Cambridge, Polity Press, 2000, Chapter 4.

Index